Until now, a majority of us did not know
that over a long period of time
many eyes have been watching over the Earthly world
beyond distances immeasurable.

The central figures of universal peace
the great angels of the cosmos
have drawn very near to us.
Resonating with the vibrations
of our world peace prayers,
they are beginning to radiate the light
of their merciful love
to all places,
coming to the aid of Earthly humanity.

Great Angels of the Cosmos
by Masahisa Goi

© Masao Murata 2002.

Original Japanese publication:
Sora o Tobu Enban to Chô-Kagaku by Masao Murata
Byakko Press 1974

English Edition:
Angels of the Cosmos
Translated by Kinuko Hamaya and Grace Roberts
Edited by David Fish and Mary McQuaid
Illustrations by Yasueki Takeuchi and Masao Murata

Published in the USA and in Great Britain by
Byakko Press
812-1 Hitoana, Fujinomiya-shi
Shizuoka-ken, Japan 418-0102
http://www.ByakkoPress.ne.jp
email: gbs1357@quartz.ocn.ne.jp
All rights reserved.

Cover design by David Lee Fish
Three Cosmic Angels Keishichi Kaneko

ISBN 4-89214-151-8

ANGELS
OF THE
COSMOS

*My Spiritual Voyage
Aboard a Living Space Vessel*

MASAO MURATA

*Translated by Kinuko Hamaya
and Grace Roberts*

BYAKKO PRESS

CONTENTS

ILLUSTRATIONS

PREFACE

Mr. Masao Murata is one of the few psychic persons in this world who can freely travel in divine and spiritual realms. He has already written several books about the contacts he has had with spiritual worlds and each of them captures our great interest and curiosity.

Quite a number of books have already been published on the subject of 'flying saucers,' 'unidentified flying objects' and space vessels, among which the works of Adamski[1] figure quite prominently. However, it is difficult to judge the authenticity of most of these works. In addition, their contents are so far removed from conventional ways of thinking that many people would find them difficult to accept.

This work by Masao Murata was written more than ten years ago, but since it was such an unusual book in terms of what was generally accepted at the time, its publication was postponed until now. However, many of us felt that the book was too good to be left unpublished. Upon a suggestion received from our publishing department that now was a good time to publish it, and with Mr. Murata's agreement, the book has at long last appeared in print.

This work is simply laden with information that is entirely beyond the imagination of Earthly human beings, with its descriptions of cosmic humans, structural details about space vessels, and much more. The narrative is also compelling. Even if you were to read a science fiction novel today, I doubt that you would find yourself in such anticipation to discover what wonders awaited you as you turned each page. The author comments that the scenes and events in this book are his spiritual rather than physical experiences. Be it a physical or a spiritual journey, this certainly is an interesting book.

Unlike other stories in print to date, I think that enthusiasts of UFOs and extraterrestrial life will find much to learn from this book.

In any event, with the growing number of sightings of space vessels around the world today, I do not think that we can casually dismiss the existence of cosmic human beings. For a long time we[2] have been in contact with cosmic humans, or, more precisely, high-ranking spirits, most of whom deserve to be called deities or divinities. While pursuing our scientific studies under their direction, we will treat this volume by Mr. Murata as a work of great importance.

I do hope that even those who are concerned only with worldly matters and objects that are visible and tangible will read this book with an open mind and, in so doing, expand their perspective of the universe to include phenomena which cannot be explained in Earthly terms.

Masahisa Goi
April 1974

INTRODUCTION

To begin with, I would like to tell you about an incident that eventually led me to write this book on space vessels. A friend had lent me a book by Adamski in which the author described the contacts he had had with cosmic human beings. I began reading it, and after finishing some twenty or thirty pages I started to feel sleepy and drifted into a gentle slumber. I do not know how much time had passed but, in that dream-like state I noticed that a woman had appeared before me. She seemed to be around sixty years old and was wearing a black dress and a black bonnet. The noonday sun was shining brightly. The lady approached me with a smooth, gliding motion. She had a beautiful face, and I felt a translucent, almost transparent vibration radiating from her.

As I looked into her eyes, my heart was enveloped in the profound wisdom they conveyed. They emanated not only intelligence and awareness, but also warmth and sincerity. I felt as if I had known her for a long time, and seeing her now filled me with nostalgia. She came closer and closer, stopping just a few steps from where I was. All at once she began to speak:

It is the first time for you to read this book, isn't it?

At a loss for words, I just nodded.

You will learn many things from it. Please read it carefully.

Yes, I will. Thank you.

As we talked, I spontaneously found myself responding to her words with feelings of deep gratitude. Little by little I grew inquisitive as to who she was, and asked if she would tell me her name.

Rosium James came her reply, as quickly as an echo.

As she continued to gaze at me with an affectionate expression, her image gradually receded from view until it disappeared altogether. The encounter was very brief, lasting perhaps five minutes in worldly time.

This incident in my dream struck me as being so mysterious that I quickly jotted down some notes about it on a nearby sheet of paper before returning to my book. As I went on reading I completely forgot about the incident. When I later returned the book to my friend, the piece of paper containing my notes was still lodged between its pages. Several days later my friend came across this slip of paper and, being curious about it, asked Goi Sensei[3] what it meant. He later told me that Goi Sensei had replied: *The woman in Mr. Murata's vision was his spiritual instructor. She appeared in order to let him know of her existence.* It was quite a long time afterwards that I learned of this.

Shortly after this incident, I began to observe space vessels flying in the sky. One day I spotted a group of them overhead when I was at Holy Hill.[4] There were more of them than I could count. Although none of the people to whom I spoke about it had shared my experience, the sure knowledge of what I had seen continued to grow within me. On another occasion, when I went outside with several of my friends to pray for world peace I sensed the approach of some space vessels. This time I wanted to take photos of them. Luckily, I happened to have a rather good camera with me. Focusing on the vessels, I pressed the shutter, certain that I had captured their images.

About an hour later more vessels appeared, approaching from various directions. All of them were medium-sized craft. Some were flying alone, while others flocked together in groups. I recall taking more than ten shots of them with my camera. A friend developed the film for me right away. Little did I know, however, that one of the most disappointing moments of my life was awaiting me. Although the scenery was in clear focus in the photos, not a trace of even one space vessel appeared in any of them! This came as a great shock to me. I had released the shutter again and again with so much anticipation! Through this experience I learned that true space vessels are made up of such subtle vibrations that most people cannot perceive them, nor can their images be easily captured on film.

Once I realized this I gave up the idea of informing people of the reality of space vessels. Meanwhile, I continued to marvel at the mystery of these wonderful objects that I had been privileged to see. Never could I contain my amazement at the sight of a huge space vessel descending vertically without the slightest sound and disturbing nothing around it, or at seeing it perfectly balanced in the air with one end touching the edge of a cliff.

At times, however, I did feel somewhat confused. I wondered if my eyes were deceiving me, or if the people around me had lost their wits. Although I had heard from Goi Sensei about differences in vibrational frequencies, I still found it discouraging to have what I knew to be a reality totally refuted by others due to a lack of proof. When I spoke about this to Goi Sensei, he replied, 'As you have seen, space vessels really exist. However the time has not yet come for proving it. Eventually, through our research in cosmic science,[5] people will be able so see that space vessels do indeed exist.'

To me, these words from Goi Sensei were more encouraging and more precious than the opinions of a million people. I decided not to care whether anyone else believed me or not. Several days passed without my thinking too much about space vessels. Nevertheless, I kept witnessing their appearance as they constantly flew in the sky above Holy Hill. I felt certain that their frequent appearances there occurred because of the hill's sacred nature.

One day I was in downtown Tokyo near Yurakucho station. The traffic lights had turned green and I had begun to cross the crowded main street at a pedestrian crossing. It was a clear, fine day, though the polluted Tokyo sky had a grayish cast to it. Looking up at the sky, I spotted a space vessel high overhead and to my right. After moving to my left, it vanished from sight. It was at this time that I realized that space vessels must indeed fly over all regions of the Earth.

Space vessels have the ability to ascend and descend vertically. They are living organisms made from fine vibrations that are beyond the range of the five senses, yet they can manifest themselves so as to be visible to human beings. They are such fine living organisms that they work like the hands and legs of the cosmic humans from other planets who travel in them. Since I had learned previously about the wondrous existence of these vessels, I did not feel the least bit doubtful or mystified by the accounts I had read in the writings of Adamski and others. I just hoped that the time would come—the sooner the better—when I could learn more about what these vessels were actually like. It had become obvious to me that some great power far exceeding our materially-oriented knowledge and capabilities was at work here.

Some two months passed without anything special happening. As we continued our world peace prayers under the guidance of Goi Sensei, I had further encounters with cosmic human beings and observed more space vessels coming close to us during our meditations. I did not expect or pray for any sort of contact with the vessels or with cosmic human beings; those encounters took place naturally while all of us were simply praying wholeheartedly for the peace of humanity. I must admit, however, that on a very few occasions I did start meditating with a hopeful feeling of continuing from where I had left off in my previous encounter; but on those occasions I was not able to see, hear, or learn anything relating to cosmic humans or space vessels.

As time went on and the number of contacts with cosmic humans kept increasing, I arrived at the following understanding: space vessels are living beings that come from planets with an extremely advanced science. Using their space vessels as mediums, many cosmic beings from marvelously advanced realms are visiting our very backward, Earthly world on a mission to help us develop and evolve our society. While keeping an eye on us, they are earnestly offering us their help through dimensions that are beyond our physical perception.

My initial ideas about space vessels were similar to what was commonly conveyed in media reports: that they were superior mechanical devices made of materials not unlike what could be found on Earth. This was a gross error, I realized. On the contrary, those vessels represented a science whose concepts lay beyond the limits of our knowledge. The way they work is similar to the way our own physical bodies work. If we think of our bodies as perfect mechanisms composed of marvelously advanced scientific instruments and precision parts, and then think of how they function when combined with our spirits, we can begin to grasp how space vessels function. It is as if they themselves were organic bodies or beings. We never think of the various organs of our bodies as separate from ourselves, do we? Likewise, when I saw a space vessel with its incredibly precise and advanced functions, I could only think of it as an organic whole. I was thus driven by an urge to write about the reality of space vessels as living entities in the fullest possible detail. I wanted people to know that, contrary to conventional belief, space vessels do not belong to a world of rough material vibrations but are living organisms developed through the science of a higher dimensional world than ours.

In approaching the subject of higher dimensional science, I searched for ways to make it understandable to my readers. To my regret, however, I could not find any suitable term for it. At any rate, even in contemporary science there is evidence that the range of waves that are visible to our human eyes is quite limited and lies somewhere between the minimum and the maximum waves. Although these maximum and minimum waves do exist, human eyes cannot perceive them. Contemporary science also testifies that what we usually recognize as existing does not cover the full range of phenomena. Humanity benefits from a variety of functions and phenomena that are imperceptible to our physical eyes, such as magnetic waves, electronic waves and electromagnetic waves.

I finally decided to tentatively refer to the science that far outdistances our own with the term 'suprascience,' which means 'spiritual science.' Although this term may not be exactly appropriate, I ask that you allow me to use it here for lack of a better term.

I do not believe that we will ever be able to attain accurate knowledge or reach a true understanding of space vessels as long as we continue to think of them as mere material objects or high tech machinery. Nor do I think that people can attune themselves to such phenomena if they are motivated only by a curiosity for the unknown.

To rectify such mistaken views, I firmly resolved to remain faithful to my conviction that space vessels are higher dimensional or spiritual phenomena. With this principle in mind, I went on writing about things just as they had been explained to me.

To begin with, I wrote quite casually. However, things did not go so smoothly. Stumbling over confusing issues, I was obliged to halt my pen from time to time. At such times, I would call out to Goi Sensei in my mind and pray for world peace.[6] While I was praying, my cosmic instructors (angelic beings) would respond from behind me, helping me to remember things I had forgotten and resolve issues one by one. The reason why I knew the inner structures of the space vessels fairly well was because they had been shown to me many times. (I will expand upon this in the ensuing chapters.) What really troubled me, though, was the type and function of each machine. Many of them were hard to comprehend. Nevertheless, I resumed writing while repeatedly asking questions of my cosmic instructors.

Sometimes, when I was absorbed in writing, I felt a sudden rap inside my head. It was as if someone were calling me to attention to reconsider the direction of my thoughts. This seemed to occur when I had not noticed that I was getting involved in thoughts of the physical world. The rap was a warning that I was straying from what I had set out to write about.

As soon as I sat in front of my desk and began to write about space vessels, my usual self would completely vanish and I would be transformed into an entirely different person. In that transformed state, I would communicate with my spiritual guides until late at night.

I did not engage in this practice for pleasure. For me, it was more a routine of strict discipline. In this way, I continued writing for two and a half years. During that time, I learned the principles of the science of the future, and they are clearly and indelibly recorded in my mind.

What I also learned during this time was that the Earth is about to undergo a major transformation. Whether humanity is aware of it or not, the position of the Earth, in terms of the dimensions of the universe, is shifting minute by minute. As the Earth keeps advancing to higher and higher planes, the time is also approaching when the science of the future, already possessed by cosmic humans, will be transmitted to Earth.

The problem is that Earthly humans are doing little to improve the state of their planet. People have been far too ego-centric in their lives, pursuing only their own personal goals and physical pleasures. If present attitudes do not change, individuals and nations alike will surely suffer widespread hardships. These will be combined with major natural disasters, causing untold agony to the people of Earth.

Today we face many unresolved problems—the problem of overpopulation, the problem of feeding the people of the world, and the problem of securing natural resources which we rely on to sustain our daily life. So far none of the politicians, scholars, or specialists in economics have come up with any workable solutions for resolving these problems. We simply make do from one day to the next, following the easygoing assumption that things will somehow turn out in our favor. As a result, the situation today seems quite hopeless. The mounting problems seem to far exceed the scope of our materially-oriented knowledge and wisdom, and no prospect of a solution is in sight. Considering all these issues, I earnestly hope that we can prepare ourselves for the dawning of a new future for Earth, assisted by the marvelous wisdom and science of cosmic humans who possess what I call 'science of the future' or 'cosmic science.'

When we create high and fine vibrations, as in our prayer for world peace, it enables cosmic humans to perform their work unimpeded. Thus, where the prayer *May Peace Prevail on Earth* reverberates, cosmic humans, or angels, are able to work energetically and effectively on our behalf. From this prayer, a wonderful science will emerge and rescue our stagnant Earthly world from ruin. I sincerely hope that the number of people praying for world peace will continue to grow so that the marvelous science of cosmic humans will become manifest on Earth as soon as possible, permitting the total rebirth of the Earthly world and paving the way for lasting peace on our planet.

Masao Murata
April, 1974

PART I

ARRIVAL OF THE SPACE VESSEL

Chapter 1

BOARDING THE SPACE VESSEL

At Holy Hill

The ninth of June, 1959, was a hot and humid day, quite typical of the rainy season. For the past two years a group of us had been getting together five times each month to pray for world peace at Holy Hill. On that day, seven of us were praying in a group. No sooner had the second stanza of the prayer been intoned by Mr. Saito[7] than I went into a very deep meditation.

For me[8], meditation starts when my consciousness leaves my physical body. This happens quite easily and naturally. It starts with that feeling we all have when we resist sleepiness. We resist only to find that when we relax ever so slightly, we drift into sleep. This is how I feel as my consciousness drifts away from my physical body. The state of separation varies from one occasion to the next and I never have exactly the same experience twice, since my inner state and the external conditions are never the same at any given moment. In addition, it is never a state of complete separation.

On that day, I was feeling quite good and went into a deep meditation instantaneously. Soon a clear yellow light began to shine in front of my eyes. The light began to grow larger and larger, and the area that I was looking at became the center of it. The 'I' that had separated from my physical body was absorbed into the center of the light and was lifted upward. As I ascended, the yellow color of the light became paler and paler, finally becoming a white light that was slightly tinged with yellow. I felt that I was flying far, far into the distance. On that day I had become almost totally separated from my physical body.

Since a person's physical and subconscious selves are linked by a spiritual thread, this enables one to return to one's physical body within an instant. It sometimes happens, though, that one is totally unaware of what is happening around oneself while one is soaring at a distance from one's physical body. For want of a better term, I am temporarily calling that condition a 'deep meditation.'

I was soaring at tremendous speed. It was a bright world of sheer white-yellow light. There was not a single object to be seen. Inside that vast space of white-yellow, I was flying like a shooting-star. The speed and thrill of it were beyond description and captured all my attention. In my spiritual body I could discern the spiritual vibrations that were incessantly coursing through the vastness of space. They resembled electromagnetic waves and I could sense differences in their strength and subtlety.

All of a sudden I plunged into a mass of white clouds. There, a scene unfolded before my eyes. I was in the garden outside the prayer hall at Holy Hill where we were now praying. In the scene that was projected, I was standing alone by a flower bed in the garden. None of the others were anywhere near me. The early summer sky was pure and transparent, without a cloud in sight. It was such a deep blue sky that it seemed to have endless depths.

Ah, what a beautiful day! I stretched out my arms and looked up at the sky. No longer was there a separate heaven or Earth; no longer was there a me standing between them. At that moment I felt that I had merged wholly with heaven and Earth in a state of perfect harmony. An indescribable feeling of warmth welled up from the depths of my soul and pervaded my entire being.

When I happened to glance in the direction of the prayer hall, I noticed someone heading toward me from the entrance. *Hmm, someone is coming,* I thought to myself. As I took a few steps in that direction, four or five people came over to where I stood. My eyes met those of the person in front and, to my surprise, I sensed that this was a very close friend. I looked at each of the others and felt the same closeness with them too. Moreover, I received the clear impression that they, too, were feeling the very same familiarity with me. Their emotions were directly transmitted to my heart.

I was utterly overjoyed but did not know what to say or how to say it. Memories of the far off past flashed through my mind one after another. I first thought that they were memories from my childhood, but I realized they must have been from a time much earlier than that. I tried to remember the names of these people and, although they were almost within reach of my memory, they would not come to the surface of my consciousness. But how happy I was to see these people again! I was beside myself with joy to be reunited with my five friends.

I was also surprised to find that all five people who stood around me held not the faintest trace of gloom or darkness. The honesty and clarity of their souls were obvious to me at a glance. I was wholly taken by the integrity that shone through in their appearance!

I do not remember what words I spoke but I found that we were naturally able to sense each other's intentions without any need for words.

Among these five friends, I will call the eldest one with the sturdiest physique Mr. M. He was about three years older than I.

We would like to invite you to come with us on board a space vessel, said Mr. M.

Really? I exclaimed. *But... but... is it possible for me to do that?*

Yes, of course it is, Mr. M replied with perfect confidence. *I will see to it.*

Mr. M may have perceived the half-doubts that I felt in my mind when I listened to his reply because he then produced a suit, which he held out to me, saying, *Here, you can put this on.*

What is it? I asked.

It's a space suit, he replied.

It looked like a captain's uniform. It was light brown and had the texture of fine silk. The inside was lined with a material that resembled rubber. The cap had an antenna-like object attached to it.

This is for you, Mr. M said as he casually handed the suit to me.

As we spoke, I sensed Mr. M's perfect dedication to his work. There was not a trace of Earthly greed about him. Rather, there was an air of angelic purity surrounding him. I was convinced that he and his four companions were angelic beings who had descended to Earth.

Mr. M then gave me a round instrument, approximately 15 centimeters in diameter and 7.5 centimeters thick. It was made of metal and was stored in a leather-like case. I had the impression that it was some sort of meter or gauge. The pointer needle and gradation marks were visible through a window in the case. It weighed about the same as any small testing device of that size. However, it had a luminous light at its center with multiple shining circles, each a different color. The colors were the same seven hues of a rainbow that appear when sunlight passes through a prism.

I quickly put the suit on over my shirt and trousers. It was much lighter and more comfortable than I would have expected a spacesuit to be. With the meter slung over my shoulder like a camera, I took a look at how the suit fit me. As I did so, the five cosmic persons took almost no time in slipping into their own spacesuits. Despite their serious and dignified appearance, I felt an immediate bond of trust and affection with my cosmic companions. Perhaps this is why I had not even the faintest sense of uneasiness over the prospect of taking a flight on a space vessel with them.

Clouds were now moving across the sky above Holy Hill, revealing glimpses of blue sky between them. At the southeast corner of the blue sky, a space vessel that looked about the size of a ball appeared momentarily. My mind was suddenly put on alert. The vessel descended diagonally from the south toward the east and quickly disappeared into the clouds.

Here they come! This thought, flashing through the minds of the five cosmic companions, resonated in my consciousness.

I was looking at the eastern sky, thinking that at last I might really be able to get on a space vessel. One of my cosmic friends came over and showed me how to read the gauge Mr. M had given me. He also gave me some information about the cap, shoes and suit I was wearing. The shoes were like soft

27

sneakers and were made of a material that felt like a cross between leather and rubber. The cap seemed to be made of leather but was very light, like nylon, and fit my head perfectly.

Like putting on glasses for the first time, I now saw the world around me in clear focus. It was a marvelous place, completely different from any I had seen before. Everything looked transparent and the hills, woods, houses, and even the roads were shining.

The space suit was light brown. The jacket and trousers were connected to each other. It opened at the front, and after putting your legs in from the middle you slipped the top part over your head. It was double-layered, with something like down or floss between the layers. It was very light and extremely comfortable.

The bottoms of the trousers were fastened with strings. The shoes were short boots and, as I mentioned earlier, were very light. As I had been instructed, I hung the small gauge over my shoulder and tried to take a few steps. Now dressed just like my cosmic friends, I could hardly wait for the vessel to arrive and pick us up.

One of my cosmic companions taught me how to read the changes in the color and positions of the light that appeared on the gauge. It occurred to me that he might be one of the persons in charge of the mechanical maintenance of the space vessel.

The Vessel Lands

A flash of light appeared in the sky as we were all looking east. All of a sudden a huge space vessel approached from above. It was shining like stainless steel and appeared to be about 30 meters in diameter. Riveted to the spot where I stood, I gazed at the vessel without even blinking. It was shaped something like the kind of straw hat that we used to wear in summer to protect us from the sun.

It came closer and closer, then landed in an instant some 50 meters east of where we were standing. Indeed, it happened in a split second. There was a gently sloping hill about 50 meters away from the front garden of the prayer hall, and its slope became steeper as one approached it from the building. The space vessel was poised there, partially touching an incline in the farmland, maintaining perfect balance. How magnificent it was to observe that huge form landing softly without a sound. Completing its noiseless descent, it looked as if it were floating weightlessly above the ground.

As I stood there astonished, Mr. M said to me, *Let's go now.* As he started to walk in the direction of the ship I quickly followed him.

With Mr. M at the front, followed by myself and our four companions, we walked single file toward the ship. When we had gone about 30 meters, someone came out of the ship. As we kept approaching, a faint buzzing sound like that of a motor running could be heard from the vessel. Mr. M, who was walking about three meters ahead of me, seemed to be exchanging a few words with the man who had come out of the vessel. Suddenly the buzzing sound stopped.

From where I was then standing, about two meters behind Mr. M and the man from the space vessel, I could see the two of them talking together. The person talking with Mr. M was a young man with an oval-shaped face. Like the five other cosmic humans, he looked Japanese and he also communicated in our language.[9]

29

Taking off his cap, the young man casually nodded to us. He had a very cheerful air about him. He was a little shorter than Mr. M and had beautiful eyes that conveyed a sense of purity and honesty. Though no words were spoken, I felt very close to him, as if he too had been a friend of mine from the past.

He was about 165 centimeters tall, taller than me but shorter than Mr. M. I was not sure whether he had just learned about my joining their flight or if he had known about it beforehand. He turned toward the space vessel and began to walk, motioning for us to follow him. As I said earlier, the vessel seemed to be floating in the air with part of its huge body touching the ground. This became more obvious to me as I came closer to it. The entire body seemed to be made of a solid metal substance that seemed rather like a cross between stainless steel and a dark-colored pure gold. Its awe-inspiring image stood out starkly against the backdrop of the slope.

Boarding the Vessel

The bottom of the vessel was curved and without legs. About two thirds of the area of the bottom of the vessel protruded downwards to form the base. The entire craft was shaped like a straw hat, with the uppermost peak being about two meters across. Before I knew it, the young man walking in front reached the vessel and a door opened automatically, as if of its own accord, revealing an entrance about one meter wide. Something resembling steps were suspended from the entrance that was about one meter above the ground. We entered one after another, following the young man: Mr. M, then I, followed by our other four companions. When we had all boarded, the door shut silently.

A soft, fluorescent type of light shone inside the room from an unknown source. There seemed to be several floors and quite a lot of rooms in the vessel. After walking along a corridor for about 10 meters, we came to an open door on the right. We walked through it into a room about 70 meters square.

At the center, there were two tables, each about one meter wide and five meters long. Mr. M sat in the main seat at the center, with the other companions seated on either side of him. I sat across from Mr. M. The young man went out of the room, nodding slightly to Mr. M.

The design of the chairs was simple but they were very comfortable to sit in. There were some thirty of them and from that I judged that the size of the crew must be approximately the same number. One question after another sprang to my mind. I did not know which one to deal with first. The young man came back to the room bringing some medium-sized drinking glasses and placing one by each of us.

The glasses were transparent and the liquid in them looked like ordinary water. However, it had a very pleasant fragrance. Inviting me to drink, Mr. M began sipping his own drink. When I brought the glass to my lips, I realized that the beverage had a consistency thicker than water. It was not an alcoholic drink, however. After taking a couple of sips, I felt greatly refreshed, and drank the rest down in a gulp. After I had been served this unusual beverage, all my earlier confusion and surprise disappeared and I felt physically invigorated and overflowing with energy.

Mr. M began to speak in a serious tone:

Now I would like to give you some basic information about this vessel. This vast, limitless universe is moving according to a certain

31

order, under one power. Ramifications of this one central power appear in a myriad of forms throughout the great universe. Not even one of the billions of stars and planets scattered throughout the universe is outside the control of this power that pervades space in all directions. We might call this power 'the Law' or 'God.' This space vessel can move freely when this power works upon it.

Though I thought I understood the logic, I could not feel wholly convinced until I had some practical examples. Sensing my consternation, Mr. M rose to his feet saying, *Let me show you a part of the central system.*

I stood up too and followed Mr. M out of the room.

The Core of the Vessel

This time we proceeded along the same corridor as before, but in the opposite direction. The corridor seemed to go around the core of the vessel which, I thought, might be a cylindrical room about seven or eight meters in diameter. As I followed Mr. M with these conjectures swimming through my mind, we came to a staircase and went up to the next floor. Again, there was a curved corridor that went around a cylindrical room, though its circumference appeared to be a little smaller than that on the floor below. After we had walked for about five or six meters, Mr. M looked back at me with a smile. A door opened silently, and we went through it into a small room. The door closed again without a sound. The room ascended a little like an elevator, lifting us up to an adjoining room.

When we reached the room, I realized that this was the top floor. It was dome-shaped, with a fairly high platform at its center. A chair was fixed to the platform, with a horseshoe-shaped desk around it. The desk was equipped with a number of measuring devices. There was a shining, white rectangular meter in the middle, with several cylindrical ones shining like florescent lights on either side of it, along with some additional devices resembling the gauge I had received earlier. The back of the chair was like a flat pillar about 10 centimeters thick and extended all the way to the ceiling. The center of the ceiling was about two meters higher than the rest of the ceiling. The walls were light gray. Mr. M explained that this was the control room. He also informed me that the captain was now taking a rest in one of the rooms downstairs.

He explained that the top of the pillar could be freely extended or retracted from the ceiling. Its function, he said, was similar to that of a powerful radar system. The energy on which the spacecraft operated could not be adequately explained in terms such as magnetic or electromagnetic waves but, for want of better alternatives, I will tentatively use these terms.

There was a cross-shaped symbol, a sort of powerful magnet used to catch cosmic or magnetic waves emanating from the origin of the great universe. The cosmic waves were intercepted within the frames of the projected cross, then passed through the surface of a convex lens. From there they flowed via the induction pillar and captain's chair into the captain's brain stem. Mr. M described these waves using terms like cosmic waves, light waves, and micro light waves. The top of the dome also intercepted cosmic waves. Looking up, I could partially see some apparatus around the top of the dome, forming the communications equipment that enabled the vessel to communicate freely with fellow vessels, mother ships, and various planets.

Several of the rectangular and cylindrical meters in front of the control chair kept twinkling and flashing in a myriad of patterns while Mr. M spoke. He explained that the central figure in the space vessel was the captain, who seemed to be mainly in charge of steering. Cosmic waves intercepted by the receiver were directly transmitted to the captain's body and mind. After being assimilated into the captain's spiritual waves, they were transmitted to the control lever, flowing next into the amplifier. The amplification room was located right below the control room.

There were a great many buttons on the desk in front of the captain's chair. When Mr. M pushed one of them, the wall of the dome suddenly became transparent, making me feel as if we were floating in the air. It was as if we were in a sunroom enclosed by glass. We could clearly see the scenery around us. Unable to contain my surprise, I let out a spontaneous *Wow!*

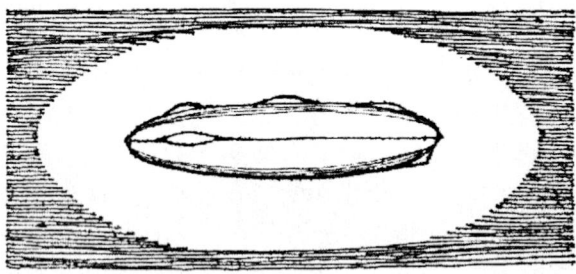

Figure 1. One type of mother ship that navigates the great universe

Hearing my exclamation, Mr. M commented with a smile, *We use this only when approaching a fellow craft, mother ship or planet. Since we can freely communicate with them while flying in space, we do not need to use it then.*

At that point the milk-white light on the horseshoe-shaped desk attracted my attention. Noting my interest, Mr. M explained, *If you push the button, you can look into the interior of the rooms on the lower three floors. They are all projected here, so you can monitor the entire vessel without leaving this room.*

My mind was still brimming with questions but Mr. M began to walk on, saying, *Next I'll show you the amplification room.*

As we approached the small room we had previously used for ascending, the wall opened silently. It shut as soon as we were inside the room and opened again after our smooth descent. We were now at the entrance of the amplification room. The ceiling was flat and the room seemed to be cylindrical, about six meters in diameter. From the center of the ceiling hung a shaft about 75 centimeters in diameter and one meter in length. The room was a little more than three meters high, from floor to ceiling, and there was a shaft holder fixed to the floor. In the middle of the shaft, a huge, yellow-white object, like a top, was spinning at tremendous speed, and the shaft quivered slightly as it hung from the ceiling. I will tentatively refer to this shaft as a gyrocompass.

At the opposite end of the room, I could see square frames that looked like boxes stacked one on top of the other, each of them containing a gauge. Mr. M explained, *That is the amplifier. The end of the control lever, steered by the captain, is connected to the top of the gyrocompass.*

The gyrocompass was spinning at a fairly high speed, making a low buzzing sound. As I studied it I estimated it to be spinning 20 to 30 per cent faster than the average 1400 rotations per minute of an ordinary electric motor. Mr. M explained, *The principle behind the spinning of this gyrocompass is the same as that of a motor where electric energy is changed to mechanical energy through the interaction of a magnetic field with an electric circuit.*

There were a number of gauges and scales on the curved wall. As I looked at them in amazement, the cosmic person who had earlier instructed me on the use of the gauge I was carrying came and stood beside me. I did not recognize him at first, since he had been behind the gyrocompass. He moved toward me, welcoming me with a smile and saying, *Since the captain is taking a rest now, light waves are extracted from the battery to spin the gyrocompass.* As he spoke, he pointed toward something on the wall behind him that looked like a square box.

I see. Is this the battery? Nodding in response to my question, he began to explain the basic theory relating to the gyrocompass and the space vessel.

The Gyrocompass and the Crystal Spheres

The cosmic person explained:

Through the captain, cosmic waves are changed into light waves. Their speed is equalized with that of the captain's spiritual waves. The captain's spiritual waves serve as the power source for steering the vessel. Through the regenerator, the light waves are converted into micro-light waves. Next, the micro-light waves are converted into electromagnetic waves through a powerful electromagnetic device. These waves are then given repelling warp. This repellence is strongest within the immediate area of the spaceship, in an area three to five times the radius of the ship, and is constantly protecting the vehicle.

Various changes in the electromagnetic waves enable the free and continuous operation of the craft. The energy of cosmic rays, gravitational force and air are also controlled by the electromagnetic waves.

You may conclude that the electromagnetic waves are the life of the vessel. In fact, however, these very important electromagnetic waves first go through various changes inside this gyrocompass. Having said this, for some reason that was not clear to me he remained silent for a while and then resumed his talk.

The theory behind the spinning of the gyrocompass is the same as that of an electric motor. Light waves coming from the captain enter the core of the compass via the transmission shaft. There is a strong magnetic pole at both the upper and lower end of the gyrocompass. Both poles have a minus charge. Although each is affected by the repelling force of the other, additional centrifugal force from the revolutions of the compass maintains the balance.

From the center of the axis of the compass, stretching outside the magnetic poles at right angles, are cross-shaped belts. At the end of each belt, two umbrella-shaped plates that connect with each other at the top spin round the axis. Right now the plates are about one meter in diameter, but they can be freely expanded or contracted by adjusting the speed of the revolutions.

The umbrellas are made of a lightweight metallic substance and have a powerful magnetic charge. Many layers of thin plates, resembling the feathers of a bird, cover the surface of the large umbrellas. No power in the universe and no cosmic waves can penetrate to the inside of those umbrellas. This is what guarantees the unrestricted movement of the electromagnetic waves. At each end of the cross-shaped belts extending from the axis of the gyrocompass, there is a crystal-like sphere about 7.5 centimeters in diameter. The crystal spheres are very sensitive and their function is to generate the perfectly free movement of the vessel, whether horizontal, upward, downward or diagonal, through the revolutions of the compass. He said only that much, not mentioning the inner structure of the crystal spheres.

The gyrocompass was revolving horizontally at that time. However, as he explained to me, the shapes of the revolutions change according to directional changes of the space vessel in flight. He added that the sensitive functions of the crystal spheres also went through various changes, depending on the mental waves of the captain.

The Regenerator Room

I thanked the cosmic person profusely and left the room accompanied by Mr. M.

Mr. M explained that we would next go to the regenerator room. We entered a small room that looked like an elevator. There were two round meters and a cylindrical device in the room. The cylinder was casting a light blue hue like a florescent light. As the door opened and shut, a ring of light about two centimeters thick twinkled inside the cylinder. As I watched, the ring moved upward and downward.

Although no light source was visible in any of the rooms we had visited, all the rooms in the craft were equally bright.

The door opened smoothly and we found ourselves inside the regenerator room. In the middle of the room was a large cylindrical tank about five meters in diameter. With a round pillar about one meter in diameter at its center, the tank was divided into seven sections. The light waves induced from the amplification room above were guided to the center of the tank. The walls of the tank seemed to be about 30 centimeters thick. The center of the bottom of the tank was about 40 centimeters higher than elsewhere, surrounding the conducting tube that hung down from above. In each of the seven parts of the tank there was a gauge fixed on the side of the central pillar.

Mr. M glanced back at me and said, *The core of this one-meter pillar is the conducting tube and it is surrounded by magnetic poles. At the bottom of the pillar, the light waves that have passed through these magnetic poles are discharged through something like a vacuum tube. The tester we have brought with us is made to react to this electric discharge.*

In this room there was another young man and he greeted us with a smile.

As I mentioned earlier, the 30-centimeter deep tank was divided into seven parts. Each of these contained a translucent, gelatinous, light blue substance. The light waves descending from the gyrocompass were discharged from the center of the regenerator tank like electric waves and dispersed into these seven sections. I was deeply impressed by the beauty of the waves emanating from the center.

The farther away from the center, the wider the sections of the tank became; each section was divided by four interception plates going from the center of the rim to the outer rim. During the entire time we were watching, the electric discharges continued non-stop. Carefully studying the discharges, I noticed they were not consistent from one section to the next.

The moment I began to contemplate why this was so, Mr. M explained, *The reason why the space vessel can maintain a horizontal position as if floating, even after it has landed, is that light waves from the battery tank are continuously being discharged and converted into electromagnetic waves. You can see the distribution of these waves in the regenerator tank.*

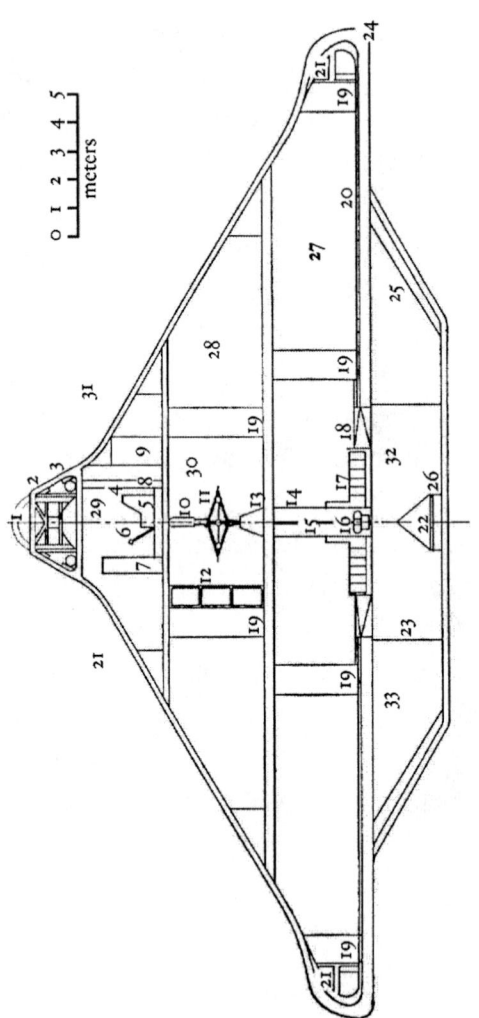

Figure 2. Cross Section of a space vessel

(1) cosmic wave receiver, (2) receiver, (3) transmitter, (4) guiding device, (5) captain's chair, (6) control lever (7) image receivers, (8) meter box (9) elevator, (10) expandable and retractable axis, (11) amplifier (12) battery tanks, (13) shaft rest (14) magnetic pole, (15) guiding pole, (16) electric discharge tube, (17) regenerator tank, (18) control box, (19) control box, (20) guiding line, (21) magnetic wave discharger, (22) telescope, (23) image monitor, (24) magnetic wave discharging tubes, (25) staircase, (26) magnetic plate for use in base hangar, (27) main hall, (28) lounge, (29) control room, (30) amplifier room, (31) regenerator room, (32) observation room, and (33) storeroom.

Pointing the tester in the direction of a gauge at the center, Mr. M turned the switch on. As he did so, a fluorescent-like light illuminated an oval plate. Next, a light ring ascended from the base. Mr. M explained, You can estimate the quantity of electromagnetic waves existing in this part of the spacecraft from the color and ascending speed of the light ring.

The Secret of the Magnetic Belt Surrounding the Vessel

Mr. M went on to say:

The energy converted into micro-light waves is controlled at the next stage. The waves are absorbed into the section of the regenerator terminal which, from the outside, is funnel-shaped and looks somewhat like an old-fashioned radio speaker. Inside the tank, the micro-light waves pass through many layers of powerful magnetic shielding like a transformer, reaching the rim of spaceship's 'hat.'

If you look at the cross-section map of the vessel, you will get a better idea. The energy of the spacecraft comes from two sources: the rim of the 'hat' and the metallic exterior. A strong emanation is emitted, especially at the rim. This emanation is accompanied by a tremendous quantity of vibrations, but we do not feel them because the wavelengths are too short and rapid to be perceived.

Shortly after, he summed up his remarks by saying:

The relationship between the individual parts and the whole is something that we commonly recognize. The outflow of energy from the rim of this spacecraft resembles the function of human skin, where each cell functions individually while keeping a harmonious relationship with the whole. Thousands of electromagnetic waves are continuously emitted from the rim, each having its own individual curve or warp. Under the control of a concentrated supervisory body, the waves function in unison, like the countless threads of a woven textile, maintaining perfect harmony with the whole.

I wondered whether there was some mechanism at the core of the vessel that expanded or reduced the size of the magnetic belt (electromagnetic waves) surrounding the craft. Though I wanted to know more details about these things, as well as the theory behind the central supervisory body, Mr. M did not elaborate further.

The words Mr. M had spoken when we first boarded the craft suddenly flashed through my mind. He had said he was going to provide me with a basic explanation as to how the space vessel operated. *Oh, yes!* I realized, *The general overview that he has given me certainly covers the basics. Thank you, Mr. M!* Thoughts of gratitude welled up from the bottom of my heart.

There is another floor downstairs, but I will show it to you another time. Having said this, Mr. M went out of the regenerator room. I also left it firmly believing that I would have another opportunity to come to this room later on. We went out into the corridor using the elevator that we had earlier used to enter the room. After walking along the corridor for some time, we came to another room. With the push of a button, the door opened without a sound. It was a room about 17 meters square. A number of astronomical maps, each measuring about two meters in height and four meters in width, were on the wall. There was a round table at the center of the room with four comfortable armchairs around it.

The Observational Television

What I noticed first in visiting the various rooms inside the spacecraft was that every room had one wall with a framed rectangular section illuminated with a milk-white glaze. The rectangles looked like picture frames embedded in the walls.

This room also had a frame about the size of a large television screen and was situated between two astronomical maps.

It looked similar to the one in front of the control lever in the captain's room on the top floor. The frames in the other rooms, however, were smaller. They were approximately one third the size of the one in the captain's room.

Mr. M began to speak while pointing at the monitor,:

This has the same function as the televisions that are widely used on Earth these days. The images received through the astronomical telescope at the center of the lowermost floor are magnified by the reflecting mirror. After being recorded and converted into micro-light waves, they are then reproduced on the screen.

With the simple touch of a switch while they are at their work stations, the crew can obtain detailed information on the movements of faraway stars and planets and their mutual planetary relationships.

If you want to observe a specific planet, you may approach it to some extent in order to investigate its conditions at close range.

This vessel is medium-sized and is used for flights originating from a nearby base or a mother ship. Some of the medium-sized vessels can conduct flights lasting two to three months while others can sustain longer flights lasting one to two years. In size, the vessels can range from as small as 30 centimeters in diameter to as large as several kilometers in diameter, each purpose-built with its own particular functions.

For instance, when it is too dangerous to approach an object, we send a small vessel that can be remote-controlled. This small vessel is equipped with extremely sensitive recording apparatus that records in detail the conditions and all vibrations of the object. The records are immediately reproduced on the television screen in the mother ship so they can be studied. When the observation has been completed, the small craft is picked up by the mother ship.

I became curious as to whether this medium-sized vessel could also send out smaller craft. No sooner did I think of it than Mr. M sensed my question and added to his explanation:

Of course, this medium-sized vessel has the ability to receive craft and it also has a store of various information disks.

The Earth's surface has been under observation for an indefinitely long period of time by innumerable large and small vessels and mother ships.

The planetary position of a number of heavenly bodies, like the Earth for example, is determined by the Law so as to maintain perfect, widespread harmony while carrying on mutual complementary relationships with other planets. This is fairly difficult to explain, but let me try. Imagine what would happen if unharmonious waves surged up on even one of those planets? For example, what do you suppose would happen if human beings on Earth, who are originally brothers and sisters, kept perpetuating a history of murder and strife, and, on top of that, endlessly continued extremely harmful experimenting with atomic and hydrogen bombs? Whether experimental or not, the radioactive contamination of the air caused by those explosions would remain on Earth for a very long period of time, disrupting the balance of the Earth's atmosphere. This would greatly affect the other planets and stars, not to mention the solar system to which the Earth belongs.

Being deeply conscious of this fact, people from advanced planets have been steadily keeping an eye on the Earth. Humanity is making a terrible mistake in continuing to conduct atomic and hydrogen explosions, which they describe as 'experimental.' From the cosmic point of view, they are like children playing dangerously with fire. When faced with adversity, it is highly probable that they might lose all logical judgment and actually use those bombs, even at the risk of causing a wholly predictable catastrophe far more devastating than anything that has occurred since the beginning of the Earth's history.

Being well aware of that danger, we have been actively working on Earth not only to save Earthly mankind from impending disaster, but also to avert the damaging effects to other planets in the same solar system. This explains the appearance of our space vessels.

How calm and tranquil Mr. M's way of speaking was. The indescribable warmth radiating from his clear eyes enveloped me completely.

At present, tens of thousands of vessels are continuously flying close to the Earth's surface to carry out their respective investigations. These vessels are active in realms outside the visual range of Earthly human beings.

Realms outside our visual range? Now, what could that mean? Noting this question as it passed through my mind, Mr. M went on explaining:

It is commonly known on Earth that electric waves speed around the planet seven and a half times per second. Though you cannot see or feel these electric waves with your physical senses, no one can deny their existence once they have been converted into pictures, letters, and sounds by way of television, radio, wireless equipment and so on. The same logic applies to the realms beyond one's visual range. I hope this helps a little to answer your question.

I know that Earthly mankind has succeeded in taking pictures of the other side of the moon by launching a cosmic stationary rocket. This is extremely helpful, not only in observing the reverse side of the moon, but also in taking a step forward in the study of the great universe.

45

Yet, in spite of all that, how preoccupied Earthly human beings have been with superficial matters only! They are eternally chasing after their immediate interests and nothing else. This is because they have been oblivious to their own true essence. Still, the success they have had with space exploration has had a very positive influence, giving hope to Earthly mankind that they might be able to go to the moon in several years, and turning many people's thoughts toward the vast universe.

To us, the 400,000-kilometer distance between the Earth and the moon seems no greater than the short distance between two outstretched arms. Yet it is extremely difficult for what is in the right hand to know, on its own, what is in the left hand. Even if the right and left hands come together and make direct contact, true mutual understanding is still difficult. This is because each side knows too little about itself, not to mention the other.

For us, everything—be it right or left—exists inside the One Being. This is because neither the right nor the left is a separate, independent being that exists all alone. It demonstrates its meaning and value only as a part of the One Being, or in its unity with the center. This is because both right and left work as outward functions of the One Being.

Though we don't underestimate these direct contacts between parts of the whole, in the ultimate sense we see them as no more than temporary phases or steps to be passed through. Yet, being convinced that direct contacts are all there is, many scientists on Earth just rush recklessly toward their object. When they reach a certain point, however, some of the perceptive ones will realize that the direct contacts are in error, since they inevitably result in collisions with a huge, thick wall that is beyond their capacity to break through.

I must admit, however, that the pragmatic method of science on Earth played a very important role in bringing Earthly science up to its present level, though it lags behind the science on other planets.

In the Christian Bible, there is a description of a seven-headed monster, with words to the effect that a time will come when the seven-headed monster will come out of the sea and trample over the Earth. This is to say that when the advances of material science reach their zenith, the world returns to its ancient, primitive condition. Civilization will regress by millions of years, starting all over again from the glacial period. Earthly mankind has experienced such regressions several times already, but...

Having said this much, Mr. M held back his words with a tense expression. I waited with bated breath for him to continue.

Oh, Friend from Earth!

Mr. M resumed his narrative:

However, you no longer have the option of repeating the same experience one more time. As the gradual shift in the Earth's axis shows, there is a shift in the control system of the Earth's relationships with other planets. One of the Earth's cycles has just been completed.

Just as with Earthly children who have slowly grown up to become adults, the path the Earth has traced for the past several hundred millions of years is coming to an end, soon to be replaced by another, new way. This is why entirely unprecedented changes are gradually occurring on the Earth's surface. This is known only to small groups of people, but the incidents are steadily increasing in scale with the majority of the population remaining unaware of them. Mysterious conditions beyond the ken of contemporary science will start taking place. These result from the Earth's cyclic

47

changes, and they may cause fear, uncertainty and confusion that Earthly mankind has never experienced before. Whether liberals, communists, or neutralists, all humanity is at risk of being engulfed in upheavals of chaos and confusion.

Since we cosmic beings are well aware of what could happen, we have been steadily praying for humanity to be emancipated from its confusion and mistaken ideas.

Earthly mankind, too, is a member of cosmic humanity. You are our friends, still in the infancy of your development and with an infant's knowledge. Oh, friends on Earth, call out to us. We will most willingly lend you a helping hand.

We will definitely go wherever we are called, to whomever is asking for our help. Though, when we appear to you, we may take a variety of forms, we will show our real selves to those who truly understand us. Then our wisdom and power will be yours.

This wisdom and power will be extremely useful in liberating many people from confusion and misunderstanding. So you need not worry. Earthly friends, if together we exert our joint efforts, before long, the most narrow-minded on Earth will come to see the error of their ways and, when they do so, they will take one great leap forward in their evolution. The dawning of a new era will come and a great illumination of mankind will be witnessed by all on Earth.

Some people have called this the 'Golden Age of Earth,' but many seem to misinterpret what this means. Some seem to take the 'Golden Age' to mean the satisfaction of people's endless, egotistic greed. The actual truth is quite different from this. 'Golden Age' refers to the time when Earthly mankind will awaken to its own true nature.

As you may have realized from watching the precision equipment of this space vessel operate and the crew members work in per-

fect order under the supervision of one leader, the captain, only when each individual makes the most of his or her own abilities can the whole function effectively and harmoniously. This is how an individual unites with or works for the whole. If you can understand this, the dawning and birth of a wonderful age will only be a matter of time. However, a birth is inevitably accompanied by some level of pain. When a major truth is about to manifest itself, it inevitably evokes conflicting views that can interfere with its emergence. This is a great challenge that Earthly mankind will have to rise above. Oh, my dear friend! Please, please be assured that the 'Golden Age' will most certainly come to Earth. Be courageous enough to face the darkness and disharmony and march forward. When you run into difficulty, just call us. We will come to your aid without fail. Please believe in this no matter what. We earnestly hope that more and more people will understand our sincere intentions and will join hands with us, my blessed friend.

Moved to the point of tears, I firmly grasped Mr. M's two hands that were held out to me.

There was a heavenly, spiritual aura surrounding Mr. M as he finished speaking, and an incandescent light surpassing all description radiated unceasingly from his eyes. Each and every portion of his message, ending with the words 'my blessed friend,' resonated to the bottom of my soul. Even now, the words still reverberate in my heart. I felt that my past had vanished away, amidst an ocean of radiant truth.

In the meantime, the young man who had entered the room earlier poured something for me to drink and then left. As I began to drink at the invitation of Mr. M, I spotted a cylinder in one corner of the room, which I had paid little attention to until now. No sooner had a light suddenly started to twinkle than a ring of light began to ascend inside it.

49

The Vessel Leaves the Earth

When I asked what the signal light indicated, how surprised I was to hear him say quite casually, *Our vessel has left Earth.* The vessel had lifted off without the slightest jolt or rocking motion. Had it not been for the ascent signal, I would have noticed nothing at all.

Suddenly wondering what might become of me and feeling a little uneasy, I could not help asking where we were headed.

Glancing at me with a smile, Mr. M stood up from his chair and walked a few steps to the astronomical map behind him. As soon as he touched the switch, the entire map seemed to go into motion with an animated interplay of contrasting lights and shades of colors. *Ah!* I exclaimed quite spontaneously.

The scenery changed dramatically. It was like the electric lights of the city that suddenly come on at dusk. Here they came on with a brilliance clearly showing the depth of the great universe through a deep stereoscopic effect.

This astronomical map shows the interplanetary relationships, with our solar system placed at the center. However, even these countless stars and planets are but a mere fraction of all that comprises the universe. I would like to add a comment here. Knowing the color of each planet or star, be it its own light or the reflected light of another heavenly body, is very important. You will find this extremely useful later. With these mysterious words, Mr. M concluded his explanation.

Just like the planets of our solar system, other planets make up other solar systems. While moving around a sun or star, the entire solar system revolves in an orbit that travels around a greater center. This is how a great solar system moves. This great solar system again serves as the component of an even greater solar system and continues to move accordingly. In this way, the number of planets and stars increases astronomically.

A shining star, like the sun which radiates its own light, and bodies like the Earth, the moon, and Mars, that receive and reflect light, form units linked with the greater center. The map is well designed to give viewers an at-a-glance perspective of this linkage with the origin of the great universe.

The space between two stars is pitch black. If you enter the sphere of a solar system, you see the particular brightness emitted by the sun. And each planet, reflecting the sun's light, also has its own particular color. This may be due to the atmosphere that surrounds each planet. I was simply awestruck by the sight in front of me, which defied all description.

Watching the screen as I stood beside Mr. M, I completely forgot that we were inside the space vessel. Looking at the panorama of planets and stars, I felt as if I had been thrown into the middle of the great universe.

Suddenly I returned from my reveries and found Mr. M standing there, still smiling. He pointed in one direction and said, *We are here.* At the lower left side of the astronomical map, I saw a small shining red dot, moving slowly with a slight trail behind it. I could immediately recognize that it showed the flight of our spacecraft. Having left the Earth, our vessel was heading towards Venus.

Mr. M briefly looked back at me and said, *We will return to Earth without going too far today.*

Although he did not say it was because there was a newcomer on board, I felt that it was implied. Watching the astronomical map never tired me. I was totally engrossed by the great relief map with its three-dimensional effects that reflected the depth and size of the great universe. As I stood there entranced, Mr. M suggested, *Let me show you the astronomical telescope,* and stepped out of the room.

The map was so intriguing that I could not take my eyes off it as I followed him out of the room.

We walked along the corridor for a little while and got on the elevator. In a short time we found ourselves on the lower-most floor.

A Telescope that Translates Languages,
Manners and Customs

It was a round room about eight meters in diameter. The central part of the floor was elevated about fifty centimeters, and was largely occupied by an astronomical telescope measuring about two meters in diameter. Various gauges surrounded it. I had the impression that there was more equipment contained in the ceiling, but I could not say for sure.

Mr. M began to speak in his usual, calm tone:

Unlike the optical telescopes that are presently used on Earth, this astronomical telescope catches and reproduces the vibrations of objects at distances unimaginable to people on Earth. Using this, a person can study a distant object as if it were at close range. Special waves are emitted onto the target object and are reflected back. Through amplification and magnification, the waves are converted into images and sound waves. I think this may give you some idea of how this astronomical telescope works. After saying this, Mr. M seemed to be contemplating something for a short while.

At this point a question arose in my mind as to whether such things as languages, social systems, manners and customs on other planets could be easily understood through the telescope, not to mention the lifestyles of people who had made exceptionally marvelous achievements.

I brought these issues up to Mr. M, saying:

I can understand your explanation of vibrations quite well, I think, but I am just wondering whether this telescope alone can enable us to understand what is happening on highly advanced planets.

Words are unnecessary for us, he replied. Do you think that spoken words can fully and truly express what a person wants to communicate? Oftentimes, they fail to convey a person's true intentions accurately. Likewise, a person's body language or the expression in a person's eyes communicates only a limited range of meaning. By means of vibrations though, we can fully communicate our intentions to one another, just as they are. A language transcending words, communication through vibrations is our cosmic language. With this, we can make ourselves clearly and accurately understood to people living on other planets, and their vibrations are also conveyed to us regardless of time and space. They are transmitted as quickly as lightning, without the risk of any misunderstanding.

Now, the vibrations reproduced through this astronomical telescope are shown as images and words. The languages, manners and customs of each country are intercepted in the form of light waves and are reproduced to match thought waves. Just as if you were tuning a radio by turning a dial, you can reproduce information that is adjusted to the particular thought waves on that planet, so there is nothing difficult about it.

Also, there are two methods of projection used through this telescope. One is direct projection on a lens and the other is projection on a screen via reflecting mirrors. You can choose either method, depending on your objectives.

53

Having said this, Mr. M suggested that I sit on a nearby chair, as he touched one of the switches on the telescope. Suddenly, the color inside the room changed dramatically. The scenery projected on the screen was absolutely spectacular, showing a portion of the great universe observed through the astronomical telescope.

Stars and Planets are Alive

Mr. M went on speaking with a quiet smile as I sat, still amazed at the scenery that had appeared on the screen.

This image is projected using the reflecting reproduction method. It visualizes the entire image of the great universe. That is, it gives us a deep and expansive, cosmic view.

With this method, you can easily understand the relationships among stars and planets both inside and outside our solar system. They move while maintaining close relationships with one another.

The explanation was so extensive and deep that, as I listened, I felt as if I were wandering in a dreamlike world. In fact, the main part of my attention was focused on the visual image rather than on the words I was hearing.

In the great universe projected on the screen, there were innumerable stars and planets, scattered in pitch dark space. As with the stars we had observed on the astronomical map, the twinkling ones, like the ones we see from Earth, were stars observed at a great distance. Others had radiant rings of light around them. When fireflies fly lightly through the sky on early summer nights, with tails of light behind them, there seem to be rings of light around them, several times larger than their luminous bodies. Looking very much the same, stars and planets have bodies of light surrounding them. And none of those bodies of light are the same color.

The stars and planets that were scattered in front of my eyes were all in a state of continuous animation, each followed by a tail of light of its own particular color. There was such variety in the color and size of the bodies, their tails of light, the lines, speed and direction of their orbits as they moved from right to left, up, down, or diagonally upward to one side or another! Observing these features that were unique to each planet, I could only feel that all the stars and planets were alive—bodies of life filled with vitality. Our notion of our planet has been based on a concept of mother Earth as a huge, solid mass of minerals covered by mountains, rivers and seas. It is hard for us to imagine that the Earth, mountains and rivers are pulsating with life and have an energy of their own. Yet the planets I was observing completely overturned this notion. I could see them in no way other than as bodies of life filled with boundless energy.

Just as human beings on Earth have stages of life, such as infancy, youth, middle and old age, the stars and planets appear to have their own stages too. Young stars, full of vigor, are extremely clear and shine whitish-blue. In astronomy class, we had been taught that the age of a star is judged by the color of its light. I confirmed that this was not incorrect. It is certainly true. The more closely I studied the colors of the stars and planets, the more strongly inclined I was to think that a star or a planet was essentially the same as a human being. I suspected that each star or planet had its own mission. This mission, in harmony with the thoughts of its inhabitants, seemed to produce the color of its light. These thoughts continued to pass through my mind.

The images on the screen constantly kept changing one after another, each revealing a fraction of the great universe.

Enchanted by the great universe that kept expanding on the screen, I felt myself wholly melting into it. I was completely oblivious to my own existence, and felt that, having become a star, I was flying through the great space of the universe.

A Human Being is a Universe

Suddenly, I returned to my usual self and reconfirmed the presence of Mr. M beside me. Smiling as usual, he began to speak:

This great universe is similar to the human body in its structure. Earthly scientists have said that a human body is composed of about 40 trillion cells. A large number of these cells band together to form an aggregate of cells which maintain a close and complex relationship with each other and together fulfill a certain function. The function which they perform is indispensable to the whole.

The stars and planets scattered throughout the universe are similar to these cells and, therefore, it is correct to say that a human being is a small universe. Cosmic humans understand that the great universe is the true body of a human being. In other words, the universe is the 'divine body' of a human being.

While listening to his words, various thoughts ran through my mind: *Which part of the human body do these stars, shining in pitch dark space, correspond to? Surely there must be worlds that shine more and more brightly as we go nearer to the center. The realm I am seeing now, reflected on the screen, must be just a fraction of the universe at its outer edges.*

As if aware of the questions going through my mind, Mr. M went on to say:

You are quite right. Conditions like worry, fear, hatred, sorrow and so on occur prior to a manifestation of truth. A truth proves to be a truth only when we have overcome those difficulties. There is no way for truth to manifest itself if it pervades everywhere from the beginning. The absolute cannot work simply by being absolute, nor can we recognize it as such. We understand what the absolute is only when it has been divided into relative entities.

Now, as you have guessed, the universe increases in brightness as you approach its center. The grand center of the universe is a vacuum, shining in whiteness.

Yes, it is the manifestation that counts. If there is only light, one cannot observe the light's existence. To let people know the light of truth or the white light of the central body, there must be darkness that contrasts with it. Then one can, for the first time, recognize the world of the light. You should not jump to the conclusion that there is nothing in the central vacuum, thinking it a void. It is a world where everything exists, a true reality. It is because everything exists in it that all is born from it. What truly exists is the absolute mind that serves as the origin of vibrations. The absolute mind is the perfect vacuum, shining white, and this is the great God.

Each human being has this perfect vacuum at the utmost depths of his or her own heart. The true vacuum is the reality of a human being. Prior to its manifestation, the true vacuum is surrounded by contrasting conditions that differ from truth, or God. Truth has thus been prevented from manifesting itself. This describes the present state of humanity on Earth. When we call you 'our young friends', we do not mean to belittle people on Earth in any way. We are simply referring to the stage where humanity is in its growth and evolution.

All of humanity is continuously proceeding along a path of limitless growth and evolution. Growth and evolution are the very essence or reality of humanity.

To attain our evolution, we have no alternative but to step through each stage one by one. There is no human population that does not evolve. Each entity of humanity is meant to experience each of these stages and, through their experiences, go on to attain their awakening. From physical, to spiritual, to divine experience, they go on accumulating experiences with their whole bodies and souls. In the midst of the flow of the great Life that has neither beginning nor end, we keep walking along the path of evolution that leads to an infinite future. This is the reality of humanity.

The Center of the Great Universe

The picture dramatically changed at the moment when he touched one part of the astronomical telescope. Just as if we had cast our sight in different directions through a pair of binoculars, the images across the screen changed at great speed. The pitch-black world changed to a world of pale white, like the sky just before dawn.

Clusters of stars zoomed into view, shining like blue sapphires. Their beauty was breathtaking. As each of these stars traced its own orbit, what was noticeable was that each one emitted its own unique color of light and displayed a short trail of light behind it.

The sky was now tinged with pink. The sight of the great, blue sky with a glow of pink was too beautiful for words. Again I found myself in awe of the sight before me.

The image changed drastically again, to scenery of sheer red like the crimson sky at sunset. The sight of the stars moving in their orbits in this dramatically colored sky was impressive indeed. They looked like spinning fireballs burning with energy. On the screen, the stars were flying, their tails of light glowing red like comets.

In my enthusiasm, I have described the planetary movements in Earthly terms, using words like left, right, upward and downward. Actually, though, there was no up or down. Nor was there any upward or downward motion. There was no way of dropping, since there was nowhere to fall. If you look at the stars flying in all directions, the direction a star is aiming in becomes the front, and the opposite direction becomes the back. Though my explanation is probably obvious even to a child, the true reality of the world I observed obliges me to set the matter straight.

The images on the screen continued to shift rapidly. From the clear, transparent brightness of a midsummer day, the light gradually changed as we approached the source of the light. I was struck by a sudden, piercing flash of light. It shone across the screen like a reflection of sunlight, through a mirror. Overcome by its intensity, I covered my face with both hands and fell down on the spot.

Fearful that the rays of that tremendous light might have damaged my vision, I timidly looked out from between my fingers. The great light had vanished, and everything was silent, as before. Yet the effects of the blinding radiance that had flashed across the retinas of my eyes had not disappeared.

I looked around and saw Mr. M, calm as usual, as if nothing had happened:

The great light we have just seen is only a glimpse of the light source of the great universe, caught by the astronomical telescope. The light source of the great universe is countless times stronger than the sun you see on the Earth. Next, let's have a look at the Earth using the direct method. At present, this vessel is flying between the Earth and Venus.

As he spoke, Mr. M busily turned a dial. After finishing the adjustment, he began to speak as he returned to the chair next to mine:

These days on Earth, people use microscopes to inspect minute objects. In just the same way, to observe a specific portion of the universe while staying inside the spacecraft, we let the object be reflected directly on the lens as if looking into a microscope. Now let's focus on Earth.

Even before he had finished uttering these words, the Earth was reflected on a lens about two meters in diameter. First looking like a gray baseball, the Earth grew larger and larger. As it grew bigger, I saw a large mass of black, but I was not sure if it was land or sea. Observing the Earth's surface through the atmosphere was not as clear as looking at a terrestrial globe; it was rather hazy and indistinct. The image gradually grew larger as if we were approaching it.

Meanwhile, it seemed as if the lens was focusing on a specific spot on Earth. It looked as if that spot was being gradually magnified. At last mountains and coastlines were clearly visible from an altitude of about 15,000 meters. Yes, they were the islands of Japan, and we were approaching them little by little. I was captivated by the images appearing on the screen.

This is a region you are quite familiar with. I am showing you this so you can see how cosmic humans look at the Earth. The scenes you will see next are related to your own actual life.

While listening to his words I looked at the scenery on the screen as if seeing it from about a hundred meters above sea level. The view moved along the coastline revealing beautiful green forests and white beaches with large and small waves lapping the coasts. I saw a small fishing village, an inlet, and a place where fishing boats were moored. There were roads and houses on either side. *Look! There you can see people, dogs and chickens!* Next I saw paved shining black roads and lines of cars traveling along them. Watching the cars that were plainly visible or partially hidden by the shadows of trees along the roadside was like looking at a miniature town. Next, I saw a fishing village. It was fairly big and had a fish market and factories. Several villages and towns like this came into view one after the other.

Finally we increased our altitude and looked over the sea from five or six hundred meters above. Fishing boats were scattered in the water, looking like birds. Among them, a cargo ship of about 3,000 tons seemed to be making its way back to port. Plowing through the waves, it headed straight for the port. Many more fishing boats and another cargo ship came in sight. It seemed that we were looking down at a part of Tokyo Bay. Forgetting that we were observing it from inside the space vessel, I had a momentary illusion that we were on an actual inspection flight of the area.

The scenery suddenly disappeared and I realized that Mr. M and I were standing in front of the telescope on the fourth floor of the basement inside the space vessel.

Well, that's all for today. Let's go back to the refreshment room, suggested Mr. M so we took the elevator to the refreshment room.

In Every Corner of the Earth People's Hearts

The images continued to flash through my mind as we made our way to the rest area. At all times, I realized, we human beings are visible to people in worlds that are invisible to us, worlds beyond our imagination. Not only do they see our each and every action but they must also see into the very

61

depths of our hearts! It reminded me of the old expression: 'Heaven only knows.' But who would have guessed at the existence of cosmic beings from distant worlds, millions of kilometers away, who always watch over us, even in the midst of our casual daily conversation!

How ashamed I felt as I thought of the childish ideas we Earthly human beings have. How often have we misbehaved in secret, thinking that as long as we were not seen, no one would know about our deeds. We have dismissed our actions as a matter of course, thinking 'Who cares as long as nobody sees? We're only human, after all!' This sort of attitude seems to have turned into an accepted way of thinking for most human beings. Before we are aware of it, ideas like these begin to exert a strong influence on our lives, and we unconsciously perpetuate this way of thinking and acting for a long, long time.

I remembered the conversations I had had with Mr. M, who seemed to have grasped my thoughts the instant they passed through my mind and then gave me detailed replies that were easy to understand. I learned that, from their bases, cosmic beings had sent mother ships and space vessels close to the Earth. Through those tens of thousands of space vessels, they must be monitoring the thoughts of all humankind on Earth and they must be well versed in the way we think. Yet, despite their knowing about our petty ways of thinking, my cosmic friends never showed any signs of it to me. This was, no doubt, because they knew how embarrassed it would have made me.

These cosmic people are compassionate enough not to cast shame on another human being. They are keenly aware that if they said something to us with good intentions but their words resulted in distressing us, that would go against the broader spirit of love. That is to say even if, by rights, something ought to be done in a certain situation, if it ends up agitating the person, what was originally a truth or a good can turn into a hindrance or a karmic[10] action that conflicts with truth. Cosmic beings are well aware of this.

My cosmic friends could easily see all that resided in the depths of my heart. They could easily draw out, from the layers of my subconscious, all my memories of things that had occurred even before my birth in this lifetime. What point would there be in trying to disguise myself in front of such enlightened beings? The only alternative I could see was to wholly relinquish my petty, small-scale self and trust in the depth of my cosmic friends' love and understanding. When I reached this conclusion, it brought me a great sense of relief.

Feeling a little tired, I sank into the sofa as soon as we came back to the sitting room.

I glanced at Mr. M, wondering how he felt. He seemed calm and showed no signs of fatigue. I felt an indescribable warmth emanating from his whole being. Reflecting on all I had seen and not able to suppress my enthusiasm, I exclaimed, *How wonderful the astronomical telescope is!*

Actually, he said, *what I have shown you is only a small part of its total function. It has much greater capabilities. I will show you more when we have another opportunity.* He then added, *Today has been an eventful day for you!*

Yes, the best day in my entire life! I can't find the words to thank you.

As he listened to me with his usual, cheerful expression, he seemed to be attentive to something on his left. Turning my eyes in that direction, I saw a rather large light flashing in a clock-shaped gauge on the wall. Looking at it, Mr. M rose and said with a smile, *Let's go see the captain now.*

Chapter 2

THE CAPTAIN SPEAKS

The Captain was a Beautiful Woman

Since I had thoroughly convinced myself from the beginning that I would never be able to meet the captain, I was taken by surprise at Mr. M's suggestion that we should go to see her. Of course, I willingly accepted and began to follow him.

We walked out of the room into the corridor and climbed the staircase to the second floor. We arrived at the doorway of a room opposite the one we had visited several times before. The door opened without a sound as Mr. M pushed a button at the entrance.

About 33 square meters in area, the room was shaped like a fan, with one end wider than the other. There was a rectangular table in the middle, covered by a deep green tablecloth made of fairly thick velvety material.

At the invitation of Mr. M, I sat in a chair at the far side of the table. As I took my seat, the other four cosmic beings with whom I had boarded the vessel came into the room. Each of them nodded to us with a smile and took a seat. Shortly after, three women entered the room, one in a black dress, one in a pink dress, and one in a rose-colored dress. With cheerful expressions, the men stood up all together and welcomed the women.

It was clear that the woman in the black dress was the captain. She was about 150 centimeters tall and was wearing an attractive, long dress. Her features were Asian, her complexion fair, her eyes and hair dark. Indeed, she looked no different from a Japanese woman. Framing her slightly round face, her short hair had a soft wave to it. With her seated in front of me, it seemed as if the room had suddenly brightened up. She appeared to be about 27 or 28 years old or even younger. The other two women looked as if they were 23 or 24. The three of them were similar in height; only the color of their dresses was different.

I had never expected an encounter with three such women inside the space vessel. For some reason, I suddenly felt like talking with them. Seeing them evoked in me a close, familiar feeling, despite the air of nobility that they all had.

The captain and I sat facing each other. To the right of the captain sat Mr. M and the four cosmic men; on the left were the two other women and the other cosmic man. When we were seated, the young man I mentioned earlier entered the room again, served each of us a drink, and left. Each of the glasses contained a pale yellow beverage. Once the drinks were served, everybody rose from their seats. A sense of tranquility enveloped the room as the captain's calm, clear and resonant voice echoed through the room:

We thank you, God, for your deep love and we pray for our beloved friend from Earth. We humbly ask that his mission may be safely accomplished so that the peace of the Earthly world may be realized as soon as possible.

All members of the party joined in prayer with their eyes closed. One minute, five minutes, ten minutes passed. It seemed as if each moment of prayer contained an eternal depth. Meanwhile, the cosmic people, whom I observed through my spiritual eyes, were shining with a transparent

66

purity, entirely devoid of selfish thought. The vibrations emitting from them were spreading like rings of waves through the room, radiating an ivory white light. I happened to open my eyes at one point during the prayer only to find that they looked no different from ordinary people.

After the prayer we all sat down again, experiencing the same tranquility that had enveloped the room earlier, like the surface of calm water.

We Cannot Ignore the Danger to Earthly People

The captain again began to speak in her clear, quiet voice:

It was a long time ago that we received divine permission to welcome you aboard this vessel. To our regret, however, we have not had the opportunity to do so until today. We are now overjoyed that our cherished wish has finally come true. Today we have shown you the inner systems of this vessel and given you information that you will be needing. I think you now have an overall idea of the basic workings of this vessel and of the universe too.

It is our sincere wish that your friends on Earth will attain an accurate understanding of the nature of God, of themselves, and of us at the earliest possible time. We have waited for such a long time for you to join our close circle of friends! Actually, I should say, to restore our long-lost friendship. We have indeed been praying for some time for this to come about. Of late we have also been keeping a close eye on Earth through the numerous methods and technology available to us.

Among the people on Earth, there might be some who criticize our initiative, saying: 'You are taking too much liberty in watching over us. We did not ask you to.' In answer to this I would say, 'When you see small children you love, so absorbed in their play that they are unaware that they are in danger, can you just stand by without saying anything? If you were in our situation, I believe you would do the same.

We cosmic humans are your brothers and sisters. We all descended from the same, one great Parent. However, while following diverse paths and going to excesses in the pursuit of self-centered happiness, too many human beings on Earth forgot about their brother-and-sister relationships with others. As their desire for self-preservation grew stronger, their consciences gradually became duller and insensitive, to the point where they brought their present conditions upon themselves.

The majority of the billions or trillions of stars and planets scattered throughout this great universe are also inhabited by human beings. Though their lifestyles differ according to their stages of evolution, the communication among the planets and stars has helped them to develop their strengths to make up for their shortcomings. This is what has helped them to develop so quickly.

This becomes possible when the population has a true understanding that people on all the planets and stars are brothers and sisters. Earthly humanity has been left isolated for a long time—like an 'orphan' within the universe—because people are not ready to understand and accept this truth. However, the day is drawing near when they can rejoin the circle of cosmic humankind in this great universe. This is due to a change in the sun itself. The earlier parental star that had been supervising the Earth and other planets in the solar system has been changed to a new one, with the agreement of the great universal God.

This change in supervisory stars, combined with recent developments in space science and technology, has turned the eyes of people on Earth toward the universe. Many people's thought habits are changing and not only from a phenomenal point of view.

Subconsciously, people are also deeply aware of the change in their supervisory star.

From now on our activities will become increasingly evident. We will begin to work with you in a number of ways. The time we have been awaiting for so long has finally come. You might think of it as the time right before a sudden afternoon shower on a summer day. With dark clouds hanging low in the sky, rain is ready to start pouring down at any moment. If lightning should flash through the sky at that time, people would expect a huge roar of thunder to follow. Just like this, right now on the Earth, there are strong signs of the dawning of a new, cosmic age, an age of the spirit.

One clear indication of this will be an increase in the number of people sighting space vessels in various locations all over the Earth. At the same time, however, it will be important to watch out for the appearance of so-called 'space people' falsely posing as cosmic beings. You must be able to recognize these self-styled impostors from low realms, whose aim is to trick people by taking advantage of their egotistic ways of thinking—a trait that still dominates the lives of a great many people on Earth.

The Activities of Cosmic Beings
Will Become More Noticeable

No matter which planet people are from, we know very well what their circumstances are and what is most important to them. We are well aware that the circumstances in which a person finds himself or herself are created by the vibrations of the person's own thought. To desire a sudden change in one's circumstances is a product of egotistic thought. But egotism can never be satisfied, even when a wish is fulfilled. What we are always hoping is that people will come to understand truth through their own experiences and circumstances.

Wherever we cosmic beings may appear on Earth, we adopt the language, manners, and customs of that country. We also make ourselves look the same as the people in that region physically. A cosmic being who appears in location 'A' does not necessarily look the same when appearing in location 'B.' You can never guide people toward truth if your appearance and mannerisms are different. It is only when you have completely blended in with the society of the people around you that you can begin to assist them.

From now on, the activities of cosmic beings will become more and more noticeable. This is because, due to the changes now occurring around the Earth, people will be exposed to a greater variety of vibrations that are new to them. In other words, they will be receiving very fine vibrations amidst the rough and coarse ones and this will bring about conditions never encountered before.

Since the fine vibrations that people are feeling are bound to find expression in one way or another, they will bring about changes in various facets of life including science, religion and art. Science will develop dramatically and there will be remarkable discoveries and innovations. In receiving scientific knowledge from advanced planets, people will start to sense how backward their Earthly science has been. They will also know that the traditional methods of proving hypotheses—which have served as their fundamental approach to research and learning—have tended to focus their attention on insignificant facts. The great, cosmic science that has been concealed behind a thick veil of mystery in this great universe until now will gradually be uncovered by Earthly scientists too. Although the scientists themselves will appear to have made the discoveries on their own, in reality, cosmic beings will have been at work within the thoughts of those people who have been bestowed with special missions, guiding them in a positive direction. The peo-

ple who are taught the mysteries of cosmic science will become guardians of the greatest power on Earth.

When I heard this, expressions like 'kings of Earth,' 'possessors of absolute power,' and 'greatest rulers' sprang to mind. Perceiving my thoughts, the captain went on to say:

They are neither kings of Earth nor possessors of absolute power. It would be a mistake to think of these people in that light. As we cosmic beings well know, only people who perform acts of deep humanitarian love will be allowed to learn those mysteries. Meanwhile, until that time comes, it will be essential for the Earth's population to free themselves of their erroneous, karmic way of thinking.

How can we achieve that? I wondered.

A Prayer Movement for World Peace

After emanating from their divine source and experiencing many rebirths, people eventually became trapped in thick shells of self-protectiveness and forgot about their identities as integral parts or entities of one divine life. Although human beings are meant to fulfill their missions on Earth cooperating with others who share the same calling, they have become blinded or impaired to such a degree that they are no longer able to recognize the very people who share their destiny even when they come into contact with them.

The only way for them to break out of their shells of karmic thought is to become reunited with God, the light of their original being. The divine spirits watching over the Earth wish for nothing more than peace in the world of Earthly mankind. Our own heartfelt desire for the peace of humanity naturally resonates from the vibrations of our hearts; our work is made easier in places where the vibrations are like ours. When many people with those peace-loving vibrations come together and unite toward one center, that center

71

will eventually become the place where our missions are accomplished.

As the number of those who pray for peace on Earth gradually increases and multitudes gather across the planet to offer their sincere prayers, humanity will witness a dramatic change. The Earth will enter a wonderful, golden age. At the prayer sites, special emissaries will reveal the science of marvelously advanced planets. Fields that had been separate, such as politics, religion, art, and science, will meld into one great current of light. This phenomenon will occur as part of the great evolution that makes mistaken views, outmoded doctrines, and antiquated moral codes become obsolete. It is nothing to fear. Be assured that all of this will occur naturally as human beings awaken to their own higher consciousness.

Total confusion may appear to reign on Earth, but the situation will give birth to a glorious, golden age.

From the depth of their subconscious memory, people will rediscover the ancient truth that they are all children of God. This awareness will allow them to see beyond their different paths to acknowledge their origin as brothers and sisters born from one great God. They will understand that their relationship with one another surpasses race, nationality, culture, and religion. How can anyone then think of warring against one's own brothers and sisters? When people begin helping each other, forgiving each other, and feeling joy in serving each other, a wonderful global nation will emerge on Earth.

Heretofore, human beings have had to work to survive, and they have had to struggle with others to do so. The development of cosmic science will dispel the dark past in which humanity has been constantly compelled to struggle. Social structures based on the systems and widely accepted ideas of the advanced planets will be adopted. Among other things, the development of science will reduce the time people work to one-tenth of the current hours. People will spend the remaining time deepening their knowledge and experience as well as cultivating their creativity.

People will also come to understand that death is like a journey. Even if a person goes on a trip or moves to a new residence, his or her true essence does not change. Death will be understood as the time when people become liberated from their feelings of attachment. The sorrow of death and separation will be completely forgotten as a past illusion.

Earth will join the advanced stars to emerge as a radiant, divine planet. The activities of the world peace prayer will spread as the motive force of this transformation.

Key Figures will Appear

The parental God, having well anticipated that the Earthly world would fall into its present catastrophic condition, assigned people various missions and sent them to many countries and regions of the world. The divine plan is to let those people wait for the right time to come in accordance with the flow of their own lives. Whether they are aware of their missions or not, these people will start working as key people in the movement toward peace. They will realize, without meeting or speaking with one another, that this movement will be the most effective way to illuminate this world that is presently enveloped in darkness. When they truly understand what their roles are, the movement for harmony will spread throughout the world like lightning. Coinciding with this, space vessels coursing through the sky will become visible to all observers and the work of cosmic humans will become more noticeable than ever. Anyone will be able to see us and speak with us.

As this intention of the parental God becomes gradually understood by Earthly humanity, personal misfortunes and diseases, as

73

well as poverty, will naturally disappear. They will not vanish all at once, though. People will come to realize that the troubles they experience are tests that they must undergo as they progress step by step. They will look upward toward a radiant world from their present state. If they face reality with new courage and hope, unpleasant circumstances will disappear before they are even aware of it.

Cosmic Beings are Waiting

The only thing people need to do is to pray for peace on Earth. This enables them to return to their divine source, the parental God. When they do so, the true nature of themselves and of humanity will naturally become clear to them.

This movement is presently starting in one corner of the Earthly world where we cosmic humans are carrying on tremendous work via the world peace prayers of human beings on Earth. This is known only to a limited number of people; at present, it is neither visible nor audible to the majority. However, the time will come when we will become visible and our voices will be heard by everyone.

How could we hold back our efforts for our beloved friends on Earth? I would most sincerely like to tell the people of Earth that we are praying that the day will soon come when we can offer our full wisdom and power to them, said the captain with deep feeling.

Seeing her eyes moist with tears like a compassionate mother, I could not hold back my own tears.

Caught up in the powerful emotion of the moment, I completely forgot about the presence of Mr. M and the other cosmic people. My whole body was enveloped in warmth. It was like the warmth felt by a child who had been lost for a long time and had finally been returned to the arms of his mother.

As our conversation ended, the captain invited me to drink the beverage that had been put in front of me. She also began to drink hers.

Taking a sip, I found that it tasted something like a pure fruit juice and had a fragrance that defied description. After two or three more sips, I became fully composed and began to feel refreshed. The young man entered the room again, this time to serve us a meal.

A Meal with my Cosmic Friends

Carrying round bowls that were half-filled with a soft, white food that looked like porridge, the young laid down a bowl along with a silver spoon at each person's place.

No one spoke until he had finished serving everyone, but no one seemed nervous or strained. When the dishes had all been set on the table, the captain began praying in silence. The rest of us followed her example. After this meditation, the captain murmured, *Thank you, God,* in a very soft voice. She looked as if she had been addressing the parental God as someone right in front of her. Her words sounded like a spontaneous expression of gratitude.

Joining the other cosmic people, I also murmured, *Thank you, God,* and took up my spoon with a strong feeling of divine protection. The food was like oatmeal and tasted very good. It was so soft and smooth that it slid down my throat and was completely gone before I knew it. It was a little warm and I felt that my face was slightly flushed.

No one was chatting or making noises with their dishes and spoons. There was a comfortable, happy feeling, characteristic of a pleasant dinnertime at home. In contrast to the mere satisfaction of our appetites that we often get from our meals on Earth, the meals with cosmic humans are a joyous exchange of love, filled with gratitude to God. Without uttering a word, we could exchange our thoughts as clearly as if they were written across our faces.

How wonderful this is! I felt. While looking at my cosmic companions in total admiration, I began to feel their kindness and love toward me. Again I felt the kind of warmth a lost child experiences when welcomed back to the fold of his family after finding his way home.

I recalled what Mr. M had said to me earlier, *Today will be a greatly blessed day for you.* He was right. I was now showered by blessings from these caring cosmic people. Their love-filled thoughts, wishing for the achievement of my Earthly mission upon my return, were felt throughout my body, reaching even to the depths of my soul.

Fruits from Venus

My heart was so filled with joy and gratitude that I did not know what to say. In the meantime, three bowls of fruit were carried to us and put on the table. The bowls were of an unpatterned dark brown and were semi-transparent. They contained three kinds of fruit: one shaped like peaches but with the pinkish color of apples, one that was golden, like apricots, and the third that was brown, like well-ripened dates. They all looked juicy and fresh, as if they had just been picked.

Mr. M explained, *These are fruits from Venus,* and urged me to help myself.

I could not help asking, *Are there fruit trees on Venus, too?* Upon hearing this, Mr. M laughed a little. I felt that the other cosmic beings were also amused at my question. No one ventured to speak, however; each seemed to be waiting for the others to provide me with the obvious response. Mr. M took the initiative:

Of course we have a lot of trees that resemble trees on Earth. The climate is similar to the Earth's temperate zone. Though there are four seasons, just like in your temperate zone we have warm days and cold days in turn, even in winter. There are no typhoons, no rainy seasons, and no droughts whatsoever. Although people on Earth use expressions like 'the wrath of nature', can such a thing as 'wrath' exist in great nature, when we are truly embraced in the arms of the great God? Should such events occur, it must be through the buildup of disharmonious thought waves which result from people forgetting their original truth. When this buildup reaches a certain point, it collapses naturally, resulting in a major misfortune. The parental God, who foresees this, prevents major catastrophes beforehand in the form of typhoons and floods. But on Venus, there is no such accumulation of karmic thoughts.

What a wonderful planet Venus must be! I exclaimed.

The Earth will become that way when harmony is achieved throughout the planet.

I do envy you. How good it would be if I could visit Venus someday!

The captain then spoke, *We'll invite you to Venus to see the bases for our spacecraft sometime. Why don't you help yourself to some fruit?*

I took a piece of fruit that looked like a peach from the bowl and cut it into quarters with my knife. The inside was white like an apple and it had a yellow-green pip, like a soybean. I took a bite of the fruit and found that it tasted like an apple. As I ate, I grew inquisitive as to how the fruits were kept fresh.

Intercepting my thought, Mr. M explained, *We have cold stores much like the refrigerators presently used on Earth. In it we put perishables like vegetables and fruits that need to be maintained at a low temperature to avoid deteriorating. With the constant emanation of electromagnetic waves, the foods can be kept fresh for some time.*

The Food Eaten by Cosmic Humans

What kind of food do you eat? I asked.

Unlike the people of Earth, we do not eat meat. Yet our life span is longer than yours. We eat mainly grains, fruits, and vegetables. Our cooking methods are also completely different from yours. In your conventional methods of food preparation, the cellular tissue of the food undergoes changes by heating or cooling it. In our food preparation methods, on the other hand, the same results are achieved by converting vibrations. We use electromagnetic waves instead of heat, replied the captain.

Though we all eat the same kinds of food in our spacecraft, when we return home to Venus we cook our own food, since we each have our own household, said the woman in the rose-colored dress.

I thought all cosmic people ate the same thing!

Amused by this notion, the woman in the pink dress immediately responded, *No, not at all. At home, we try to be as creative as possible and are always trying to improve ourselves.*

The captain, for instance, is the mother of two boys. Her husband is a civil engineer and she herself is an expert in the study of cosmic magnetic waves, continued the woman in the rose-colored dress.

Education on Venus

I next asked the captain, *How do you educate your children, and what is the educational system like?*

She replied:

It very much resembles the educational system on Earth, although all our education is public. One goes through a number of stages, and advances to higher and higher grades in developing one's own abilities. The education of an individual is divided into infancy, childhood, youth, and lifelong stages. The television sets currently used on Earth can only project programs that are broadcast from TV stations; on Venus, however, one can easily see and hear whatever one wants, just like playing a record on a record player. Thus, the educational system is organized to give individuals different assignments to match their abilities and learning pace. We do not need to see the results of a lot of tests or homework assignments to confirm a student's ability. The level of understanding is manifest at every moment as soon as learning has taken place. Should there be any difficulty in a student's understanding, however, various supplementary methods are used.

Unlike the educational system on Earth, we do not adopt uniform methods of learning. At all times, a person's heavenly mission takes priority. From an Earthly point of view, this might create great differences where some students might be seen as high achievers and others as low achievers. In our view, however, these differences have nothing at all to do with the 'superiority' or 'inferiority' of the students. We see nothing wrong with differences in performance, since we know very well that differences show themselves in the process of bringing out each person's own mission.

Some Earthly philosophers have called life 'a drama,' but a drama cannot be played only by the main actors. A drama becomes complete only when people in a variety of roles come together. In the

79

same way, no matter what our role or mission is, what conforms best to the divine will is for us to do our best in accomplishing our own given tasks. We are well aware that our souls can rise to greater heights only through the achievement of our own missions.

On Venus we do not have unharmonious thoughts such as envy, jealousy, hatred, sorrow, resentment, and other negative feelings that are still found on Earth. Children there grow up in all innocence and with a joyful sense of freedom.

In addition, we cosmic humans are given lifelong education in the accumulation of knowledge and experience. One of these practices involves visits to other planets aboard mother ships and space vessels. We improve ourselves by seeing other planets and learning about their good points and their shortcomings.

Some people also visit extremely distant planets to learn about more advanced science or to acquire superior technology. Those people contribute to the advancement and improvement of society on Venus or other planets.

Surely there would be no such thing as the 'hell of exams' that many children on Earth have to endure to get into a good school? I ventured to ask.

Though each person has his or her own mission from heaven, these missions are not imposed on us by an external force. We sense them intuitively, and we each have our own personal freedom. If we did not have freedom, life would be quite fatalistic, devoid of human will, spontaneity and brightness. How could we carry out our individual missions to the fullest under such conditions? Since people on Venus have a strong sense of their own missions, no one dreams of choosing an unsuitable way. Nor do we adopt the method of selecting a person's school based only on their test results. Promotion to higher grades occurs whenever deeper understanding is attained, the captain replied.

How do you store water in the space vessel? I asked, suddenly changing the subject.

This time, the specialist in technical maintenance informed me: *A certain amount of water is constantly held in reserve inside the vessel. We also generate more when there is a need for it.*

How about water used for cooking and the staff's daily use? How do you dispose of it after each use? I asked.

For cooking and washing inside the vessel, we use the vibrational separation method utilizing electromagnetic waves. So, instead of washing with water, we use special electromagnetic cleansing devices. In addition, unwanted matter is broken down, deoxidized or restored to its original state by electromagnetic waves. While you burn rubbish on Earth, we return the elements to the air or to their original state without leaving a trace.

The Population of Venus

What is the population of Venus compared with that of Earth? I inquired next.

This question was answered by Mr. M:

I understand it to be about one twentieth of the population of Earth. People on Venus have a longer life span than human beings on Earth; consequently we have fewer children than you do. There is no region or person on Venus that experiences hardship from having an overabundance of children.

Aren't there any diseases or misfortunes on Venus?

Disease and misfortune on our planet are essentially different from what is experienced by Earthly humanity. The suffering of people on Earth, experienced within the thick shells of their karma, is in itself a manifestation of the distorted ideas that Earthly humans have generated; it is too shortsighted to define an experience as good

81

or bad simply from its superficial manifestation. That would be like seeing the tip of an iceberg and mistaking it for the whole. We cosmic beings are well aware that the invisible part is the real 'iceberg.'

Though various changes do take place in the course of human evolution and development, the misfortunes on Earth originate from mistaken thoughts, or from attaching oneself to various things and occurrences. In the course of evolution, we also experience some occurrences and events that are comparable to what you experience in the Earthly world, but they are not accompanied by the emotional vibrations of sorrow, pain and so forth. In our case, evolution occurs quite naturally.

Are There Any Other 'Orphans' in the Universe?

I suppose there must be a great variety of stars and planets in the universe. Are there any, apart from Earth, that would also be considered 'orphans' of the universe? I asked.

This time the captain responded to my question:

Among the billions and trillions of stars and planets scattered across the great universe, some are located at distances beyond our reckoning and situated at unimaginably high evolutionary stages. With their wonderful wisdom and power, they are pursuing their own missions. From those at that elevated position down to the youngest planets that have just been born, there are an uncountable number of stages. Even as we speak, new stars are being born and old stars are disappearing, having completed their missions. This unceasing movement and evolution reflect the reality of the great universe.

I think you can now understand that there are planets at earlier stages of development than Earth. It is also important to understand that during the evolutionary process of each planet, its spiritual and scientific levels do not necessarily coincide with those of other planets. There are planets with advanced science but extremely low spiritual levels. On the other hand, there are planets with high spiritual levels and limited scientific development.

The expression 'orphan' of the universe does not really mean that the Earth or any other planet is left isolated. It just describes the state of a planet that has been unable to communicate with other stars and planets due to its lack of understanding of the system of the great universe. However, this is just a temporary condition; a world beyond your imagining will soon flourish on Earth as well.

An inexpressible feeling of joy and hope welled up inside me as I listened to the captain speak. A chance glimpse of her face in profile revealed to me her eyebrows, nose, mouth, slightly round features and dark wavy hair. Together they all imparted to me an impression of intelligence radiating from within. How powerful, youthful and full of vitality she was! Her physique was like that of a ballet dancer. It was hard to believe that she was really the mother of two young boys. Yet, at the same time, from her translucent fair skin and eyes that looked at me with a warm expression, I sensed the kind of compassionate love that naturally emanates from a mother.

Her black dress was made of a thick crepe-de-chine fabric and had a round, embroidered white collar that stood in stark contrast to the rest of her dress. There was a jewel about the size of a small bean decorating the neckline at the collar and it sparkled in shades of white and blue. It looked like a sapphire and changed into a various hues as she spoke.

The dress had three-quarter length sleeves and was fastened at the waist with a thin black belt made of a material that was neither a natural fabric nor leather; it looked like nylon. The rectangular buckle at the front seemed to be made of a semi-precious stone like sardonyx. The other two women, on the other hand, had oval buckles inlaid with several sparkling jewels.

The skirt of the captain's dress was neither straight nor flared, but fell in folds like natural waves. There were no rings on her delicate fingers. None of the three cosmic women seemed be wearing makeup. It seemed quite unnecessary considering the natural beauty of their faces.

Cosmic People Know their Own Missions

None of the cosmic people smoked. It seemed that the men and women alike were closely linked with one another and merged together at a common center. The extent of each person's wisdom, derived from their respective missions, seemed to be expressed through the work that each was doing.

I felt that they must all be doing their best in carrying out their missions and thought how happy I would also be if I could work in such a world. At that moment, I heard a voice from the depths of my soul that said, *Know your own mission!*

Oh yes! I remembered that I needed to convey all the information I had learned here to the people of Earth in as much detail as possible. Simultaneously, the various things I had been shown and taught after being invited to the space vessel rushed through my mind like a rapid stream. I suddenly became eager to go back to Earth as soon as possible to convey this information to the people there.

In the meter at the entrance, the ring of light went out in one section and was descending. The captain spoke once more: *The vessel is approaching Earth. It is time for us to bid our farewells. Next time, we will give you a guided tour around the base of our vessels.*

When will that be? I inquired.

We will let you know with our thought vibrations. It will be in the near future, she added.

A Return to Earth

The cosmic people simultaneously looked at the meter at the entrance as the light ring in it suddenly went out altogether. It was obvious that the vessel had landed on Earth. The landing was smooth, without the slightest jolt.

I suddenly felt reluctant to say goodbye to everyone.

We have landed and must say goodbye to you now, said the captain as she rose from her seat. The other members also stood up. I showed them my heartfelt appreciation by bowing deeply.

Walking in front of me, Mr. M then guided me to the exit of the ship. As I looked back, I saw the captain and crew members sending me their blessings. Moved almost to tears, I bowed again and left the room. Mr. M walked down the corridor a few steps ahead of me. I followed him, hurrying a little. Without using the elevator, we walked around the corridors and staircases until we reached the exit. The door opened quietly and the scenery of Earth all at once became visible. As if looking at the Earth for the very first time, I found the fresh green of early summer truly breathtaking. Disembarking ahead of me, Mr. M began to walk toward the prayer hall taking big steps. After walking fifty or sixty meters, he stopped and said, *I'll say goodbye to you here. We will be able to meet again soon.*

Again, so filled with emotion that I could not say a word, I expressed my gratitude by bowing over and over again.

I stood in the same spot to see him off as he made his way back to the vessel. He turned to look back at me once and then again. Arriving at the entrance of the vessel, he turned back one final time to wave goodbye to me before going inside.

Seeing a flash of light, my eyes shut involuntarily. When I reopened them, the vessel was no longer there. The grass and crops in the fields were swaying from side to side though there was no wind. Looking up at the sky, I spotted a small space-craft, but it disappeared the next instant.

As I continued gazing at the sky, my consciousness gently returned to my physical body, which was seated in the meditation Hall at Holy Hill; I was praying for world peace with the other people there.

PART II

THE SUPRASCIENTIFIC BASE

Chapter 3

BOARDING THE SPACE VESSEL AGAIN

Visiting the Bases of Space Vessels

The bases of space vessels are roughly classified into three types. First, there are natural bases which take advantage of natural mountains. These are used for medium-sized craft and their hangars. The second type are artificial bases. Ranging in size anywhere up to tens of kilometers in diameter, these are the most impressive and elaborate of the three and have the capacity to hold craft of all types and sizes. The third type are combined natural/artificial bases which are constructed by carving into the sides of natural mountains. These bases are used for large mother ships.

I would like to describe in as much detail as possible what I saw of these three types of great bases: how they looked, what there surroundings were like, and the nature of their interior mechanical facilities. Incidentally, I would also like to mention how impressed I was by the brightness and spontaneity of the captain and the two women accompanying her on board. They shone with bright intelligence, radiant health, keen sensitivity and a pure, wholesome beauty. Even now, whenever I recall them I cannot help but wish that I had the ability to draw or paint their likeness so I could convey to others the wonderful qualities they possessed.

I would also like to write about the captain's husband and his work. He is an urban planning engineer and travels on special high-performance space vessels to very distant, advanced planets to study various aspects of their science and technology. However, I will leave that for a later occasion as I resume the report of my experiences.

A Flock of Space Vessels above Holy Hill

It was early September 1959. The sinking sun above the forest at the western side of Holy Hill tinged the scattered clouds with a brilliant crimson as if to remind us of the wonders and vastness of the great sky. The clouds kept changing constantly, appearing and disappearing only to reappear in a different form. The ever-changing nature of the great sky, I felt, was not unlike that of our own Earthly human world. With the setting of the sun, the crimson clouds and their beautiful patterns would vanish from the great sky without a trace, like the dance of a heavenly maiden.

The mystery of the great sky at dusk made me feel as if it were communicating some great truth to those of us who looked up at it. Tomorrow was to be one of the days we would pray at dawn. We were lodging at Holy Hill that night in anticipation of our sunrise prayers for world peace under the guidance of Goi Sensei. With the red sky behind me, I hurried to the prayer hall at Holy Hill.

There were people here and there in small groups in the fields after the rain. The tomato vines that had been laden with fruit until recently were now almost entirely withered and had only small underdeveloped red tomatoes remaining on them. It would not be long before the green leaves of the daikon radish would sprout in the fields.

While passing the village shrine and walking under its tall leafy trees, the trees somehow attracted my attention. Looking back at them, I saw three space vessels flying between the crimson clouds as the sun was setting. Flying horizontally from right to left in formation, they vanished from sight into the clouds. As I was still staring at the sky where they had disappeared, one vessel suddenly reappeared and, ascending at an angle of about 35 degrees, changed to a horizontal course and disappeared once more into the clouds.

As I walked further on, the road descended into the woods. I walked through the woods and climbed the hill. The afternoon sun had already set when I arrived at Holy Hill. However, I could clearly see innumerable space vessels flying overhead in the sky still tinged with crimson. Space vessels are constantly flying above Holy Hill. Since they fly outside the range of human visibility, however, they cannot be detected by most people. Nevertheless, the time will come when they will be visible to everybody.

I remembered that during my first flight the captain had promised to show me around the bases. This memory awakened in me the notion that one of these space vessels might very well land the next day to take me to the bases. On the other hand, I remembered the dangers of entertaining such expectations. As Goi Sensei repeatedly told all of us, whatever we needed to know would be taught to us at the time we needed to know it. I also reminded myself that we are always guided by our guardian divinities and spirits as well as the cosmic beings. So, whether I would be taught or shown anything tomorrow was entirely beyond my control; it all depended on a bigger plan. However curious I was to know what lay ahead, what was meant to happen was beyond my reasoning and ego.

91

The deep and lofty mysteries of the universe cannot be taught or learned while the thoughts of personal ego remain within us. These truths originate from realms that transcend the personal ego or worldly attachment. As long as we human beings on Earth maintain our coarse vibrations, we will not be able to harmonize with the fine vibrations of cosmic beings. The gap in our wavelengths is too great. Through my own experience, I knew that it was when the vibrations of the cosmic beings and ours met that we were taught and allowed to experience wonderful things for the very first time.

Everybody who wants to watch television or listen to the radio knows that they have to tune their dials to the wavelengths of the respective broadcasting stations. However, when it comes to space vessels and cosmic beings, many people see them only as curiosities and not as phenomena that we should seek to understand.

Fundamental Conditions for Communicating with Space Vessels and Cosmic Beings

My report was partially carried in an article concerning space vessels in the December 19, 1959 issue of the *Tokyo Journal*. Following its publication, I received various comments and questions from people all over Japan. The existence of many active researchers of space vessels greatly encouraged me initially. After reading letters from people in various places throughout Japan, however, I felt that the majority of the people did not understand that the most fundamental condition for accepting space vessels and cosmic beings was for the thought waves of human beings on Earth to change. People were more interested in finding out new interesting trivia about cosmic people and space vessels than they were in making serious efforts to learn about them.

The recent increased sightings of space vessels in a large number of places was due to fine, powerful waves emitted amidst the rough waves of the phenomenal world. The release of these waves resulted from efforts on the part of cosmic persons to transmit the principles of their science to the Earthly world. That science manifests itself in a number of ways; it causes both phenomenal changes as well as spiritual changes by reaching the very depths of the human heart. However, these are only fragmentary appearances of the fine waves of cosmic science; to receive them fully requires efforts on our part. We must purify our coarse waves and uplift our thoughts. How can we do so? The answer is to practice our usual prayer for world peace. This is because the prayer for world peace is the very tool that purifies and refines our vibrations to the level of the world of space vessels and cosmic beings.

When many people say the words of the prayer *May Peace Prevail on Earth* in unison, wonderful vibrations will become concentrated in the places where they pray and it is there that the space vessels and cosmic beings will be able to do their work effectively. As a result, everyone will someday be able to see with their own human eyes cosmic persons who are essentially no different from us. People will also be able to hear them speak in languages that are the same as their own.

I would like as many people as possible to know that all they have to do is transform their vibrations, and that the way to achieve this is to pray for world peace.

Welcoming Cosmic Friends

Emerging from the night's sleep, the sky above Holy Hill greeted the new day by resuming its state of constant change. With Goi Sensei at the center, we started to recite the prayer for world peace facing the eastern sky where the sun would rise. No sooner had Mr. Saito intoned the first stanza than I fell into a deep meditation as I usually do.

The eastern sky before sunrise was filled with a dim light. However, when we started our meditation, it suddenly became bright as if the sun had already risen. The light became stronger and stronger, shining even more brightly than direct sunlight in mid-summer. With these conditions, I sensed that we had completely transcended our physical bodies, blending into the infinite light. At the same time, our consciousness of self (ego) gradually vanished and we entered into a body of light that shone like the sun.

Suddenly, I felt myself colliding and blending with the light source. Next, I felt myself expanding limitlessly, in oneness with the light that was radiating to immeasurable distances. There was no knowing at all how much my awareness would expand. I felt that I would be limited only by the scope of my own consciousness. There was nothing but light everywhere. It was a world of sheer light, totally surpassing any description I could give here.

I could feel myself drifting. I have no idea how many seconds or minutes I remained in this state. I then found myself standing in front of the prayer hall at Holy Hill. Basking in the brilliant morning sunlight, I was calling out to the great sky.

As if anticipating the arrival of my closest relatives, I became excited about welcoming my cosmic friends. Even without seeing or speaking with them, I was receiving strong vibrations that they were approaching me. It was not a vague feeling that they might come; it was a feeling of absolute certainty. I was only awaiting the moment of their arrival.

The Space Vessel Lands at Holy Hill

The September sun was shining above my head. When I looked up at the sun and found a small object crossing its rays, I intuitively recognized it as a landing space vessel. Unlike the first time I encountered a vessel, my heart did not beat violently. I stood calmly watching the sky after the vessel had flown away. Before I knew it, however, there was a huge object unexpectedly approaching me from behind. By the time I caught sight of it, the vessel was already on the ground.

It appeared in the space of an instant. A medium-sized vessel, it was of the same type that I had boarded previously and it had that same particular overhanging peak, which, I could sense, was now emitting extremely potent electromagnetic waves. The sight of its great, stately form, poised horizontally as if floating in midair over the slightly sloping farmland, was impressive indeed. Probably because of the angle of the sunlight, the cosmic wave receiver at the top of the vessel was twinkling brightly.

I did not approach the ship immediately. Quietly watching it, I walked slowly towards it. I was aware that, at the time of landing, electromagnetic waves are reduced to a minimum, and those emitting toward the entrance and exit cease completely.

When I had walked about 10 meters, the door facing the prayer hall opened silently. At the same time, landing stairs with three steps were lowered from the vessel. Mr. M appeared and, watching his footing, descended the stairs. I could see his smiling face the moment he stood on the ground. The brown space suit, the ankle-length boots, his slender physique and his familiar oval face rekindled feelings of nostalgia within me. I do not remember exactly what I said but I remember shouting out to him as loudly as I could while waving with my right hand high in the air.

Waving back at me, Mr. M hurriedly approached. As the distance between us narrowed, we both began to run to each other. Mr. M grasped my extended hand. As I shook his hand firmly, I could feel tears of joy running down my cheeks. Although I had a great many things to say to him, the sudden joy of our reunion drove them all from my mind.

People are waiting for you on the vessel, Mr. M said in his soft, quiet manner.

I see. Thank you. Thank you, was the best I could respond. I did not know what else to say. That was all I could say to express my gratitude to my cosmic friends.

The two of us began to walk side by side. Without saying a word, we were able to understand and communicate with each other as if there were an electric current flowing between us. Overjoyed by the reunion, I could not tell whether my feet were really touching the ground. As I approached the vessel, I could feel strong electromagnetic waves. The waves were so strong that I felt as if I had received an electric shock in my hands and feet. Completely unlike the previous occasion, I felt the impact of the waves being emitted even though they were indirect and of minimum intensity.

Boarding the Space Vessel Again

As we got closer to the space vessel, Mr. M walked in front of me. The door shut as soon as we climbed the stairs and entered the vessel. The interior of the vessel was an entirely different world. Away from the potent electromagnetic waves, the brightness of the sun, and all other Earthly influences, the space vessel seemed to be a universe unto itself. The corridors were the same as when we had walked through them before. Another wave of nostalgia and familiarity again took hold of me. We went up the stairs to the third floor and stopped in front of the door to a room. Briefly glancing back at me, Mr. M asked, *Do you remember this room?*

Isn't it the room where you keep those wonderful cosmic maps?

That's right, answered Mr. M as he pressed a button to open the door. The luxurious sofas looked the same as before. *Now, please be seated.* Motioning for me to take a seat, he also sat down.

Once seated, I was at a loss what to do next. I had an endless number of questions about the space vessel. I wanted to ask about the method of gradually reducing the wave frequencies, the relationship between the crystal sphere and the captain's brain waves, the functions of the telescope and various other meters and devices. These were only a few of the things I wanted to know. What also ran through my mind like a ticker tape was an endless stream of questions about the mysteries of the great universe, including an insatiable desire to know as much as possible about the stars and the planets. I did not know where to begin. Aware of what I was going through, Mr. M watched me with a warm, understanding expression. He responded to my unspoken questions through his eyes: *Yes, I know very well all that you want to ask. I will answer each of your questions one by one as the need arises. I understand how you feel but there is no need to be in a hurry.*

A pleasant smile spread across his handsome face. It released my heart from the tension of the moment, and I found myself smiling too, encompassed by the soft, quiet atmosphere that Mr. M created.

Do you remember the promise you made to the captain the last time you were here?

I have been thinking about it ever since, and today I had a strong feeling that you would be coming for me.

Communicating through Telepathy

It is because we were communicating with you by telepathy from the vessel.

Now I understand why I felt so sure that I would be able to see you today. Is it possible to keep communicating by telepathy this way in the future too?

If you can attune your wave length to ours, I am sure you will be able to receive our messages at any time. They will be reflected onto your own mental waves. You may even find that your problems are solved immediately. We do not give you instructions through signals or words that we transmit from our side. Instead, we send you fine waves that blend into your own spiritual waves. Through this method, messages are transmitted directly and naturally like a spring that flows from one place to another. So, without consciously recognizing the introduction of new ideas or thoughts, the receiver writes, speaks and does things motivated by an irresistible inner drive.

If each communication were to take place through a system like making telephone calls as you do on Earth, you would need to confirm everything that was relayed to you through an additional cognitive step. You would have to mentally process what was meant by the words of that communication. If you had to verify whether the transmittal was correct or not each time, your actions would be somewhat delayed and awkward. This is why we communicate through direct transmission to a person's spiritual waves where understanding is always accurate. We will communicate this way with you in the future too.

I asked Mr. M: *It sometimes happens that something we have casually written or said in our daily life takes us by surprise, and we are amazed at how wonderful it is. I feel that this kind of thing might be the result of the special waves you have been sending us to bring about changes in our way of thinking. If so, what an incredible teaching method it is! Can't this method be practiced by humanity on Earth too?*

Many people on Earth block out our fine waves with the coarse waves they emit. This is why they do not feel anything. We are keeping an eye on Earthly humanity at all times, and we try to guide people whenever we can. However, they do not seem to make any effort to try to find out about us. In fact, the number of people who know about us is extremely small. This is the present state of Earthly mankind.

I think coarse waves make it hard for people on Earth to achieve perfect communication with each other through telepathy. However, coarse waves do respond to and interact with coarse waves.

As we talked, I forgot that I was aboard the space vessel; it was as if we were in a room in a quiet mountain villa somewhere. I noticed a meter beside us. It was moving incessantly and seemed to be registering the condition either inside or outside the space vessel. Seeing my attention focused on the meter, Mr. M explained: *The vessel is now leaving Earth.* He then stood up and walked to the other end of the room. I stood up and followed him. I walked five or six steps, looking at the astronomical maps on both sides of the room. Then I noticed that the ceiling rose at an angle.

No sooner had Mr. M pressed a button than a window about 50 centimeters in diameter appeared on the side of the slanted ceiling, looking as if it were floating. Simultaneously, the brightness of the outside entered the room and I could see that we were flying through a sea of clouds. As if running in a rapid stream, the clouds flew by one after the other. The next moment we seemed to have entered into a huge cloud mass which cut off our view of the dynamic sky.

The Windows of the Space Vessel

We are flying in the Earthly sphere. It is just like flying in one of the latest jet planes. An airplane will crash if it runs out of fuel, but a space vessel would never meet such a fate. No one ever imagines such a thing either, said Mr. M.

I did not know there was a window hidden in this type of vessel. Some of the space vessels that I see from the ground have windows while others don't. Why is there a difference? I asked Mr. M.

Both vessels with windows and those without look the same from the outside. There is no major difference in their inner structure. Whether their fittings are visible or not, all space vessels are meticulously equipped with everything they require for their efficient operation.

The lifestyles of cosmic people are not necessarily the same from planet to planet. Just as each planet has its own heavenly mission and its fixed orbit, people live according to the circumstances on their own planets. For instance, many of the houses on Mercury and Venus are cylindrical. They are shaped like the 'pao' found in Mongolia on Earth today. There are no windows at all if you see the house from the outside, but from the inside you can see out in what-

ever direction you wish. Space vessels made on these planets have no windows. This is because the space vessels cosmic people build reflect the lifestyle and architecture of their environment. On other planets, you can see construction methods similar to those followed for buildings on Earth, but the shapes of the buildings might be cylindrical. Many of the buildings constructed in this way are truly marvelous and immense. Space vessels and mother ships construct-ed on these planets have windows easily visible from the outside.

I see. I understand very well what you are saying. It surprises me to know that such a deep relationship exists between planets and their space vessels, even right down to the windows. I felt an inex-plicable sense of awe learning about the relationships between space vessels and planets. As soon as he had finished speaking, Mr. M pressed the button beside him; the window once more became a part of the ceiling. I realized that it was impossible to discern that there was a window in the room.

The Key to Wisdom Hidden in a Button

Returning to his chair, Mr. M went on speaking in his usual quiet manner:

It is not possible to grasp everything about the systems and per-formance of the mechanical facilities and meters in space vessels through observation alone. As you can well imagine, there is a limit to the knowledge and understanding that can be gained through the visual senses alone. By actually experiencing the functions first hand and then seeing the results, you will for the first time gain an insight into the logic behind each specific manifestation. You will also understand how precise and sophisticated each mechanism is. The key to deep wisdom can be hidden in a button that no one even notices. Such things cannot be understood through mere observa-tion.

The members of the crew of a space vessel are all highly experi-enced and have considerable depth of knowledge in their field of work. Their experience is enhanced with each position they hold. After gaining experience in one position, they move to a position with even greater responsibilities. Initially, instruction is given by the captain as needed. It is as if the person were working in tandem with the captain. However, as time goes on and people's under-standing of their work increases, the captain takes a back seat and gradually assumes the role of an observer.

Since the captain can see with ease all the positions on all the floors through three monitors in front of her, she knows at all times what is going on in any part of the vessel while she is operating the steering post.

For a certain period of time, the members of the crew undergo basic training at bases on a number of planets. After completing their training, they are assigned to various types of vessels and mother ships. They need considerable training to be able to handle and operate all the various space vessels which are built for differ-ent purposes and are, therefore, equipped with different devices and mechanisms.

The Crew Members and Passenger Capacity

How long does it take to become an independent crew member?

Each person has his or her own mission to fulfill, which natu-rally determines the role the person is to assume. The expression 'independent' is commonly used in judging people in the Earthly world, but I cannot say it is necessarily correct to say that a person who has satisfied a given standard has become independent.

The activities inside a space vessel are roughly divided into four departments: waves, navigation, transformation, and oscillating magnetic waves. In addition to these, there are activities relating to the specific mission of the vessel or mother ship and various cosmic people come on board to undertake these. For the main activities, however, there are only these four separate departments. Some people complete their duties having worked in only one of these departments while others learn about two or three departments. Still others will gain experience working in all the departments of the vessel and then go on to gain further experiences on other vessels and mother ships to attain an independent status. Therefore, the independence of a crew member cannot be judged merely by the length of time in months or years that he or she has worked. Those who are able to serve ably and wholeheartedly in their given positions will be truly happy in fulfilling their individual missions.

Just as missions differ from person to person, each person is given their own specific position. Cosmic people understand the joy of contributing through a given position and feel an abiding sense of gratitude for being able to do so. They also know that having an understanding and acceptance of their mission proves that they are ready to ascend spiritually to a new and higher stage.

About how many crew members are on this space vessel?

The normal capacity is 32 persons, but we sometimes fly with a much larger or smaller crew. It all depends on the distance of the flight and the degree of experience of the crew members. When the ship flies with a small crew, we sometimes each assume responsibility for more than one position. We also have guests on board occasionally, answered Mr. M.

How many passengers can this medium-sized vessel carry? I asked.

Mr. M replied: *Unlike craft such as mother ships that are designed and constructed to carry large numbers of cosmic people between planets, this vessel is used by cosmic people with specific missions, for the attainment of those missions. However, if need be*

103

it can accommodate up to five times the number of cosmic people it usually carries.

As we were talking, a light began to shine in a meter beside Mr. M. He smiled and stood up. I, too, stood up and followed him. Although he said nothing, I knew what he was going to do. We left the room and started walking along the corridor. As we walked, it occurred to me that I might be meeting some other cosmic people today. Climbing the stairs, we went to the upper floor. Mr. M turned to me with a smile as I stood in front of the entrance to a room that I remembered from my last visit.

A Welcome from the Entire Crew

Mr. M pressed the button and the door opened without a sound. I was surprised to find 17 or 18 cosmic people in attendance. Among them were those I had met on my previous visit, including the three cosmic men, the captain, and the two cosmic women.

The rectangular table with its thick dark green tablecloth and its chairs were all familiar to me. The cosmic people stood up together to welcome us. Suddenly I felt a shining brightness emanating from them. Entering the room after Mr. M, I bowed deeply to express my appreciation.

I was greeted by a shower of welcoming smiles and blessings from the cosmic people as I approached the table. I suddenly felt nervous in front of the captain, who was standing in the center of the room. I bowed to her and attempted to express my heartfelt appreciation: *Ma'am, thank you very much for the kindness you showed me on my last visit.*

The captain returned my greeting with a smile and began to speak, *You need not be so formal. We are all friends, you know.*

Let's relax and have an enjoyable conversation today. The captain continued to smile. In the background, I could hear cheerful words of agreement from the other cosmic people.

Standing in front of all of you, I couldn't help but feel nervous, I said, touching my head with my hand in a gesture of embarrassment.

With a smile the captain suggested that I take a seat. She also sat down. I sat opposite her with Mr. M taking a seat beside me. The rest of the cosmic people gathered around the rectangular table on both sides of us.

When we were all seated round the table, the captain began to speak in her bright, clear voice, *Do you remember the promise we made here last time?*

Yes, I will never forget it. In fact, to be honest, I could not help becoming impatient, wondering when I would be invited to come here again. I spoke to Goi Sensei, who reminded me that the timing all depended on your plans and was beyond my control. At such times, I would pray the prayer for world peace whenever and wherever I felt impatient. When I did so, my consciousness would merge with my spiritual self and my impatience would disappear. I would then feel a bright light enveloping me. I melted completely into the light and, once inside it, could clearly see images of you and the vessel. I could also hear your voices. So, I always felt near you when I prayed the prayer for world peace.

As I continued to relate all these experiences to the captain, a delighted expression spread across her face.

The Sixth Wave

We are always watching over you whenever you pray for world peace. In addition, we are working extensively in your prayers and at the places where the prayer is prayed. This is because in those

105

places we can radiate fine waves having various functions into the coarse waves on Earth. Through those prayer sites and through the spiritual bodies of the people who are praying, fine waves flow out and spread through the Earth to gradually purify the karmic thoughts of the Earthly world. Everything that the eyes can see, the hands can touch and the heart can feel, whether with or without form, consists of waves. The time will come someday when the law of waves and vibrations is understood by the whole of Earthly mankind as being the foundation of all things. This will occur in the not too distant future. As I have said many times, waves are the basis for the formation of all things. So, I think you can understand the reason why we attach so much importance to waves.

In general, the waves radiating from the source of the great universe or the great God go through seven stages of transformation. The number seven stands for completion. When the seven transformations have been perfectly achieved, we attain unification and a return to the original oneness. As of now, the Earthly world has experienced five transformations. The waves produced by these five basic transformations are all coarse waves which are unable to create fine and sophisticated things. The sixth transformation of waves, which will occur along with the cyclic change of the Earth within its solar system, is brought about by a very fine and subtle wave. When this wave has become thoroughly integrated with the existing five waves, the seventh vibrational change will take place for the very first time.

Thus, with the emanation of a new, fine wave amidst the rougher and coarser ones, the seventh harmonized world will emerge at least partially. Needless to say, the world in which we cosmic people live is a high, deep, and purified world where the seven waves are completely harmonized. Now I think you can understand how the vibrations ought to be in places where we can do our work.

I would like as many Earthly people as possible to understand this fact because, through the sites of the world peace prayer and the spiritual bodies of those who pray, we can let fine spiritual waves gradually permeate the Earthly world which is now engulfed in the coarse waves of karmic thought. The larger the sites, and the more spiritual and divine the wavelength of those who pray, the more powerfully the prayer works. Its waves have the capacity to perform extremely deep and important functions that are far beyond the imagination of Earthly mankind.

In accordance with the plan of the great God, sites of prayer for world peace will gradually expand over a wider area. At a certain point of time, an epoch-making incident like a natural calamity that far exceeds the imagination of Earthly people will take place. It will be an incident that compels a 180 degree change from the dense, resistant karmic thoughts of self-protection which Earthly humanity has allowed to build up over the past millions of years.

People of all political allegiances, friends and foes alike, will be completely stunned by it. Totally at a loss what to do, they will have no choice but to simply stand by and watch. It will be a phenomenon far beyond any they could imagine. When it does occur, it will be at the time when the fine waves spread most intensively and permeate the Earthly world. This will be the beginning of the emergence of a new world.

At a time when the confusion in people's minds is at an all time high, the truth contained in the prayer for world peace will begin to be understood and its vibrations will spread to every country of the world. It will be at this very moment that all the divinities and spirits, ourselves included, will simultaneously commence a grand work. Heaven and Earth will tremble and shake and a new and peaceful world will be born. This is how heaven will be realized on Earth.

When will this heaven on Earth be realized?

Needless to say, it will depend on the number of people who pray the world peace prayer. It is essential that as many people as possible pray at as many prayer sites as possible. It is not only the external action that counts; internal conditions also need to be met.

Yes, I quite understand. Thank you very much for explaining the vital role of the world peace prayer that we pray every day.

I felt as if my whole body and spirit were being absorbed into each word spoken by the captain. My heart filled with gratitude and admiration, I said a few awkward words of thanks.

The young man who had served us food and beverages during my previous visit had entered the room without my noticing, setting down cups of what looked like tea and leaving the room.

Cosmic Persons From Jupiter and Mercury

All the other cosmic persons in the room gave their full attention to the captain as she spoke. It seemed as if they had been harmoniously united with her, becoming one with her words, or rather, their vibrations.

We have some people with us today that we want to introduce to you. Of the three women on my right, two are from Jupiter and one is from Mercury. The gentlemen on my left are also from Jupiter and Mercury. As the captain introduced them to me, I greeted them with a bow, and they also bowed to me slightly.

One of the two ladies from Jupiter seemed to be around 40 years of age. She was wearing a vermilion jacket mixed with brown. She appeared to be about 160 centimeters tall. Her hair was cropped short at the neck and, unlike the captain's, had no wave in it at all. She had a very prominent nose. Her reddish hair and innocent eyes made a distinct but harmonious contrast. She seemed to be a strong person. Unlike the thin, light material of the dresses worn by the captain and the women in the rose and pink dresses, her jacket was made of a material that looked like a nylon knit. The collar was open-necked and heart-shaped and she wore a thin chain necklace. The chain was silver and had an oval-shaped bronze pendant hanging from it. In the middle of it was a beautiful small, shining pink jewel. She was also wearing a pair of dark navy blue slacks.

The other woman from Jupiter, who looked similar to the first, was around 35 or 36 years old. However, she was a little shorter and had unusually large eyes. She wore a dark green jacket.

The lady from Mercury, who was sitting next to them, had a very graceful appearance. She had an oval face and long, very beautiful reddish hair that touched her shoulders. She was about 24 or 25 years old and was wearing a pink dress with deep pink vertical stripes. The dress had a round collar and four pearl buttons down the front. I was very much impressed with her beauty and grace as she listened attentively to the captain's words with both hands placed on her knees. The skirt of her dress was flared and the material looked more like a summer twill than a thin silk and had a pattern similar to those we see on Earth.

On the captain's left sat a man from Jupiter. He was about 165 centimeters tall and looked about 55 or 56 years old. His features reminded me of portraits I had seen of the American President Lincoln. I had the impression that he was taller than me and thin, even though he was dressed in a fairly thick, dark gray space suit. His eyes were not big but looked very warm.

The man sitting next to him, also from Jupiter, appeared to be about 35 or 36 years old. He had the physique of someone who does a lot of physical labor. He had a roundish face, a well-shaped nose and medium-length hair combed to the back. The next man, who was from Mercury, seemed to be the eldest of all the cosmic persons there. About 160 centimeters tall, he had a round, fairly flat face and slightly sunken eyes.

While listing to the captain's speech and feeling different vibrations from each of the new cosmic friends, I could not help but wonder why these people were on board the space vessel.

The captain began to speak again: *The cosmic persons who are aboard today will be good friends with whom you can discuss various things when you visit their planets and bases in the future. This is why we have invited them to this vessel. We hope you will build a friendship with them.* The captain then nodded slightly at the cosmic persons on either side of her. The six cosmic persons nodded back at her with a smile.

I was so moved by her warm consideration that my eyes felt moist with tears. *I would appreciate your kind guidance since I know nothing at all,* I said as I bowed in their direction. At that time, the man from Jupiter who looked like Lincoln spoke to me in clear Japanese: *We will show you around when you come to Jupiter.* Completely surprised, I stared at him with my eyes wide open. Smiling at me and speaking to me with his eyes, he asked, *Did my Japanese surprise you?*

He seemed to be suppressing merriment. Truly nonplussed, I could only exclaim, *Yes! I was indeed surprised at your Japanese.*

Hearing this, the cosmic persons simultaneously burst into laughter. This seemed to break the ice and we began to feel comfortable with one another.

The atmosphere was like that of a reunion of very close classmates who had once studied together under the same teacher but who were now working on different planets. The captain was the teacher and the other cosmic persons were the students.

As we drank our tea, joyful thoughts were exchanged at high speed. I saw indescribable beauty in the cheerfulness and warmth that pervaded these cosmic persons and the happy, appreciative thoughts that were continuously exchanged among them. This kind of atmosphere seemed to be typical of such gatherings.

The light in the meter beside us began to blink again, signalling our approach to a base.

Observation of the Base from the Vessel

A series of seven or eight rings of light moved continuously downward in the meter which was housed in a transparent glass tube about 20 centimeters in length. It was very beautiful to see the rings of soft light in a vivid shade of violet disappear as they descended to the bottom of the tube.

Mr. M, who was beside me, began to talk to the captain: *I would like to show him the base from the sky before we arrive.*

Please do. We will now go back to our posts.

With these words, the captain stood up and all the other members did also. Headed by the captain, the cosmic women went out of the room. Mr. M and I left the room after them. We walked down the corridor to the left, descended the stairs, and turned right. Going down the familiar staircases that led to the bottom floor, we arrived at the room that houses the astronomical telescope.

111

Mr. M walked along the corridors and the staircases so quickly and smoothly that it looked as if he were gliding along, but he never left me behind and continued to pay careful attention to me.

Descending the stairs, he looked back at me briefly. Soon the familiar astronomical telescope came into view.

I learned a lot of things from this astronomical telescope. I know it is a magnificent instrument, I said.

Let's observe the base today through this telescope. Inviting me to take a seat, Mr. M seemed to have pressed a button after checking various parts of the telescope and the attached meters.

In a matter of seconds, just like on a TV screen, an image was projected fully onto the lens, which was about two meters in diameter. It seemed to be focused on the part of the planet where we were about to land. I could see green plains. The landscape was not like the sea of green of a tropical rain forest observed from an airplane at seven or eight hundred meters altitude; it looked more like a mountain village in the temperate zone. Gradually, the telescope shifted its focus.

The scenery on the screen began to change rapidly in accordance with the flight of the space vessel. It was just like watching television on a large screen. It was easy for us to make everything out clearly. Mr. M began to speak:

The base we are to arrive at now is located on what people on Earth call 'the other side of the moon,' the side that is little known to Earthly people. On the moon, there are many kinds of bases for various types of space vessels and mother ships. There are also cosmic people living there to maintain the bases. The scenery coming into view on the screen is the green belt on the other side of the moon. As you see, there is an expansive green forest. You can also see rivers flowing in the forests. When you see this, don't you feel as if you were flying above the temperate zone of Earth?

Exactly. I was almost under the illusion that we were indeed observing the temperate zone of Earth. To be frank with you, I cannot help being confused by the reality of all this. We Earthly human beings have many misconceptions about the moon. We have long believed that it has no air and that neither animals nor plants could live there. As I look at the screen, I now realize how inaccurate our information was. I can see no difference between this and the landscape of the Earth.

You are right. You are correct in saying so, except for one fundamental difference. Everything that you see, feel and touch on the moon—for instance, the water and air that are considered to be non-existent on the moon according to studies on Earth—consists of particles that have not yet been discovered on Earth. Based on these particle structures, plants can grow and cosmic people can live here. Although the results we see are similar to what is observed on Earth, the processes are different. I mean, the elements behind materialization are different. Without understanding this point, you cannot know the reality of the moon, said Mr. M.

I replied, *The distance of 38,000 kilometers between the moon and Earth is quite insignificant from the point of view of the universe. How in the world then can we explain the fundamental differences between two celestial bodies which are so close to each other?*

Well, do you remember the comment I made the last time we were looking at this telescope and the mobile astronomical map? Of the stars and planets that are living in our universe, some are in their infancy, others in their youth or middle age, and others are in their old age. A general astronomical survey makes us feel that each of the stars and planets resembles a person. On the Earth too, when some great person dies, people sometimes describe his or her passing as 'the loss of a bright star in the heavens.' Perhaps you remember what I said before, that it is not fanciful at all to think of an individual planet as an individual human being. Even though a person is close to you in your daily life, you cannot say that he or she is the same as you, can you? In the same way, it is not correct to judge other stars and planets in the universe by applying to them the law of materialization that prevails in the Earthly world, answered Mr. M.

Doesn't it make interplanetary trips for cosmic people pretty difficult? I asked.

That is a good question. You are quite correct. The reason we can freely enter and leave worlds that are controlled by fundamentally different elements is that we can easily change the waves we emit to adjust to each star or planet. However, while we have frequent communications with planets having similar waves to ours, we have difficulty in approaching planets with coarse and violent waves. You could compare us to the ayu, sweet-tasting fish that live in clear mountain streams but cannot live long in muddy water.

The screen shifted constantly as I listened to these explanations. On the green plain, there were mountains and rivers. On the high mountains, however, there were no trees to be seen. The changing screen gradually began to monitor a mountainous district, and one mountain after the other came into view. It was a chain of steep ranges. As I watched closely, I could see something that resembled small plants at the bottoms of valleys.

A Hangar for Mother Ships

Look closely at this mountainous district.

When I looked in the direction Mr. M was pointing in, I saw some gentle hills among the mountain ranges. The foot of the hills gradually connected to the plain. I then saw something like a round volcanic crater on the top of a hill.

This is one of the bases for space vessels. Mr. M said.

Do you land in such a place?

You will find out when we actually go down, Mr. M answered with smiling eyes. I felt that our vessel was actually flying slowly above the base. I realized that this was an operation undertaken expressly for my benefit to teach me various things about the base.

The peaks of steep mountains were reflected on the lens.

Oh! What are those? I exclaimed excitedly. I noticed horizontal tunnels which resembled large caves on the sides of two of the mountains.

They are hangars for space vehicles or mother ships.

How do you house such enormous vessels as mother ships?

I will show you later. The easiest way for you to understand is to actually see them being docked.

As several caves came into view, the scenery of the mountainous district continued to change. The horizontal tunnels were all of different heights and sizes. Little by little, I became increasingly preoccupied with my emotional reactions to what I was seeing, wondering: *However could they undertake such huge construction projects!* and so forth. When I looked at Mr. M to see his response, his face was as tranquil as the autumn sky.

What on earth is the matter with him? I thought.

Although he must have been perfectly aware of what I was feeling, Mr. M chose not to communicate with me with either his words or eyes. Then it dawned on me that when one gets too carried away with one's own emotions one can easily fall into a self-centered, unharmonious way of thinking. Upon taking note of this I was able to regain my former calm.

A Gigantic Artificial Base around the Control Tower

When the mountain range began to show gaps between the peaks, I noticed a particularly magnificent mountain between the ranges and a plain; it was something I had never seen before. Its shape was entirely round. On top of it, there was something like a volcanic crater shaped like a seven-pointed maple leaf. Taking a closer look, I realized it was not a volcanic crater. However, it did not look like a sand hill or a rocky mountain either, and it seemed to be covered entirely by some grass-like plant.

This is a base for space vessels and mother ships, said Mr. M.

I almost mistook it for a volcanic crater. Although shaped like a tree leaf, it doesn't seem to be on a natural mountain. It has such a regular shape that it must be an artificial construction.

You are right. It is an artificial base constructed for the arrival and docking of space vehicles in hangars. There are a variety of arrival stations with innumerable hangars for various types of space vessels. Medium- and small-sized mother ships are housed in hangars that look like caves in the sides of the mountains. The entire base is connected by various automatic road belts and elevators that enable the transportation and storage of machinery, daily necessities, food, construction materials and other supplies. Eight main automatic road belts surround the seven arrival stations. In the middle of the junction where these intersect, there is a control tower that oversees the entire base. The base is equipped with numerous facilities. Do you see that cylindrical structure under the control tower that looks similar to the buildings on Earth? It has many floors and rooms and is used to foster friendship with cosmic people from various planets. We entertain them there and have discussions and meals with them during their stay. The interior facilities are really marvelous. Now look at the sides of that valley.

As I looked in the direction where Mr. M was pointing, I saw seven radial ridges extending from the exterior round ridge to the center. Inside the valley between two of these ridges, a mother ship stood stationery, hovering in the air. I uttered a low cry of surprise when I saw it disappear suddenly into the middle of the mountain.

I was watching the valley where the mother ship had disappeared as if it had been sucked inside. In a short time, it came out and disappeared again into the other side of the mountain. There seemed to be various kinds of hangars. When a mother ship came down to a valley for landing, it could enter or exit from the entrances on either side. I guessed the hangars were designed like that.

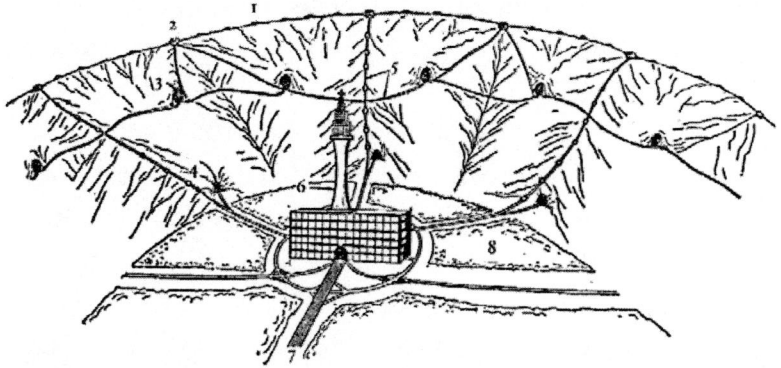

Figure 3. Bird's-eye view of the artificial base: (1) vessel hangar, (2) vessel landing pad, (3) mother ship entrance, (4) automatic roadway entrance, (5) automatic roadway, (6) command tower, (7) automatic roadway—trunk line, and (8) orchards.

I had a sudden desire to know more about the base and was nearly overwhelmed with excitement when Mr. M said in his usual soft-spoken manner, *I will show you around the artificial base so that you can take a good look at it after we disembark.*

Even before he finished saying this, the scenery began to change rapidly. It felt as if the vessel were flying above the border between the plain and the mountain range at an extremely high speed. I saw several natural bases on the way.

In observing all this I noticed that our vessel was flying according to the instructions of Mr. M, varying from rapid to slow, from high to low, right to left, and even briefly hovering motionless in the air. Mr. M began to speak: *Even without using mechanical equipment we constantly keep in touch with the captain. This is because we can communicate by means of telepathy.*

While he was saying this, the movements on the screen suddenly began to slow down. As I watched closely, I saw a mountain the shape of a round hat between two other mountains. On top I noticed an arrival station for space vessels similar to ones I had seen before. I realized that the vessel was flying slowly above the base so that I could observe it carefully.

The Arrival Station and Automatic Road Belts

This base for space vessels was located at the end of a mountain range. It was connected to the mountain range on one side and directly merged with the plain on another. On the remaining two sides, it detoured around the mountains and came out on the plain. The mountains in the area near the plains were much lower than those in the main range and were gently rounded. On the peak of one of these low, rounded mountains was a volcanic crater shaped like a plate. I could feel the vessel descending and, as I watched, the plate-shaped crater rapidly widened. It was fairly expansive, and now looked like a large bowl or baseball stadium. There were a number of steps leading down into it and the entire bowl shape was sectioned into concentric circles which diminished in size as they descended. In the center of the bottom circle, I could clearly see a pure white cross which looked as if it were floating in the air. It was shining brilliantly, reflecting the light of the radiant sun. *Oh! What a wonderful base!* I exclaimed to myself.

Surrounding the arrival station at the top were four ridges extending in the four directions. One joined with the mountain behind it, about halfway up, while another ridge merged with the plains. The remaining two ridges disappeared from sight into distant valleys among mountains. On three of these four ridges were what appeared to be pitch black asphalt roads; the roads looked as if they had two parallel rails. At places along the parallel rail-like roads were sudden swellings that made the meandering road look like a snake that had swallowed eggs at intermittent intervals.

Taking a second look at them, I noticed that they looked like doorbells. They were placed at fixed intervals and were of various shapes and sizes. The sight of them and the two black parallel rails on the ridges was impressive indeed. I now realized that we were approaching the base. After we had descended repeatedly to observe these bells while flying slowly above the central ridge, I caught a glimpse of a space vessel taking off from one of them.

The roof opened at the middle like the rapid shutter of a camera, and the space vessel that had apparently been on stand-by emerged smoothly from inside. No sooner had it appeared than it disappeared from the lens.

When I looked at the base after the vessel had flown away, there was a white cross shining at the base. Like the other arrival plates, it looked like a small stadium with several steps. As I was studying it intently, the roof again shut smoothly like a camera shutter, and now looked no different from the other bells. I saw Mr. M beside me, smiling as he watched me observe. He then began to speak.

Figure 4. Aerial view of an artificial base (with a dish-like landing site).

Automatic Road Belts and Hangars on the Base

We thought it would be easier for you to get a rough idea of the bases if you saw them from the sky before we explained how they worked. This is why we have taken the time to first show you the different kinds of bases. We will now show you the arrivals, hangars, and communications one by one. But I suppose that you already have some questions about what you have seen so far.

If you do not mind, I would now like to give you an overview of the systems of the bases. First of all, I will start with the arrival stations. The arrival station where we are to touch down now is designed to house five types of space vessels of different dimensions. There are larger hangars constructed to house larger space vessels and smaller ones for smaller vessels. However, this type of station is the most common and therefore it is the type that is constructed most often.

The white cross at the center is the magnetic plate for landing. It is designed to come in contact with the magnetic plate for touch down beneath the vessel. Through mutual magnetic attraction, the two magnetic plates lock together and keep the vessel stable during the docking process. Next, the two parallel black lines that appear to flow out of the arrival station on the summit of the mountain consist of upward and downward lines. At first sight they may look like conveyor belts that you have on the Earth, but their system is totally different. That is, the automatic road belt does not move continuously as a whole. Instead, a person or a thing on the belt activates electromagnetic waves in direct proportion to the gravity of the object, making it move in a fixed direction as if it were flowing. Operating on a principle very similar to the way a bell works on Earth, the continuous movements of attraction and repulsion create the movement necessary to transport objects from one place to another on the road belt.

Our vessel was rapidly decreasing in altitude. Mr. M, who was busy adjusting the telescope, glanced at me and said, *We will continue the observation at zero magnification.*

The image on the screen shrank as if the vessel had suddenly climbed. However, it soon began to regain its size. The steps of the arrival station could now be clearly seen. People on the road belt looked as if they were moving in gliding motions, as if skiing on the road.

Suddenly, I noticed a space vessel just above the arrival station. No sooner had it appeared than it touched down as if locking itself to the station. It was a marvelous sight. It landed instantaneously as if it had been sucked into the mouth of a giant.

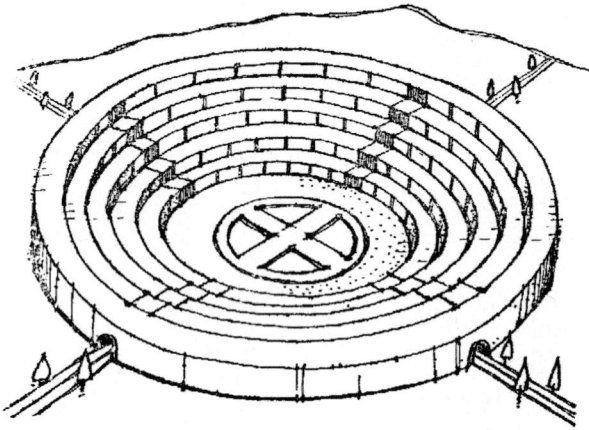

Figure 5. One type of landing site for space vessels: A building shaped like a baseball stadium with all floors made of glass.

In a short time, cosmic people began to leave the base from exits on three sides. They entered the automatic road belts and instantaneously they too appeared to be gliding from one place to another. The entire sight before me demonstrated, I believe, the perfect harmony of nature and technology. I felt that great nature, technology, and human beings had perfectly merged into one, each fulfilling its own role.

Shortly after, the space vessel left the station and disappeared. Oscillations of light indicating the landing of our vessel began. Simultaneously, the image reflected on the astro-nomical telescope vanished from view.

Chapter 4

THE LANDING

Arriving at the Moon Base

As the flashing lights began to signal our arrival at the base, my eye caught sight of another unusual meter. In shape and appearance, it looked like a pink plate, around the center of which an object was swirling rapidly and continuously. Intriguing as it was, I had no idea what it signified.

So far, we had not felt even a slight jolt as the space vessel commenced its landing. Nevertheless, I realized that subconsciously I had been feeling a bit anxious about the whole procedure.

Then it happened. A sudden mild jolt rocked the vessel slightly. The moment it did, the blinking of the lights ceased. Only the swirling motion in the round meter with the pink base continued as before. Mr. M remained seated as he monitored the equipment, and I was only able to catch a glimpse of his face in profile.

Observing his tranquil, handsome face in profile, I could not help but feel that the calmness he possessed was a reflection of his deep wisdom and abundant experience. Another interesting quality of his that I had noticed was that he was constantly smiling and always seemed to be at ease around me. I somehow got the feeling that he could feel this way because he already knew everything about me. While intently monitoring the movements in the various gauges, meters and mechanical equipment that were unfamiliar to me, he seemed to be fully aware of my apprehension prior to landing. In fact, he seemed to be aware of all the thoughts going through my mind. As he sent a smile in my direction from time to time, I felt that he was constantly trying to reassure me and put me at ease.

He did not speak to me however. Instead, his communication was of a nonverbal nature. It was quite effective. It penetrated my mind without the slightest possibility of misinterpretation. It was a communication that left no room for doubt or ambiguity. In response to those clear vibrations, my heart resonated from its depths.

A green light came on in another meter and Mr. M began to speak: *We have landed. Let's disembark and take a look at the base.*

With this, he stood up from his chair. We climbed the stairs and went out into the corridor. It looked the same as before except on one side of the passage there were two lights side by side; one was a soft green color and the other yellow. Although I had passed through this corridor a number of times before, I had never been aware of these lights.

Observing the lights, Mr. M turned to the left. The vessel had four entrances. The green and yellow signal lights indicated which of these we were to use.

After we walked about a quarter of the length of the circular corridor, the same green and yellow lights now appeared on our right some two meters ahead of us. Passing in front of them and proceeding about four or five meters, I turned to look back at the lights but they had already been extinguished and I could not locate them. We then came to a passage on the left leading to an exit. Arriving at the exit, I noticed a transparent door made of a material that could have been glass. The door opened automatically and we went inside. As soon as we entered, it closed again. Standing behind the closed door for a short time and waiting for it to reopen, I heard a light buzzing sound above my head. We seemed to be in a type of elevator. Looking up, I noticed another green light near the ceiling. Once more the door opened and we went out into the corridor. I suddenly felt as if I had become lighter, as if liberated from the weight of my body. The stiffness in my shoulders disappeared and my neck and shoulders now felt loose and relaxed and easier to move. As I walked, I felt as if my steps were lighter than usual. Looking back at the door we had just passed through, I noticed that it had closed again.

The Grand Hall in the Arrival Station

Walking into the corridor, I saw a few cosmic persons but they did not pay any particular attention to us. After walking for another five or six meters, we came upon an automatic walkway that was carrying people up and down to different levels. It was like an escalator on Earth. Without getting on it, Mr. M went around to a door on our left. It opened and shut again automatically after the two of us went through it.

The center of the room was like a great assembly hall. There were numerous rows of tables and chairs. The tables were made of what looked like a translucent type of plastic. They were grouped in units, each unit being formed of two rows of tables that faced each other. Running through the center of these units of tables were conveyor belts about 30 centimeters wide.

The interior of the room was a soft cream color and was as bright as day although there was no visible source of light. The temperature was neither hot nor cold; it was as if the room was

127

controlled by an air conditioning system. In fact, the air was so fresh and invigorating that I felt both physically and mentally refreshed. Shaped like a baseball stadium, the sides of the room were made of what appeared to be transparent glass, and a corridor ran alongside them. We seated ourselves in a couple of chairs by this windowed area.

Let's have something to eat. While we do, I'd like to tell you as much as I can about the base and its facilities, said Mr. M.

My head was already swimming. Everything I had seen or heard about was entirely beyond what I could ever have imagined and I could now only stare at things in a semi-dazed state. Probably recognizing how overwhelmed I was, Mr. M had decided it would be best to have something to eat and drink before he went any further with his narrative about the base.

Each and every object that I stared at in amazement was indeed unusual. Although dazzled by it all, I was beginning to get a picture of the lifestyle of cosmic humans. At the same time, I did not cease to be surprised by the enormous difference between their lives and those of human beings on Earth.

Mr. M pressed various buttons on the table in front of him, setting off a series of illuminations on the signal board located at the right corner of the table. To begin with, the two colored lamps located in the middle, and all the lights to the left and right of them, lit up all at once. Next, when he pressed some buttons along these rows of lights, the lights began to blink. Next, I remember seeing him press one button on the second row from the left, one on the second row from the top, and another on the fourth row from the top on the right. After he finished doing this, he looked up at me momentarily and started to speak in his usual quiet manner.

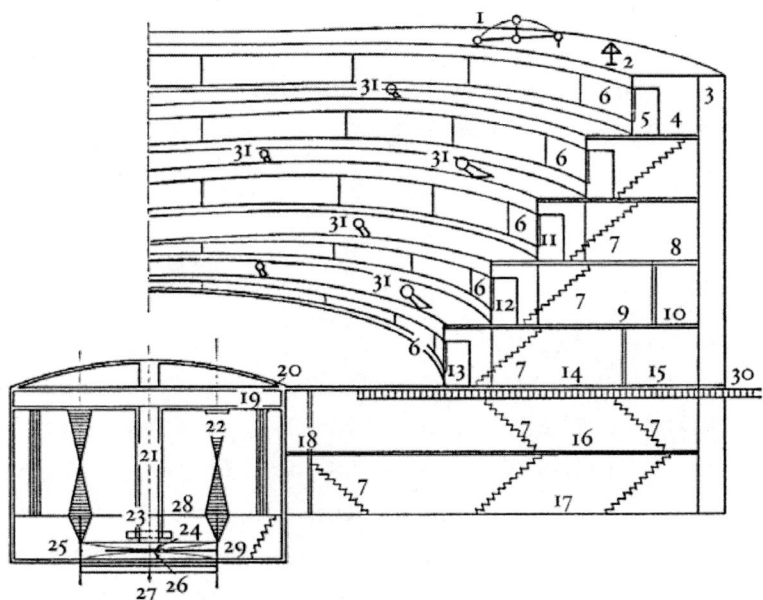

Figure 6. Cross-section of a landing station: (1) cosmic wave receiver, (2) two-way antenna, (3) elevator, (4) cross section, 5th floor, (5) entrance, (6) window, (7) staircase, (8) 3rd floor, (9) 2nd floor (10) kitchen, (11-13) corridors (14) 1st floor, (15) kitchen, (16) basement, 1st floor, (17) basement, 2nd floor, (18) basement corridor, (19) landing pad, (20) cross-shaped plate, (21) extension device, (22) wave controller, (23) automatic controller, (24) magnetic plate, (25) attraction/repulsion equipment, (26) repulsion plate, (27) wave guidance/reinforcement, (28) machine room, (29) wave control room, (30) automatic road belt, and (31) landing control machine.

The Landing Station: Five Stories High
With a Three-Storied Basement

As we observed from the sky, this arrival station can accommodate five different types of space vessels. It consists of five floors above ground, each floor dedicated to a different type of vessel. As you see, cosmic people occupy each ring-shaped floor. The people on a given floor belong to a specific space vessel. They are always aware of the whereabouts of the vessel that they are to board, thanks to the signal lights that indicate the movements of all the vessels. This is how they track the activity of their own vessel as they wait at the arrival station. In addition to the five floors above ground, there are also three floors underground.

As Mr. M spoke, two glasses that had been moving along the conveyor belt stopped in front of us. Mr. M casually took them off the belt and placed them in front of us. The belt then began to move again.

You must be thirsty. Please help yourself. This is a beverage particular to this base. Mr. M then lifted his glass and emptied it. I was thirsty and had actually wanted something to drink so I took a sip. I found it so good that I also emptied my glass in no time. The drink tasted very much like fruit juice but it was perfectly transparent and colorless, like water. After finishing my drink, I felt completely refreshed. It was as if a sudden surge of energy were shooting through my body.

Seeing that I had regained my energy and alertness, Mr. M resumed his narrative: *The transparent glass plate in the windows is much like the plate glass that you have on Earth. It is important to keep the area completely sealed since strong electromagnetic waves are at work in this arrival station. With this insulation, the area is completely free of electromagnetic waves. The building was designed and constructed making use of all the latest scientific knowledge. Its primary purpose is to facilitate any necessary adjustments in waves. There are also three basement floors beneath the cross-shaped white magnetic plate that you saw at the center. The third floor is a magnetic tank. The magnetic plate can be raised or lowered as far as the second floor to accommodate the various sizes and shapes of the vessels. The height and diameter of space vessels are not necessarily proportionate to their overall size, so the free* upward and downward movement of the magnetic plate adjusts itself to the specifications of the various vessels.

When a vessel takes off, it does not rely solely on its own force; instead, it shifts to a flight mode that relies mainly on electromagnetic waves radiated from the magnetic plate. When a vessel arrives at the landing pad, on the other hand, the captain's task is to get the very center of the vessel to make contact with the center of the cross of the magnetic plate on the landing pad. When the central point of the cross coincides with the central point of the space vessel, the landing is considered perfect. This is rather difficult for captains who do not have a great deal of experience, so assistance is given. On each floor I think you can see a number of devices that look like long arms pointing upward towards the sky at an angle of about 40 degrees. When the vessel comes into contact with these, it can easily align itself with the center of the magnetic cross plate.

There is also a wave adjustment room at each exit. Nobody can leave without passing through one of these. When you enter the room, special electromagnetic waves act upon you and adjust your vibrations so that you may make a comfortable transition to the environment outside the vessel. When this process is complete, you are ready to enter the arrival station and the door will open automatically.

On the fifth floor, just above the cross-shaped magnetic plate, there is a control room as well as three other rooms for observation and communications. The administration of the arrival station is conducted in these four rooms. From here necessary instructions are relayed to each floor, communication is maintained with vessels in flight, and liaison is conducted with the central control room of each base.

After relating this to me, Mr. M paused a little. There were 12 or 13 cosmic persons in the grand hall where we were. As they sat here and there in small groups chatting and eating, I got the impression that they were waiting, perhaps for the arrival of their vessel.

There was a signal board near the ceiling in the middle of the grand hall. It was visible everywhere inside the room. There were ten round signal lights fixed horizontally in three lines. It seemed that the ceiling was also equipped with various mechanical devices, the purposes of which, needless to say, were unknown to me. Even the chairs we were sitting on seemed to contain various devices and mechanisms for purposes that were beyond my understanding. I found a number of buttons on the side of the chair facing the table. I noticed that each was different in color from the others. Seeming to be aware of my observation, Mr. M resumed his explanations.

Creation comes from Variations of Light

As the captain said, everything that exists in the whole universe is made from variations of light. These variations of light create rays outside the range of what is discernible to humans. It is impossible to study each and every one of these invisible rays, distinguishing one from another according to its functions. If we were to see all of these rays in their own forms just as they are, we would understand that the varieties and intricacies defy verbal expression.

Instead of analyzing these variations of light, we study them based on a concept we refer to as 'sub-light;' that is, we grasp the contents and functions of light in the form of waves and classify them according to their fluctuation and intensity. Although this is a concept understood by Earthly scientists, the waves that they have been able to discover constitute only a small fraction of the whole. They are not yet aware that there are still a great number of waves with different functions that they have yet to discover. In other words, a wave of light has two fundamentally different aspects. It is as simple as understanding the front and back or the surface and interior of an object. If we were talking about a human being, for instance, it would be the physical body and the soul. Likewise, light has two fundamentally different aspects. We could say that all light rays that have been discovered by scientists on Earth, even those that are not visible to the ordinary human eye, have been identified according to their 'surface,' or superficial side. Based on their observations of the superficial or phenomenal aspect of light waves, they conclude that these are rays of certain wavelengths. However, they have not perceived the full picture. This is just like jumping to the conclusion that the whole of a human being is the physical body alone.

While the physical body certainly constitutes an important part of a human being, we are all aware that there is more to the human existence than the physical aspect. And, of course, we are fully aware that the part that has the power to control the physical body is the true human being, and the true power is the power that comes from within. When this power is separated and works in various forms, those forms become waves with their own characteristics, such as the waves of a person's intellect or the waves of a person's will. They are living waves that are constantly at work in people. The true body of a human being is made up of waves of intelligence. However, that intelligence is not without warmth or brightness. It is a deep and expansive wisdom that is perfectly free and manifests itself in various forms. In other words, works of love and sincerity can be understood as waves of intelligence emanating from the supreme wisdom that lives within.

Mathematics as the Foundation of Cosmic Science

These waves are constantly at work inside the true or divine body of a human being. So, it became necessary to devise a means of differentiating the myriad waves that make up the whole. In mathematics as currently studied on Earth, you express a nearly infinite range of numbers as combinations of numbers from one to zero. However, we do not use numbers or signs. Still, the basis of the present cosmic science is mathematics. Cosmic science cannot be understood without mathematics. Now, the mathematics we have is many times more profound, more complex, and more encompassing than Earthly mathematics. Suppose Earthly mathematics were to express the contents of a proposition as a simple plane; cosmic mathematics would express it in cubic proportions including height and depth as well as the simple surface dimensions of planes.

I think you can now understand that there are living numbers, numbers that are dynamic, and numbers that quantify characteristics and intelligence.

Let me explain the basis of this mathematics. We subscribe to the principle that all things existing in the universe are composed of waves, and these waves come from a source of light which, in turn, radiates from the One Source. This light was split into plus (+) and minus (-) forms. Once split, these pluses and minuses further divided into other plus and minus forms respectively. Thus, repetitions of these separations and connections created all that we see, hear and touch. When one wave crosses with another wave and merges with it, a form and color are manifested. This is why colors can be thought of as 'pronouns' of waves or 'sub' waves. It is these colors that we cosmic beings regard as the basis of mathematics.

Instead of using numbers the way you do on Earth, we differentiate things using colors. If the functions and essential nature of things were to be expressed only in terms of numbers, would you be

134

able to comprehend that essential nature intuitively and would you be able to show it? This would be possible only for those who had undergone special training in mathematics; it would also be of little practical use for most people. On the other hand, we cosmic people know the nature of things at a glance through color variations, which indicate the classification, relationship, interaction, progression and other properties of things.

Rather than pursuing an explanation with words, I will show you an actual example on an announcement panel at the front of one of the tables here.

With this, Mr. M pressed a button on the front side of the table where he was sitting. In the right hand corner of the announcement board were twenty signal lights that looked like miniature bulbs arranged in two rows with two larger bulbs at the center. All of the lights came on simultaneously, each emitting light of a specific color. This was exactly what happened when he had pressed the button to order our drinks. While I was watching the board intently, Mr. M pressed a different button with his right hand. The colors of light began to change one after another. One light made changes ranging from the number 1 to 0. Seeing these changes in color, I wondered what was causing them.

Surmising what was going on in my mind, Mr. M resumed his explanation: *The color variations in the signal lights on the announcement board are caused by a wave separator that works by applying the laws of wave separation and connection by electromagnetic waves. The sophisticated functions of the board produce ten kinds of variation quite easily.*

I wanted to know about the nature of these functions, along with even a partial explanation of the laws of separation and connection. Unfortunately, Mr. M did not disclose that information.

The round signal lights on the announcement board at the center of the grand hall were changing color constantly, like traffic lights. They were repeatedly going on and off in groups; the colors and positions of the lights that were on kept changing constantly. Mr. M, who had been watching the changing signal lights on the board, explained their meaning to me: *A small-sized craft is approaching and will land soon. A medium-sized vessel is also on standby. At the moment there is quite a lot of other communication being received from various vessels.*

Let's have something to eat, suggested Mr. M as he pressed various buttons in succession beneath the announcement board at the corner. The lights changed color, to one similar to electric lights on Earth. When he finished pressing the buttons, he turned them all off.

The Life of Cosmic Human Beings

How do you pay for meals here?

When I asked this, Mr. M looked back at me briefly and smiled with his soft, quiet eyes, but he did not answer at once. After a while he replied: *Exchanging daily necessities with money may have been necessary for Earthly mankind in their process of evolution. However, since we understand that each person's necessities for living are provided by the parental God, we have no need to struggle for our own requirements; in other words, we have no need to protect ourselves. So, money has no value at all in our society. We know that each person's heart is far more valuable than money or things.*

Can you get whatever you want without paying money?

Yes. Various kinds of meals are prepared on this base, for instance. But none of us is so rude as to order unnecessary food.

According to our Earthly way of thinking, it seems as if an easy life is guaranteed here even without working.

You are right. In a way, we can lead a free and easy life even without working. But there is not one single person among us who is without an awareness of his or her heavenly mission. Since each person knows the role he or she is to fulfill in this world, there is no one who would forget or neglect his or her daily duty. Clothing, food and housing are all supplied as needed. How could we neglect to appreciate it, much less harbor complaints or dissatisfaction? So, there is no reason why unnecessary strife should occur. Contributing to the great universe with happiness and gratitude is our basic way of life. Our daily life follows the most natural progression. It simply flows. We never attach ourselves to past occurrences.We let the past disappear. There is no retention of turbulent energy. That is why we have nothing like natural disasters or violent storms.

Occasionally, leaders from highly evolved planets visit us aboard their wonderful space vessels to teach us portions of their advanced science. Each and every one of their words at such times permeates the depth of our souls. They also teach us the evolutionary process for our planet's ascent to the next realm.

As I listened, a meal was brought out and placed in front of us.

Food and Beverages of Cosmic Human Beings

I took a look at the dishes that had been delivered to our table. There was a round dish of what appeared to be rice, covered with a white sauce. Cooked vegetables, dried fruits, and something like a vegetable salad were also placed neatly on the conveyor. There were two of each dish, two drinks, one large bowl filled with fruit, and what looked like a coffeepot for each of us.

A signal light was blinking at the right corner of our side of the table. It reminded me of a doorbell on Earth. I felt a constant, steady vibration from it. It was as if it were saying: *The meal you ordered has been delivered. Please remove the dishes so that we can deliver our next order.*

Mr. M swiftly moved the dishes to the table. When he had finished, the conveyor started to move again. Mr. M efficiently arranged the dishes in front of us. I felt I was learning about his character little by little as I watched him organize everything so neatly; the distance and space between the dishes and other tableware were arranged in a precise, balanced manner.

Sorry to have kept you waiting. Please help yourself to your first meal at the arrival station, he said with a gentle smile.

Thank you, I said, and wondered where to begin. Since Mr. M took the dish of rice first, I tried it too. It was actually not rice at all, but something as soft as rice and that looked like bread and cream. It was pure white. I took a mouthful and found it so tasty that I ate the entire serving at once. After eating all of the cooked vegetables and other food, I felt a little thirsty and wanted a drink of water. Mr. M poured a semi-transparent liquid from the coffeepot-like container into the glass in front of me.

The vegetables tasted as if they had been sautéed in oil. In the fruit bowl, there were three different kinds of fruits: one kind that looked like oranges, another that looked like long, thin bananas, and a third kind that resembled apricots.

Feeling satisfied after the drink and dessert of fruits, I began to feel completely relaxed. When we had finished our meal, Mr. M pressed one of the buttons lightly and the conveyor immediately stopped. Except for our glasses, he put all the dishes back on the conveyor and pressed another button. The conveyor began to move again, carrying the dishes away to the kitchen on the other side of the hall.

Preparation of Cosmic Food

Looking in the direction of the kitchen, Mr. M resumed his explanations:

The conveyor flows into the kitchen at the other end. A number of cosmic people are working there. The various ingredients are stored in the basement and carried up in an elevator. The kitchen is equipped with various machines that operate on electromagnetic waves. In an extremely short time, the kitchen staff can make a wide variety of dishes as they are ordered by cosmic people. The facility is capable of preparing various kinds of meals for a large number of people. Orders taken at the tables are automatically transmitted to the storage area downstairs in the order they were placed. The necessary ingredients are then sent to the kitchen to be prepared as requested. The whole process is extremely quick and efficient.

The cooking is done in an oven-like device shaped like a rectangular box. Before the ingredients are placed inside, specific instructions are given so that only the required stages of preparation will be carried out and only the necessary equipment will be turned on. The finished dishes come out onto the conveyor never having been touched by a human hand. However, no matter how sophisticated a device it may be, the cooking machine is not what ultimately decides the quality of the food. It is the subtle adjustments of the equipment and the loving thought put into it that are most important. Loving thoughts are an essential ingredient of cosmic meals and these are transmitted from the cosmic persons who are putting their best efforts into their service. How could the cosmic people who eat the food be happy only satisfying their appetites, while ignoring the warm and energetic vibrations of those who prepared the food? They naturally appreciate the loving thoughts of the kitchen staff; there is no reason why they should have complaints or dissatisfaction. For cosmic people, partaking of a meal is a wonderful exchange of loving thoughts that permeate the hearts of friends, families and other people as they dine together.

Hearing Mr. M's words, I felt as if the meal I had just eaten had become new life and power inside my body, compensating for the energy I had lost earlier. An indescribable feeling also came over me as I somehow sensed that the loving thoughts of the cosmic persons who had prepared my meal were going to continue to be at work within my body.

The Arrival of Other Space Vessels

There was a sudden flash of light that put all my senses on alert. The fuselage of a huge, dark vessel appeared outside the window.

A vessel has arrived, said Mr. M.

Where do you think it's from? I asked.

Most likely from very far away. A fairly large number of cosmic humans are aboard this craft. They departed from Saturn and have been visiting a planet outside the solar system. The craft is one of the larger types among the medium-sized space vessels. It will take off soon after changing crews with the cosmic persons waiting on the floor just above us. Because this craft has a very important mission, it always continues to work without interruption. It'll be departing soon.

Listening to Mr. M speak as he read the various lights on the announcement board, I felt that he must know everything about the space vessel that had just arrived.

How quickly the people arrive and leave!

The cosmic people who frequently travel on space vessels can finish their wave adjustments as they board and disembark. This is why they can change crews so quickly.

Now that he mentioned it, I remembered our wait in the room with the buzzing noise. I recalled how the door did not reopen until after the green light had come on.

They are taking off now.

When I heard Mr. M say this, I watched the vessel commence its departure. No sooner had it ascended in a floating motion than it disappeared from our sight. I continued to watch the station after the vessel had taken off and noticed that the white, cross-shaped plate had been elevated by two meters. As I watched to see what would happen next, the huge arrival plate returned to its original position as if it had been absorbed into the floor. The entire process happened quite smoothly and naturally.

Several cosmic people were now coming into the dining room. A group of young men and three young women sat at a table on the other side. They were brimming with the energy and optimism of youth. They must have ordered beverages because glasses and pots were moving on the conveyor in their direction. At that time, Mr. M announced, *Another vessel is landing. This time, a rather small one.*

It landed at the center as if it had been drawn into it.

This is a craft that flies within the territory of the base. It has quite a few passengers in spite of its small size. The vessel will depart soon after receiving supplies here. The cosmic people most

141

likely will not disembark. This type of vessel is quite a handy vehicle, almost like a sky taxi.

I would love to have the chance to go on one.

Automatic Road Belts and Transfer Vehicles

Why don't we do just that. First, we need to go on the automatic road belt, replied Mr. M as he rose from his chair. I followed him out of the room although I still wanted to see more of the systems and facilities inside the arrival station. Going down the stairs to the exit, we came to an automatic road belt. Seen up close, the road belt looked quite different from what I had seen from the sky. What had appeared from the sky to be two dark rails were actually two parallel dark gray lines that lay flat on the ground.

Mr. M had gone into a room at the entrance to the road belt and had come back carrying what looked like a large collapsible chair.

What is that? I asked

It's the transfer vehicle we are to use.

Figure 7. Automatic transfer vehicle.

At this, he skillfully assembled the device by snapping the pieces together. Watching him set it on the tracks, I realized the four projected legs had been designed to lock into the grooves on the inside of the tracks. When he pressed down on the vehicle, it yielded by about 15 centimeters like a spring. The four legs fit into the tracks so snugly that the car stood firmly in place. It looked like a small automobile but the two seats actually faced each other. Each seat was able to accommodate two passengers. With a top that could be pulled out like an awning, it gave the impression of a covered wagon. Without the top, it looked a bit like a jeep. It was designed with convenience and versatility in mind and could be assembled in various forms. In the middle of the floor, there was a slight protuberance that looked like a round, flat bell. When Mr. M pressed it lightly, a rod glided up smoothly. Upon his attaching a conveniently placed handle to it, it became a perfect steering stick.

After assembling the vehicle, Mr. M went back to the entrance to wash his hands. He invited me to do so also. At a device that looked like a washbowl, he pressed a button with his foot. White vapor-like steam spouted out with a hissing noise. The vapor then seemed to be absorbed into a pipe from the drain. Mr. M finished washing his hands in what seemed to be no more than a second or two. Following his instructions, I also extended my hands and pressed the button with my foot. I felt neither warmth nor coolness; it was as if my hands had been bathed in some kind of gas. When I looked down at them, I noticed that my palms were now spotless.

How amazing this is!

It's a kind of electromagnetic cleanser, Mr. M explained to me.

I now felt ready to board the assembled vehicle, which was basically just like an open sleigh. The two of us sat side by side. The seat cushion was comfortable and the controls had been adjusted without my even noticing it.

Here we go! said Mr. M enthusiastically and the car started to move very slowly. It then picked up speed but ran very smoothly, as if gliding. It was like a boat moving smoothly across the surface of the water. I felt no resistance at all. We came to the exit of the arrival station. There was a large transparent gate which opened silently when our car arrived in front of it. The outside air was chillier than I had expected, causing me to tense up a bit.

Proceeding on the flat road for about 10 meters, we came to a slightly descending slope. The mountains of the base began to draw near, creating a strong visual impression. The mountains looked dark and steep but grass and flora that resembled alpine plants were visible in the nearby valleys.

The parallel automatic road belts, like two rails, had a green strip between them beautifully covered with grass.

As I sat with Mr. M on the moving transfer vehicle, I felt almost as if we were driving along a paved road in the suburbs of a city.

Let's go faster.

Even before Mr. M had finished saying this, the car started to slide straight down the road belt that followed along the ridges of the gentle slopes. In a cylindrical dial located among the various meters and gauges, a swirling ring of light suddenly began to rotate. Its color kept changing as the number of rotations increased. The car's velocity seemed to be indicated not by numbers on the meter but by the speed and colors of the rotating lights. I felt that the speed we were travelling at might have been 120 or 130 kilometers per hour but there was no resistance of the type that would have been felt on Earth at such a speed. I felt no numbness in any part of my body from the direct contact with the air. There was just a comfortable resistance that one might feel at a speed of 30 to 40 kilometers.

Adjusting to Differences in Gravity
and Atmospheric Pressure

Why, I wondered, is there so little resistance? Could it be that things such as gravity, air, water, minerals and plants here were fundamentally different from their counterparts on Earth? I could not help but think so. As if attempting to answer my question, Mr. M began to speak: *If you remember what I said earlier concerning the composition of the water and air on the moon, you will realize that they consist of molecules that have not yet been discovered on Earth. Therefore, I think you can appreciate that air and water here differ fundamentally from the air and water that you have on Earth.*

Then, gravity here is also very different from that on Earth, isn't it?

Yes, it is. It is about one third of the gravity on Earth.

Is the atmospheric pressure much different too?

Yes, it is. The difference in atmospheric pressure is felt as the difference in air resistance.

Doesn't the difference in atmospheric pressure cause difficulties in sustaining human life? Wouldn't it cause breathing problems and various difficulties for normal human functions? Can you explain this?

There is nothing so adaptable as the human body. Space vessels are equipped with facilities where cosmic people can train and adjust to constantly changing waves as they get off and on vessels. In fact, we went through these adjustments without knowing it. As I told you before, the arrival station is a training room for the harmonization of waves and makes use of the most developed scientif-

ic knowledge. Everything we did while we were there, each moment we spent resting, having meals, observing things and enjoying ourselves was time required for the harmonization and acclimation of our bodies. There was not a moment wasted. As for advanced cosmic beings, they can come and go through these facilities with ease since they require no adjustments.

In hearing these thoughtful explanations my heart filled with gratitude toward Mr. M. At the same time, I felt embarrassed about the amount of time that was required for the adjustment of my waves at the base. After living amidst the coarse vibrations on Earth for such a long time, I had no idea how coarse my own had become.

A fairly large building in the shape of a bell came into view in the middle of the road belt on which we were driving. Running at tremendous speed, our vehicle looked as if it would crash into it when all of a sudden we came to a left and right fork in the road. We passed by the building in an instant. It felt like being on an express train that passes through the local stations without slowing down.

Storing Important Equipment and Facilities

Is that the hangar of a space vessel? I asked.

Yes. We avoid leaving space vessels, mother ships and other important equipment and facilities exposed to the elements as much as possible. This is another difference between Earthly science and ours.

Is it to avoid deterioration in the performance of machines due to corrosion and oxidation?

Yes, but that is not the only reason. Cosmic science is based on the selection of waves. We select and use only the necessary waves out of the numerous phenomenal manifestations caused by the sep-

aration, unification and crossing of waves. In my first remarks about the interior of the space vessel, you may remember I told you that the umbrella-shaped cover of the gyrocompass at the center of the craft was made of layers of thin metallic plates. I explained that these plates were charged with a strong positive current and that no cosmic wave could penetrate them. Because of this, we are able to assign it with specific capabilities such as separation, amplification and deviation. The more sophisticated a machine is, the more vulnerable it is to the influence of waves. Space vessels are very sophisticated precision machines, so we keep them underground to protect them from the waves that freely penetrate the great universe. In this way, we can shut out specific waves.

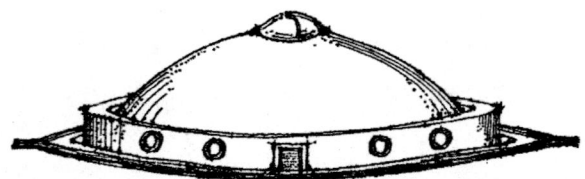

Figure 8. One type of hangar for space vessels

Now I can understand why the roof of a hangar opens and closes instantaneously like the shutter of a camera when a space vessel has landed or taken off. I presume there are many other underground facilities.

Yes, there are. The facilities of an artificial base are, for the most part, situated underground. There are underground factories and general services like the type you would find in a city. There are a few other reasons for having underground facilities, but I will explain them to you when we actually come to them.

As we continued to talk, we passed by several hangars. The mountain ridge where we were now sloped gently. We could see various trees in addition to those planted along the road belt. We came to a fairly large hangar.

Shall we take a brief look at the interior? suggested Mr. M as the vehicle arrived in front of the hangar and stopped at the entrance as if it had been drawn to it.

The Collision-Free Automatic Road Belt

Now, let's get out, said Mr. M as he swiftly alighted from the vehicle. Following his cue, I got out from the other side.

Let's remove the vehicle from the road so we don't hold up traffic. Could you please lift the other end?

The two of us lifted the vehicle very easily and put it beside the road. At that moment, I felt someone coming from the rear. It was a cosmic person driving down from the base aboard an automatic vehicle for a single passenger. In the blink of an eye he passed in front of us at a tremendous speed. I could not help but imagine an accident occurring on this road.

By the way, you should know that collisions never occur on these automatic road belts. Electromagnetic equipment automatically stops a vehicle if it fails to maintain a certain distance from the car in front of it. This is why we never have what you call on Earth 'traffic accidents'. We never even imagine such things. Earthly people do not realize that traffic accidents as well as other unexpected disasters are already latent in the world of waves prior to their actual materialization. You will never be able to rid yourselves of accidents and disasters as long as you keep seeking phenomenal causes after phenomenal results have actually materialized.

Then, are there no violations of any rules in your world, not to mention collisions caused by a disturbance of waves or a movement in the wrong direction?

Well, I can't say that we are free from such things entirely. Let me explain how things work. A base is divided into several districts, with each district under the supervision of a control unit. This unit is equipped with a sophisticated sensor that keeps a constant watch over the flow and interaction of waves in its area. If it detects anything irregular, no matter how insignificant, it radiates strong corrective waves to ensure that harmony is maintained at all times. When a space vessel flying from some other planet approaches, the unit chief pays particular attention to it. If, for some reason, the unit chief feels the situation might be beyond control, he or she will ask a supervisor for assistance. Nevertheless, such situations rarely occur.

It seems we live in a 'supradimensional' cosmic system, if I may call it so, that goes beyond my reckoning of time and space.

The great universe in its limitless expansion has one source at the center. Innumerable waves originating from this center repeatedly interact with each other vertically and horizontally and, in the process, create various forms with various characteristics. Manifestations of these forms and characteristics include the stars and planets scattered throughout the galaxies as well as the mountains, rivers, grass and trees that are found on the planets. But none of these entities continues its ceaseless activity outside the unseen great universal system or law. Among these living things, we human beings are given the greatest freedom and the highest wisdom. This is because we human beings came into existence for the purpose of manifesting the divine mind that creates this vast universe.

As we talked we were standing in front of the hangar. Mr. M pressed a button on an announcement board setting off a series of illuminations, with several signal lights on the announcement board in front of us blinking in different patterns. I somehow got the impression that the lights were actually communicating verbal signals.

Here is the answer. There is no space vessel in this hangar at present since the vessel is in flight. We are welcome to come in and have a look. The door will open in a moment.

As Mr. M said this, a green signal light above the entrance came on. The door immediately opened without a sound.

A Visit to the Hangar

Mr. M proceeded inside as if he had been waiting eagerly for this moment. After taking some four or five steps, we found an inner, transparent door through which we could see the circular shaped interior of the hangar. It was so bright that it was hard to believe that it was actually indoors.

The transparent door opened silently as we stopped in front of it. Beyond it were a main entrance with two side entrances, one at either side of it. The inside of the hangar was like a small athletic stadium and consisted of three ring-shaped floors, each wider than the one below it. It was similar to the arrival and departure station, but here we were also able to see the outline of the ceiling shutter system. We came to the central hall before I knew it.

The inner hall was much smaller than what I had imagined from the outside. It seemed to be approximately 40 meters across at the widest part. Looking up at the beautiful, transparent, shining ceiling, I sensed someone behind us. Turning around, I found Mr. M and a cosmic man from the hangar speaking. Seeing me, the man bowed politely.

We just felt like seeing your hangar on our way down from the arrival station at the summit. Are you sure we aren't inconveniencing you with our sudden visit?

Not at all. You are most welcome. And you seem to have a guest from afar. There is nothing special here, but please take your time and have a good look at things to make your visit worthwhile.

The warm, spontaneous and sincere welcome from this cosmic person did not fail to touch me; I felt as if I had been invited into the home of a close relative.

I appreciate your kindness, I said, bowing to him sincerely and quickly adding the awkward comment, *How amazing the ceiling shutter is!*

As you know, we cannot leave it open for a long time. But I will show you how to open and close it since the vessel to be docked here won't return for a while yet, he said as he glanced at the announcement lights on the opposite side of the entrance.

The cosmic man walked towards the entrance. No sooner had he touched a button than a light buzzing sound like that of an electric discharge could be heard from the center of the ceiling. A hole then appeared in the ceiling. Next, there was a snap and a sound as if something had been sucked inwards. This was followed by another light buzzing sound. After this series of sounds was repeated several times, the great ceiling was almost fully open. With the last snap, as if something were being fastened in place, the ceiling was fully open. The cross-shaped arrival plate at the center reflected the shining white sunlight. It had taken only a few minutes for the cosmic man to completely open the ceiling.

The ceiling consisted of four main beams, eight medium beams and 24 auxiliary beams that supported the larger ones. Just like fishing rods, they became gradually thicker closer to the base. Between the beams were thin boards which gradually rolled back with a low buzzing sound as the ceiling opened. Not wanting to miss even a second of this amazing process, I could not take my eyes off the ceiling.

What a wonderful system this is! I exclaimed spontaneously when he had finished opening it.

Please also watch carefully as I close it, he replied. He seemed to have pressed another button. After a clatter, the ceiling began to close with a buzzing sound. It measured about 40 meters in diameter, and shut almost instantaneously, as it had done earlier.

A Hangar Designed by People from Saturn

What is inside? I asked Mr. M, but the cosmic man at the hangar responded first:

A hangar is one place where cosmic people carry our their missions in life. Anyone, young or old, man or woman, who needs to stay in this hangar is able to do so as long as he or she wishes. In addition to the storage and machine rooms, there are many private living quarters and rooms for communication, entertaining guests, and dining. The hangar consists of three floors above and one floor beneath the ground.

I would never have imagined that many cosmic people were living in a hangar like this, without windows. But as soon as I came here, I was impressed with the marvelously sophisticated nature of the building.

You wonder why there are no windows? The reason is that this hangar was designed by people from Saturn. Many other hangars on this base have also adopted this style. Buildings on Saturn have no windows but have a free view of the outside whenever necessary. I guess it may be difficult to understand this just through a verbal explanation. I think we can truly know something for the first time only when we actually experience it.

How do you get the energy necessary to support this hangar?

I think you know the principle by which a space vessel flies. This hangar operates according to the same principle. But since it doesn't fly, we do not use a gyrocompass to reduce the vibrations of the waves that come through the captain's body. The coarse waves intercepted by the cosmic wave receiver are transformed through the multiwave separator into the energy we need.

At that moment, the lights stated blinking on the announcement board at the entrance. Mr. M seemed to have noticed it.

We might be in the way if we stay too long. Maybe it's best to say good-bye now.

Yes, of course.

I agreed to leave the hangar as Mr. M suggested, even though there were still many things that I wanted to know.

We are sorry if our sudden visit has caused you any inconvenience, said Mr. M in appreciation of the cosmic man's kindness.

Please feel free to stop by anytime.

Grateful for his words, we left the hangar turning back to wave good-bye a number of times. He was a tall man about 50 years of age and had pure, innocent eyes like those of a child. The sight of him sending us off with an endearing smile left an indelible impression on me.

Boarding the Automatic Transfer Vehicle Again

We soon boarded the transfer vehicle again. The road belt brought us to a plain curving sharply to the left. We took in the scenery on both sides as we descended in the smoothly running vehicle. I noticed more trees and green grass around us. It was like a mountainous area in the temperate zone of Earth. Taking a closer look, however, I realized that the plants were more like those in a subtropical region. At that time, I saw another automatic vehicle coming up the road belt from below. One other vehicle was also running just ahead of us. As we were about to pass the ascending vehicle, Mr. M raised his right hand a little. The other person held up his hand in reply.

As we approached the plain, Mr. M reduced the speed of the vehicle. As I wondered why, I noticed that the road converged with others. It was not an ordinary intersection; it was a roundabout where a number of road belts came together. One could enter and choose one's direction from a number of roads branching off it. The roundabout seemed to operate on a system where vehicles proceeded toward the middle in a clockwise fashion, giving priority to the vehicles on the right.

Our vehicle exited to the left and went onto the plain. Although the road belt and the avenues were truly splendid, the plain was a breathtaking wilderness. Because it was not utilized, I wondered whether there was any problem with it. Mr. M spoke as if explaining the reason: *There is a lot of uncultivated land on the base. We have an abundance of land considering the size of our population. Also, since we have a much more advanced technology than that of Earth for cultivating plants for our sustenance, there is no need for fields on the sides of mountains. I will show you a marvelous farm.*

The vehicle continued to traverse the flat plain. In a short time, we came to a forest.

Oh, a river! I exclaimed in surprise.

The vehicle slowed down as it crossed a bridge over the river. The river seemed to be about fifteen meters wide. Its clear water was flowing gently and the pebbles at the bottom were clearly visible through the crystal water. Various plants were growing lushly on the banks. I felt like drawing a picture of the pristine river flowing through the middle of the lush green plain.

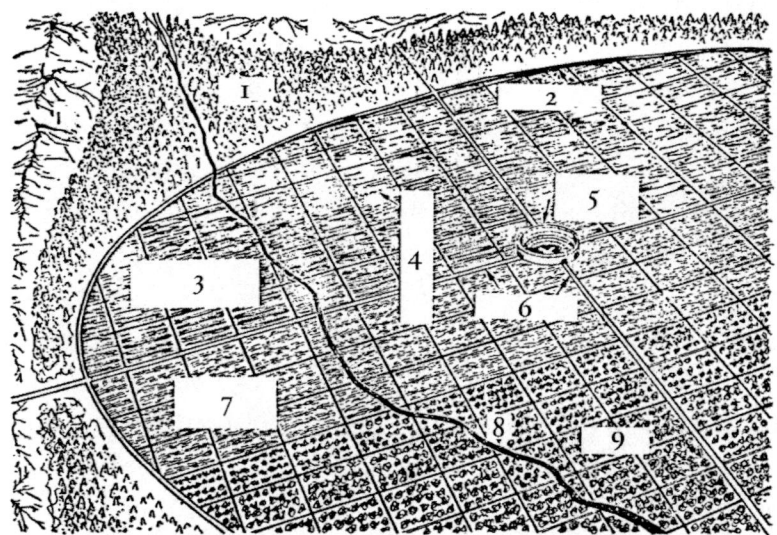

Figure 9. Green fields and farms: (1) fields, (2) mountains, (3) farmland with crops resembling wheat, (4) automatic roadway for farm crops, (5) traffic circle arrival pad, (6) automatic roadway trunk line, (7) river, and (8) orchards.

A Grand Farm

Continuing on our way through the forest, we came to a hill. In spite of the gentle slope, there was no change in the way the car ran. Reaching a flat summit, Mr. M reduced the speed and said, *Look at that!*

I turned in the direction he was pointing and found scenery that was absolutely spectacular. The vista of a great farm spread out before my eyes. The automatic road belts also spanned the countryside in an intricate network. The central

155

hill was positioned as if it were the control center of the area. The rectangular blocks of farmland and the plants were of a verdant green. As all these sights appeared before my eyes, I was so overwhelmed by the grandeur of it all that I almost felt dizzy.

Let's go to the central hill and enjoy the scenery on the way, said Mr. M.

Looking down from the top of the hill, I saw crops planted in a wide area across the vast plain. There was green everywhere. A self-running road extended into the green from the top of the hill. On its way, it crossed with another road at a mildly elevated roundabout.

Green fields and farms

The plain was covered by a network of main road belts as well as by farm road belts that served slightly different purposes. They intersected at level crossings and there were no roundabouts. Stretching out on either side of the roads were crops that looked very much like grain. We crossed a river on the way and came to a roundabout. On our right in the distance we could see what appeared to be fruit trees that were now green with a thick covering of foliage.

At a central roundabout, a horizontal road belt leading to the mountain range intersected with a vertical road.

The crops appeared to be well cared for even though the fields spread across a wide area on the vast plain. Questions automatically surfaced in my mind one after the other, such as: How do they take care of the crops? How do they cultivate and fertilize the fields? How do they harvest their crops? Other things I wanted to know were: Are there owners of the land or not? How do they cope with damage caused by heavy rain, draught, typhoons, blight and insects?

Management and Control of the Farm

How is such a wonderful farm managed? Is there an owner for each block of land? Do you adopt a tenant farming system or collective farming?

Mr. M appeared to be contemplating something for a while. Although he seemed to be looking at the roundabout ahead of us, I knew his mind was on something else.

Well, none of us fails to recognize that everything, from the farmland, to the dwellings we live in, to the daily necessities for maintaining family life, is given to us by God. We accept it as a matter of course. Thus, we do not think of land as something that is owned. People who work in agricultural positions contribute to the cultivation, processing, managing and storing of agricultural products. These people own neither land, nor houses, nor even daily necessities. What they do have are equal opportunities and the freedom to make the most of their lives through the work they are doing at present. How well they accomplish their work will depend on how they exercise their originality and creativity.

This vast farmland, for instance, is divided into several blocks, each managed by one leader. Through further subdivisions, a certain area of land is managed by a group of several people. In addition to these people, there are also people in charge of giving technical training in the use of machines and equipment, and giving other instructions on how to raise crops.

When they are short of labor at harvest time, many people come to assist them as volunteers. On these occasions, we not only harvest crops but also hold great thanksgiving festivals in appreciation of the divinities that have nurtured and protected the crops.

Everyone is eager to participate in these feasts at least once in their life to celebrate the harvest season and express their gratitude to God.

At the thanksgiving festivals held each autumn in the mountains and fields, people dance and sing as if in response to the vibrations coming from heaven. I guess it would be hard for people on Earth to imagine such a scene.

Also, since we have no coarse vibrations here, such as those which cause floods, storms, or damage by blight and insects, none of us even thinks of such things.

We arrived at the roundabout as I was listening to Mr. M talk. It was fairly large and was located on a small hill. We entered the roundabout, which was about half the size of the arrival station in the mountain. It was not high but operated on the exact same system. We returned the automatic transfer vehicle there and decided to take a sky taxi.

Boarding a Sky Taxi

This arrival station did not seem to have equipment for wave adjustment, which meant that arrivals and departures could be managed quite easily. We went to the waiting room on the second floor and took a seat. In a short time, a small space vessel arrived. There were quite a few passengers getting on and off. The vehicle had two separate entrances and two exits.

The craft ascended as soon as we finished boarding it. Mr. M began to talk about the sky taxi as he walked along the corridor: *The central floor is the main part of this vehicle, with floors for the control room and the battery tank attached beneath it. The core of the vessel is comprised of the machine room surrounded by private and other rooms for the crew. Outside, the corridor is divid-*

ed into compartments for passengers. It is quite compact on the whole and the corridors are not very wide. Let's go into this room.

With that, he pressed a button; the door opened silently. It shut when the two of us had entered. The room seemed to be able to hold about five or six passengers. Inside was a fine table. There was a television for observation, a signal board and some other equipment. There were also many buttons of various colors, but I had no idea what they were used for. We sat facing each other as Mr. M told me about the sky taxi:

Unlike long distance aviation vessels, this vehicle flies short distances. The flight time is short and the speed is not particularly fast. Because of this, its internal structure is totally different from that of long distance vessels. It is short in height in comparison with its diameter, and passenger compartments take up the entire external part of the circular cabin area. Each room is furnished with a direction indicator and a communications machine. After boarding, passengers enter their own designated rooms and state their destinations. By doing so, they can be notified when the vessel is approaching their arrival stations. Until then, they can watch on the television in their compartment various events at the base or at nearby planets. Since this vessel doesn't fly at a high altitude, why don't we open the inner window and take a look at the outside?

With this, Mr. M rose from his chair and went to the side opposite the entrance. As he pressed a button, two round windows, each about one meter in diameter, appeared. One was near the ceiling and the other near the floor.

A Grand Construction Site

These windows cannot be seen from the outside, but they are made to command a good view from the inside. This taxi is flying at full speed at an altitude of some two or three hundred meters. The expansive plain at the end of the mountainous area is as beautiful as a painting, don't you think?

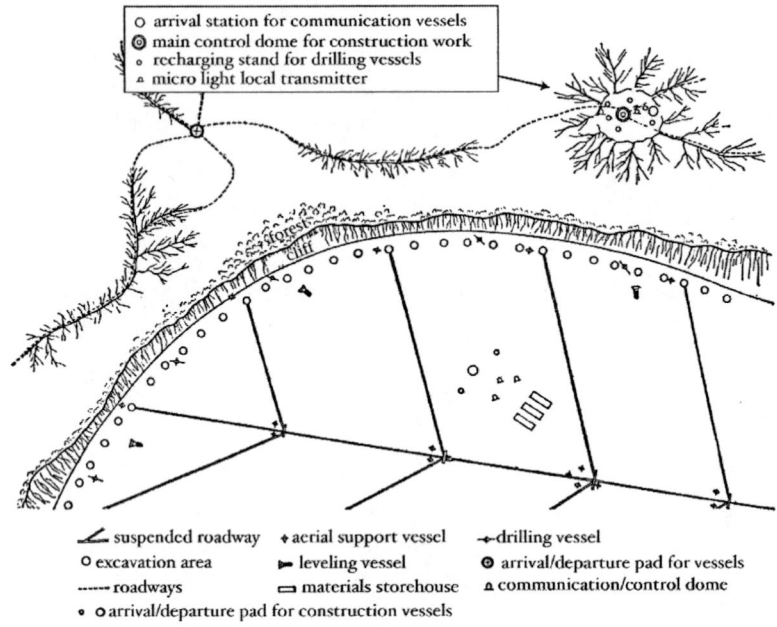

○ arrival station for communication vessels
◉ main control dome for construction work
○ recharging stand for drilling vessels
▵ micro light local transmitter

Figure 10. Aerial view of the construction site

When I looked down, I saw automatic road belts stretching out in every direction on the plain. Inside them were roundabouts of various sizes; the large ones contained stations for space vessels. I was fascinated by the marvelous view. Then I saw a fairly large engineering project underway near the end of the green plain. It looked as if large mountains were being removed to make some kind of dome. Not able to suppress my curiosity, I asked, *What is that?*

Mr. M smiled and said: *That is the construction site of a small artificial base. We cannot see well from here, but they are doing the work using various machines and special vehicles. There are many*

*engineering work sites in the base. Let's get off at that site and take
a look at the work.*

Mr. M returned from the window and communicated with
the crew by pressing a series of buttons on the direction indicator panel. The two main lamps on the board changed color
and started to blink. Reading the response, Mr. M pressed
another button and the lamps went off simultaneously.

Aerial View of the Construction Site

*They have replied that they were making a stop there anyway,
because there are some cosmic people going to the work site.*

As we continued our conversation, the sky taxi arrived at a
roundabout beside the work site. I was riveted to the window
watching the activity there: there were special road belts for
the engineering work, vehicles shaped like helicopters to support them, and excavating machinery digging into the Earth.
Spinning gently like tops, these excavating machines dug
through the Earth using the radiation of strong electromagnetic waves. They were working like huge drills, churning away
into the ground. When a machine completed the work at one
place, it shifted to another. In addition, there were special
vehicles that lifted several tons of soil at a time, transporting
it to automatic vehicles.

The workers were carving away at the mountain at a marvelous speed using the advanced mechanical equipment and
extensive facilities that had been set up there. Approaching
the site, I was unable to say for sure what was happening due
to my lack of knowledge of the technology being used and the
construction going on.

There was a fairly large roundabout at a small hill nearby.
Our sky taxi landed inside it. We went to the entrance and, as

we waited, the door opened silently. After that we found our-selves in the waiting room on the second floor. Like other sta-tions, this one had a transparent protective glass plate that completely covered the windows on the side facing the arrival area. As elsewhere, this glass shield seemed to be there to block out the strong electromagnetic waves emitted during the arrival and departure of a space vessel.

Going down the stairs and making our way to the road belt, we found many automatic transfer vehicles ready to depart. This made me realize how large the number of passen-gers was. We headed for the construction site in one of the vehicles.

Road Belts in the Sky

There were not many tall trees in the mountains here, but there were various types of tall grasses growing amidst the sparse trees that were scattered here and there. The trees looked very much like cedar trees on Earth. Observing the mountains on the right, we headed straight for the engineer-ing work site.

As we approached, I felt various vibrations through my body. The atmosphere here was similar to an engineering work site on Earth. When I happened to look up, I was over-whelmed by the expansive view of the road belt in the sky. So impressive was the site before my eyes that I was absolutely speechless!

The road belt connecting the arrival station of the space vessels and the engineering work site branched out into sever-al lines. We chose one that passed over several gentle hills to get to the site. As we came close, a spectacular vista appeared before our eyes. It was an indescribably great view of the road belts built for the exclusive use of the construction work. These were the very ones that we had previously observed from our sky taxi.

Oh, what an amazing sight! I could not help saying aloud.

Those are the road belts for the engineering work. At first glance, they look as if they are supported by legs on the ground, but they are actually suspended from the sky. They are hung from special space vehicles that look like tops. Depending on their weight, the belts are supported by either two or four vehicles. The leg-like objects are actually conveyor tubes that transport the soil to the mobile road belts.

Almost before I was aware of it, our vehicle came to the hill where the soil was being excavated. We got out of the car and walked in the field amidst the grass and trees, which had leaves similar to those of the oak trees that we see on Earth. We arrived at a cliff where the soil was being removed. The cliff was about 50 or 60 meters high. As I approached it, I worried that the ground beneath my feet might crumble at any moment. I looked back at Mr. M and found him smiling as he surveyed the work site.

You need not be afraid that the ground will collapse beneath your feet. It does not occur naturally. Particles and clods of soil are broken down through radiation of specific electromagnetic waves. An announcement is made beforehand to the cosmic people all around the site prior to using these coarse waves. It is similar to a sonic communication system that you might use on Earth where a canon or bell might be utilized, but here we communicate with presonic vibrations.

I see. And where does this road track lead?

You cannot see it from here, but it continues to the construction site, where an artificial base is being built.

The road belts radiated outwards like a network of veins crisscrossing in the sky. Together with the vessels in the sky from which they were suspended and the funnel-shaped excavation works at the end of the road belts, they formed an expansive circular pattern. Small space vessels shaped like children's tops were flying busily from hole to hole like butterflies flying from flower to flower. On the ground, fan-shaped machines were performing work similar to that of bulldozers. Behind them were a number of cylindrical buildings. Behind these buildings were numerous rectangular structures that resembled tool sheds. At the center of the road belt network was a cylindrical building.

As I surveyed the work site around me, a number of questions sprang to mind. For example, what would happen to these gigantic sky bridges if they were attacked by violent winds or heavy rains? I was curious to know how the construction crew would deal with such matters.

When I glanced at Mr. M, he looked back at me with his usual smile. His eyes possessed such depth that I could honestly say I had never seen a human on Earth with comparable eyes. Their reassuring look communicated the warmth of a very caring person.

A Base Free of Storms and Earthquakes

You don't have to worry about such things since, unlike on Earth, there are no violent winds or storms at all on this base.

I realized that I was unconsciously basing my judgments of everything here on my experiences on Earth. This was, no doubt, a result of my past lives spent in the coarse vibrations on Earth.

I see. You told me before that you had no natural disasters such as storms, earthquakes, or extreme heat or cold.

That's right. All phenomena that have come into being in the Earthly world are based on the repeated mutual interaction of the five types of coarse waves of Earthly humanity. These phenomena are mistakenly regarded as true reality. The accumulation of people's mistaken ideas regarding these phenomena, mixed with the light of the great God, have produced the present Earthly world of truth mixed with illusion. When mistaken perceptions and illusions accumulate, they eventually reach a critical limit where they automatically materialize in the form of major natural disasters that cause widespread misfortune to humanity. Needless to say, the great God is well aware of these impending disasters before they happen and tries to issue warnings before irreparable damage occurs. These warnings are manifested in the form of violent winds or floods. If the situation is left unchecked, however, a major calamity several times greater in intensity will occur.

Take rain, for example. Unlike on Earth, we never see a sky full of heavy black clouds completely darkening the sky, as if to overwhelm the Earth. Rainfalls here occur when rain is needed but we never see black clouds that block out sunlight to the point that it becomes as dark as night during the day. Here, rain falls in such a way that everything looks as if it has been covered by a thin mist. Furthermore, the rain does not continue to fall day after day. It comes in the form of a light shower lasting for only a very short time.

Please remember what I told you about the composition of molecules of water, for instance. Here a water molecule includes features not found on Earth. Also, because Earth is enveloped in thick of layers of distorted ideas (thought waves), something of a given content and size will weigh about three times more than its coun-

165

terpart on the moon. Unless you keep these basic differences in mind, you will find it extremely difficult to understand what you experience at the base.

These basic differences make all the scientific knowledge you have acquired on Earth completely irrelevant here. You need to learn the fundamentals all over again from the start. Otherwise, you will be forced to acknowledge as reality conditions that are totally inconceivable to you when you see them at work in the construction site and other places. Take, for example, that sky bridge. The reality of it floating high in the air and continuing to rise in the distant sky beyond our sight speaks for itself.

His ardent efforts to impart all these understandings touched my heart. I was moved by his very caring ways and could hardly say anything, other than just nod with a simple *Yes*. A sky bridge? How could such a thing really exist? But there it was right before my eyes. I was now seized by the desire to learn whatever I could about this superior science.

Floating Space Vehicles Supporting Automatic Road Belts

I understand that there are special vessels from which the sky roads in the air are suspended. Are they manned by cosmic persons?

No, not at all. Those vehicles are entirely unmanned. All the steering is done at the control center using special waves, just like a remote control system.

What do those things that look like wings do?

On the opposite mountain, there is a control center that is supplied with a wide range of equipment to supervise the entire work site here. The vessels from which the sky roads are suspended are not able to intercept sufficient cosmic waves to provide the buoyancy required to support the weight of the roads. To provide the vessels with the required buoyancy while keeping their size to a minimum, the control center transmits cosmic waves to them that are downgraded to pre-electromagnetic waves. The parts that look like wings are actually wave receivers which pick up waves radiated in specific directions. The surface of the wing is covered with a number of extremely sensitive receivers similar to the compound eyes of an insect and these can be thought of as serving as 'the eyes of waves.'

Aren't people affected by the electromagnetic waves beneath a buoyant vehicle?

When you first saw the medium-sized space vessel, you learned that its ascent, descent, diagonal and level flight movements were entirely managed by the crystal sphere in the gyrocompass. This is because the angle of the emission nozzle of the electromagnetic radiator and the quantity of the electromagnetic waves to be discharged are controlled through the extremely powerful and sensitive functions of the crystal sphere. Thus, the electromagnetic waves surrounding a space vessel maintain the best conditions for the flight by constantly changing shape. I'm afraid the relationship between the buoyancy arising from changing distances between two points of intersection and the speed cannot be explained easily, but strong buoyancy is obtained by radiating electromagnetic waves in a pyramidal shape or by shrinking the distance between the points of intersection. With buoyant vehicles, for example, the electromagnetic waves are scattered, since no speed is required. Even so, the cosmic persons working at the site are dressed in electromagnetic wave protection suits.

How many hours does a person work at the site?

The work continues without a break throughout the day and night with cosmic persons working in six shifts.

Does that mean that they work for four hours each day?

Actually, I have not yet explained to you about our time here. Time on Earth and time here at the base are totally different. The best way to understand it is to think of our time as being equivalent to half the length of yours.

As I listened to Mr. M's explanation, a number of small vessels kept flying about in the air above the vast engineering work site. They were landing and taking off quite easily.

How do those vessels shaped like tops crush the soil?

Those vessels are manned. Working relentlessly without a minute's rest, people are busy monitoring the progress of the excavation, receiving instructions from the control center, and constantly maintaining communications with the cosmic persons at various places in the work site. However, their vessels are not equipped with facilities to receive cosmic waves; they only have the ability to receive and discharge electromagnetic waves. So, they have been designed to store energy. The vessel converts the energy into the roughest of vibrations, which it discharges. Those vibrations crash into the soil with the same impact as bullets shot from a gun, crumbling the soil instantaneously. As a result, the soil returns to its original state of single particles. Both the axis at the core, the single leg, and the thin, long head can be freely extended or contracted. After each shift, the vessels fly up to the control center on the mountain where they are recharged with energy. They then fly back to the work site with a new crew. There are ample facilities at the control center to allow up to ten of these vessels to be recharged at a time. When waves are to be emitted in designated directions, weak electromagnetic waves are emitted first. When these come into contact with an object, some of the waves are absorbed while others are sent back immediately. In this way, the position of the receiving host can be detected.

When a top-shaped vessel is in flight, the head and leg are retracted so it flies just like an ordinary space vehicle. It is safer for us to stay away from the work site since we are not dressed in elec-tromagnetic wave protection suits.

Looking down, Mr. M seemed to be contemplating some-thing and remained silent for a while. He then walked back to the automatic road belt saying, *Let's go and see how the construc-tion of the artificial base is progressing.*

Grass of a type unfamiliar to me and about a meter high covered the area. Interspersed among the grass were red, yel-low, and purple flowers. Among them were birds that looked like quails taking flight.

Oh, birds! I uttered in surprise. *Do you have birds on the base too?*

Yes, birds and small animals live in the base, but there are no birds of prey that you see on the Earth.

Do you also have domesticated birds?

There are birds closely resembling canaries and parakeets. They are all cared for with our loving thoughts.

While walking through the tall grass in the field and exchanging these remarks, I suddenly became aware of the lightness of my own movements. Until then, for the most part, I had been aboard a space vessel or a transfer vehicle inspecting the various sites on the base. This was my first time to walk in the mountains and fields, and I now noticed that my body was very light and movement from one place to another required almost no effort. I tried to jump a little and found myself lighter than I had expected; I could jump well over two or three meters.

Next, we boarded a transfer vehicle and made our way quickly to the arrival station of the space vessels. There was not a cloud in the sky over the base. It was as clear and deep as an autumn sky. Space vehicles of various sizes and shapes could be seen flying in the sky. Each flew at a different speed, like jet planes in the stratosphere.

Measurement of Time at the Base

Entering the arrival station, we proceeded to the uppermost floor. Sitting in a chair in the waiting room, I noticed that the lights on the announcement board at the center were blinking on and off as usual; but because I had not yet learned how to interpret them, I was not able to tell what they were signaling. Watching the blinking patterns, I noticed six lights beside the board. The one at the left end was shaped like a gourd. It was as if two lights had been fused together to form one. As I watched them, they began to change color. On close inspection, I noticed another extremely small light on the side. It was busily blinking at fixed intervals and was the same color as the two connected lights.

What is it? I could not help but ask.

It is a device which measures what you on Earth refer to as time. In other words, it serves the same purpose as a clock. It's about eleven o'clock now according to Earthly time.

So, is the day here also divided into 24 hours?

A day is divided in two halves, just like AM and PM on the Earth. However, the first and second halves of the day are respectively divided into seven units and each of these units is further divided into 70 smaller units. These smaller units are again further divided into 70 units. The final one-seventieth unit is somewhat shorter than one second on the Earth.

The base here, like the Earth, has its own measurement of time. In the world of vibrations, time serves as the horizontal rule. Without time, or the horizontal rule, the vibrations, or the vertical rule, cannot be determined. The point where time and vibrations intersect with each other is understood in cosmic science to be the starting point of a planet. The vibrations originating from the great source of the universe, in other words, the One Being or the great God, undergo changes in their waves as they become further removed from the great God. In other words, the further removed the waves are, the coarser they become. However, becoming further removed does not mean being further away in terms of distance. Distance is decided by the thought waves of humanity living on the planet. It is not something determined through calculations of time and space. Among the trillions of stars and planets scattered throughout the great universe, none of them has a rule of distance identical to another. Each planet has its own reckoning of time which corresponds to its vibrations—in other words, its perspective. The heavenly position of a planet or its heavenly mission is shown by the point where its vibrations and time intersect with each other; on this basis, the planet endlessly pursues its own activities and evolution. The more evolved or spiritualized humanity on that planet becomes, the briefer its time and smaller its space. The time when we become one with the great God will be the time when we arrive at a world without time or space. It will be the absolute world or the source of vibrations where all dualistic contradictions are transcended.

How long will it take us to become one with the great God?

The evolutionary stages differ from planet to planet in time and space and are almost countless. In fact, it is impossible to count or measure their number. It's no use thinking about it.

I am led to believe that human beings living in a world too detached from the great God will not only find themselves backward in their evolution, but will also be faced with difficulty in achieving it.

You are right. Initially, the great God planned a unilateral evolution of all humanity. However, since many souls had forgotten about their true identity as offspring of God, and had gotten lost while pursuing their own confused thoughts, the great God sent forth additional, special waves to guide and protect humanity. These are the angels who still continue to protect, guide, and stay in close contact with all human beings.

Mr. M explained these deep principles smoothly and steadily, starting from a simple signal light on the announcement board at the space vessel arrival station. To me, he looked like an embodiment of love itself. And though elucidating a profound truth, his each and every word was calm and natural, as if he were speaking about everyday occurrences. I thought he was a living example of what we refer to as a person with a 'constantly calm heart.' At that time, an unusual light was illuminated on the announcement board.

The Main Control Center and the Governor

A sky taxi is arriving. It is a large sized vehicle belonging to the Twelfth Control Center.

Does each sky taxi belong to a specific control center?

The bases on this planet, as on other planets, come under the control of one main control tower that incorporates two sub-control towers, each assisted by seven control offices. This is the fundamental organization of the social system of this planet. In addition to the 14 control offices, there are countless branch offices and liaison offices. From the various types of space vehicles to each kind of machinery and equipment, there is nothing that does not come under the jurisdiction of one of these offices. The administration of this planet is based on this fundamental social system. A general assembly is attended by the chiefs of the 14 control offices as well as by officials from the sub-control tower. However, final decisions are ultimately made by the governor. The governor of this planet is fully experienced in living on a marvelously advanced planet over a long period of time and possesses superlative wisdom and an infinitely loving mind. The governor is dedicated day and night to the evolution and betterment of humanity on this planet. In addition, none of the cosmic human beings at this base fails to understand that his or her mission can only be achieved through assistance from the parental sun that supervises this planet.

A sky taxi arrived with a bright flash of light. Many cosmic human beings alighted from the vehicle. After they had all gotten off, a green signal light came on and the cosmic people who had been waiting boarded the vehicle. We got aboard it too. Once everybody was on board, the door shut automatically without a sound. The vehicle seemed to have taken off as we were walking along the corridor. As soon as we entered our compartment, Mr. M began to communicate with the control center. I pressed a button and opened the window to look down at the ground. We were flying at an altitude of some 1000 meters. The vessel did not accelerate much during the ascent, waiting instead until it leveled off. While it was at a low altitude, it also flew at a moderately slow speed. I thought this might be because someone was monitoring the engineering site from the sky.

After completing his communication, Mr. M said, *The next stop is the artificial base.*

We got off the sky taxi even before we had time to sit and look down from the sky. I felt that we were just like commuters who take a bus for only a single stop.

Arriving at the Artificial Base

Flying across the sky at great speed over the artificial base under construction, the sky taxi came to an arrival station located some 120 to 130 meters above sea level. From outside, it looked no different from an ordinary arrival station. What was special about the artificial base, however, was that, unlike the arrival station on a natural base built as a single, autonomous entity, this station also seemed to function as an antenna of a scientific plant. Its enormous size reminded me of an athletic stadium. The entire base seemed to have been constructed as a part of an extremely large-scale plan.

There were passages leading to the underground base both from the first floor and the basement of the arrival station. Especially conspicuous at this base were the various meters and signal lights as well as signal boards that provided at-a-glance information on the operations and general state of the internal systems. In addition, there were various other facilities that we had not seen at other bases.

After alighting from the sky taxi, we went directly outside without going down to the basement. Following Mr. M, I walked out of the building at a brisk pace.

About 70% of the circular hill had been completed while the remaining 30% was still under construction. I happened to look up and noticed that a network of automatic road belts connected the entire engineering site, extending to the construction site passing above our heads.

This hill was not a rocky mountain with rugged rocks exposed on the surface but was composed of gentle slopes with ridges that seemed to be designed to converge at regular intervals toward the center. At a glance, I recognized that it was an artificial hill. Its perfectly harmonized, neat shape gave that impression.

Stepping outside, I found several automatic road belt tracks. Rather than one or two arrival stations on the hill, there were many. They seemed to be classified into large, medium and small stations. With these impressions passing through my mind, I started to follow Mr. M. After walking for a short while, he stopped to talk to me, looking up at the road belt extending high in the great sky.

The soil excavated from the engineering site is carried along that road belt suspended from the sky to the construction site. Based on Earthly measurements, the distance it is transported is about 10 kilometers. Let me explain the order in which things are constructed at this base. First, the control tower, which is the central building of the base, is built. Next, the surrounding artificial mountains are constructed starting from one end. Finally, the construction goes along the main road belt returning at last to the starting point, bringing the large circular shaped artificial base to completion.

This particular base is divided into five sections above ground and one section under the ground. Some sections are several floors high while others consist of a single floor. These sections have a huge capacity to house medium- and small-sized mother ships. The caves that look like entrances to tunnels at the sides of the hills are entrances for the mother ships. The interior is equipped with various machines and devices to move and maintain the balance of the mother ships. Except for the automatic road belts and elevators, the entire base is maintained in a condition similar to that of an airtight room. This is done by using equipment to control the air pressure, ventilation, temperature and humidity. There is also equipment to absorb waves emitted by various machines and multi-separators of cosmic waves that are intercepted at seven different points. In addition, by-products that are produced in the process of separation, such as reduction, harmonization and repulsion, are utilized for various purposes. A countless number of machines of various kinds, such as large-scale separation equipment and storage tanks for the energy produced, have also been carefully and ingeniously installed in perfect order and carry out their respective work. The base as a whole functions as a model workplace where those united around the same purpose show an exemplary ability to accomplish great tasks. This artificial base is fulfilling a major role as one of the important organizations within our society.

Superior Construction Materials

What are the main materials used for the construction of this base and how are they produced? On Earth, a major part of a project like this would be the assembly of the steel frames combined with various other materials based on geometrical calculations. Could you explain what happens here?

Well, the main construction materials that are currently used on Earth are steel, cement, bricks and wood. In the distant past, say, thousands of years ago in Earthly time, we did use materials derived from minerals and plants using processes such as refinement and extraction. Today, however, bases like the ones you have seen are built with compound materials developed through our more highly developed science. They do not depend on minerals or plants as sources of raw materials. Instead, light waves, gas, heavy gas, liquids, semi-solid and solid bodies produced during wave separation procedures are utilized. These materials are used mainly in a process we call 'time quality change,' or 'stiffening,' during which other additional characteristics, such as durability and tensility, are introduced depending on the specific uses of the material. To give one example, we do not shoot heated rivets using air hammers when we construct the framework. Instead we use a heated compound liquid which flows along 'guides' that serve as molds. When the liquid compound is ejected from the guide, it turns into a semi-solid body upon making contact with the air. Thus, materials in various shapes are produced according to the shape at the end of the ejector.

Different types of vessels fly over the construction site. Among them are some that transport tanks of the liquid compound. They remain in the air ready to deliver the tanks to the required spots. Suppose we were to make an 'I' shaped beam 50 meters in length. The material sent out on the rollers along the guides connect when one end meets with the other at the point of the leg. The two link together as if they were glued with adhesive. This compound material or synthetic steel, if I may call it that, is several times stronger than the steel you have on Earth yet has only one fifth the weight. Let's get on a transfer vehicle and go down to the site. Rather than spend time listening to my explanation, I think you would understand the process better if you saw it in action.

Mr. M began to walk in the direction of the transfer vehicle. The hill inside the completed portion of the base was covered with what appeared to be a lawn. Looking at it, a person would think it was nothing more than just a wide, gently sloping hill that could very well have been part of a golf course.

On the Way to the Central Control Tower

The hill was covered by road belts that spread vertically and horizontally to form a network. Within the network were roundabouts, level crossings and lines that connected the inner areas with the surrounding areas. Some transfer vehicles stood ready for use on the sidings. At the roundabout on the hill, the road belts converged from four directions and there were signs that seemed to indicate the destination of each belt as well as information regarding connecting routes.

Let's go to the central control tower. We'll be able to get a lot of information there. It also overlooks the entire base so I think it probably commands the best view in the area.

Heading for the control tower, the vehicle we were on went straight down a ridge that ran toward the center. On the way, we could see entrances for mother ships in the hillside. Viewed at close range, they were enormous. I had imagined that they would most likely be in the shape of a horseshoe, but I was wrong. They were elliptical in shape and no two of them were alike. As I observed them, I became entirely absorbed in thought concerning the docking of mother ships in these hangars. For example, I wondered whether mother ships moved on their own power in the hangar and, if so, how they dealt with the electromagnetic waves. If, on the other hand, they moved through some external power source, I wondered what that source would be. I also wondered about the air pressure divisions in the entire base, about how they disposed of contaminated gas and supplied fresh air. One question after the other sprang to mind. If, for example, special waves were generated through the activity of various kinds of mechanical equipment and combined with each other, what effect would these have on the entire base? Also, if the idea was to seal off the air from the outside, this would be impossible to manage at times of entry and departure of such gigantic objects as mother ships. The same problem would also apply to people coming and going as well as the arrival and departure of automatic transfer vehicles. There were so many issues to contemplate. Lost in thought, I almost forgot that I was aboard a transfer vehicle.

Mr. M began to speak in a contemplative tone, as if talking to himself:

The systems and facilities of the artificial base are, I think, too intricate for you to grasp fully at the present time. Rather, I will show you the facilities in operation and comment on each of them as we go along. I think the best method is to experience the reality of the base and its science through the senses of sight, hearing, and wave vibrations.

These words brought me back to the present moment. Our vehicle continued to go straight towards the control tower. Mr. M seemed to be intently watching the tower, and it occurred to me that he might be communicating telepathically with the chief of the control tower. I could not help but feel that he had a particularly dignified and lofty air about him at the time.

Passing over a ridge, the transfer vehicle was now running along the plain. Beautiful fruit trees were planted at regular intervals on both sides of the road belt. It looked like an apple orchard; the trees had not grown too big, but their growth looked vigorous and promising. I assumed they had been planted at the time when the base was constructed. I could not see any fruit among the fresh green leaves on their branches, but this may have been because the trees were still immature.

The Control Tower

The control tower was almost completely surrounded by a road belt forming a roundabout; the road belt also ran through the center of the tower in the shape of a cross. Mr. M reduced the speed of the transit vehicle as he drove into the center of the tower. The word 'tower' tends to give the impression of a structure that is tall and thin, but as we entered the control tower I felt as if we had been absorbed into a huge building.

179

When we reached the center, we found several road belt tracks with a large number of cosmic people boarding and alighting from vehicles. The place was as busy as the lobby of a large hotel. There seemed to be many elevators both large and small.

Let's go up in an elevator and I will tell you more about the construction site.

Do you ever use all of these elevators?

When cosmic people from other planets arrive at this base in mother ships or space vessels, it is our custom to invite them to the upper floors. We have quite a few rooms ready for their entertainment, including a large banquet hall that can accommodate several thousand people at one time. There are also lounges, small conference rooms and meeting rooms for groups who come here on various missions. When large groups of visitors arrive from distant planets, all of these elevators are fully utilized.

The ceiling of the tower was dome-shaped and extremely high. Announcement boards and lights were visible everywhere. A cosmic man approached us as we were going to the elevator. Mr. M handed him the automatic transfer vehicle. The man quickly folded it. He did this with all the vehicles for all the cosmic people who streamed in. After folding them, he stored them all away.

We boarded a medium-sized elevator. When all the passengers had finished boarding, the door shut automatically. What was interesting about this elevator was that it felt very soft and light inside, not like the cold feeling of being in an iron box made of hard metal.

Chapter 5

AN INTERVIEW
WITH THE GOVERNOR

Going to the Top of the Control Tower

I think we should now go meet the governor. We'll have to go all the way to the top of the tower, said Mr. M as he pushed a button. With a light click, a green light came on. Various other lights on the display board also flashed on and off briefly.

Before I was aware of it, the elevator had stopped and the door had opened. We went out into a corridor that was very brightly lit. Its pristine white walls made everything look clean and fresh. As we came to the end of the corridor, there was a large window overlooking the base. I now realized how high we had ascended in the space of a very short time. We were so high up that it made me feel dizzy to look down at the landscape below. We were able to get an expansive view of the mountains where the artificial base and the construction site were located. I felt as if I could almost reach out and touch them. As I was studying details of the scenery below, Mr. M suggested that we proceed to our meeting with the governor.

I feel so nervous that I am almost shaking. There are so many things I want to ask.

There is no need to be nervous. The governor is very helpful and will explain everything in a lucid, considerate way so that you will be able to get a clear picture of what goes on at the base. He knew about you long before our meeting, said Mr. M with a smile.

Oh, is that so? was all I could say. I found Mr. M's words mysterious if not perplexing. As if my body had separated from my soul, I walked behind him in a daze.

Turning to the right onto a corridor that was painted a shining white, we arrived at the entrance to a room. Above the door was an insignia formed by seven small overlapping rings. These seven rings formed a circle around a shining yellow-white center. The arrangement of the circles looked very much like the aperture of a camera. Needless to say, I had no idea what it signified. The door to the room receded from the corridor and was positioned at the end of a series of transparent, sky-blue, glass-like frames. As Mr. M pressed a button, a series of flashing lights appeared on the display board. Presumably after reading the response, Mr. M looked back at me with a slight smile.

It was my guess that the governor had answered something to the effect of, *I am waiting. Please come in.* My mind suddenly flashed back to my earlier observation of Mr. M on the hill. At that time, I had surmised that he was probably using telepathy to communicate with someone in the tower. I now began to believe that Mr. M may have already received the governor's consent at that time.

The Meeting with the Governor

The door opened silently. The room inside was quite spacious. In front of a large desk at the center of the room sat a person who seemed to be the governor. Mr. M went straight to where he sat. I followed him promptly so as not to lag behind.

The governor was seated in a chair with his eyes closed, and seemed to have been deep in prayer. As we approached, he discontinued his meditation. Even before Mr. M had the chance to give a polite bow, the governor rose from his chair with a cheerful smile and greeted us, *Welcome to the control tower.* He signaled with his eyes to a young man at the entrance as he motioned for us to be seated in the chairs beside him.

The room was circular and very bright with windows on three sides. The entire hill of the artificial base was visible from here. It looked miniature, as if it could fit into the palm of my hand. There seemed to be 14 or 15 cosmic persons in the room. Each of them had a fairly large desk. On each desk was a box containing meters of various sizes. Beside these were several very thick books with dark blue covers. There were also several other books that appeared to be used for keeping records. It surprised me to think that even cosmic people kept records. I also saw various styles of pens that resembled fountain pens. Some of them had buttons on them; others were plain without any buttons at all.

A Conversation with the Governor

Mr. M began to speak to the governor: *It must be quite a lot of work to manage the construction of the base.*

Actually, I am filled with gratitude as I watch the construction progress day by day, thanks to the sincere efforts of the people working here, the governor answered.

Such an enormous construction project must require careful attention since you use various scientific materials and large-scale machinery and equipment. In addition to the immediate work, there is also the consideration of long-range future plans. It must be quite a task to supervise all these aspects, commented Mr. M.

The construction work is divided into various sections. The work proceeds in stages but they are all part of an integrated process.

183

Although there is a person in charge of each section, the entire work progresses with a consistent flow. The final results of the various stages of work are brought together at this control center so we can oversee the entire workflow from beginning to end just by being here and monitoring the situation. What we do here basically is check the current work to make sure that there are no errors. So, in effect, there is no need for us to exert ourselves or to feel stressed. Our main task is simply to carefully oversee the general flow of the work. Above all, we feel a strong sense of gratitude to the people who are working at the construction site.

As I listened, I could not help but wonder how many years a project like this would take from start to finish.

From start to finish, how long will it take to complete this artificial base? I asked.

Using an Earthly measurement of time, it will take about two years, replied the governor a friendly tone. Dressed in a deep indigo space suit, he was about 170 centimeters tall and appeared to be about 57 or 58 years old. He had a slightly thin, oval face and his hair was jet black and showed no signs of graying. My first impression of him was of an experienced physician one might meet on Earth. He had a gentle manner and his eyes conveyed a feeling of real warmth and and affection. Each word he spoke held a deep wisdom, and he had the ability to speak in a way that any listener could understand. He had a pure, clear complexion and his calm, gentle attitude communicated an indescribable sense of dignity and nobility.

Each of the fourteen or fifteen persons working in the control room seemed to have his or her own special role and position.

What method of communication do you use between the construction site and the control room? I asked.

We keep in constant touch with the persons in charge of each of the sections at the construction site using a device similar to the wireless telephone you have on Earth. For example, the spacecraft that distribute the condensed thermal liquid compound to the construction section have the ability to continuously gauge the quantity of the compound liquid inside the tanks. Therefore, as they observe the progress of the entire work, these spacecraft can give orders to the transport vessels that bring the liquid compound from the factory. Also, when they supervise the fabrication of the frame joints, the conditions and time required for setting are recorded using special wave reactors. In this way, we constantly supervise the frames under assembly so that the required balance is maintained at all times.

What is the capacity of this base for housing medium- and small-sized mother ships? I asked.

The base is designed to house a total of 47 medium and small mother ships.

Where do the cosmic persons who designed this artificial base come from?

Cosmic people from Venus designed it. However, this base is not intended to be an exact replica of an artificial base on Venus, since this base has its own particular planetary vibrations. This base was designed so that its missions would be achieved in tune with its own vibrational frequencies. In other words, it is basically the same as a base on the planet Venus but operates somewhat differently. Why don't we go take a look from the observation platform on the top floor of this control tower?

With this, the governor stood up. We also stood and then followed him out of the room.

As we walked along the corridor to the left, we came to a staircase. Ascending the stairs, we arrived at the observation platform. It reminded me of the mast of a large ship. A huge cylinder projected high up from the center. Just below the top of it, I noticed equipment for emitting special waves. Underneath this, I also saw various other types of equipment, but I had no idea what functions they performed. The control tower that served as the center of the artificial base below us was designed so that the entire surroundings could be observed easily.

The governor went to the center of the observation platform, raised his right hand above his head, pointed to the sky and then rested his hand on his chest, pausing for a few moments of deep meditation.

I somehow got the impression that his movements were meant to represent the unification of heaven and Earth in prayer.

Observing the Construction Site from the Tower

The cloudless blue sky had a depth and clarity that were refreshing and energizing to both body and soul. Standing at the top of the control tower at the center of the base and immersed in quiet prayer, we felt that our entire bodies were being purified. We felt incredibly light and transparent. I wondered what season it was now at the base in Earthly terms. Because of the brisk, refreshing air, I surmised that it must be autumn.

From the control tower, the mountains looked like gentle hills in perfect harmony with the surrounding environment. Covered with grass resembling a lush, green lawn, the hills of the base expanded in front of my eyes as beautifully as a picture in a dream. Large and small spacecraft were busily coming and going. From where I stood the network of automatic road belts on the ground and the road belts extending radially from the control tower looked pitch black and shining. They stood out in bold contrast to the otherwise unbroken expanse of green countryside. Both large and small transfer vehicles were running along these road belts. Turning my attention to the construction site where work was now in progress, I could see the frames of the main buildings being constructed. In some ways the methods seemed to be similar to the way steel frames on Earth are assembled during construction. Twelve to thirteen spacecraft remained hovering in the air, each carrying heavy looking tanks of a liquid compound. Very small craft were also working busily, making use of their lightness and freedom of movement to assemble the guides from which the frames would be molded. I could also see cosmic people working both on the beams that had already been constructed and on the guides.

The work started from an underground level. It seemed that the construction was divided into several stages that were completed in succession until reaching the final stage. At the final stage the frames, which looked like intricate latticework, were covered by what looked like thin sheets of rolled steel. They were next covered by soil and sand transported on the sky road belts. When this cover reached a certain thickness, another craft came and sprayed a special liquid as if moistening the surface to bind it together. It was just the way concrete is made on Earth. Finally, the surface was covered by a fairly thick layer of a different type of soil to finish the surface. Special leveling and solidifying machines were also in operation. I surmised that automatic road belts and hangars would be constructed following the completion of this project. The steps that comprised the construction of the artificial base became clear to me as I watched. I suddenly interrupted my observation, taking a deep breath of air and then exhaling; I felt as if my body had become empty. I had completely forgotten that the governor and Mr. M were beside me and that I had come to the observation platform on the top of the control tower to listen to important information to be imparted by the governor.

The Governor's Words

The governor began to speak quietly:

No matter how hard we may try to understand it, the love of the great God far surpasses anything we can imagine. That love is deep and all-embracing. The supreme cosmic beings who govern our base are themselves watched over and guided by their own guardian divinities. These beings surpass any of us on the base in their wisdom and abilities, and they work to fulfill their high, divine missions. These cosmic beings, who have been given the responsibility of guiding the leaders on the base, come from highly evolved planets with an extremely advanced cosmic science. They, in turn, are guided by further elevated cosmic beings. I want you to know that in higher realms there are cosmic persons who have wonderfully evolved lifestyles and are engaged in noble, excellent pursuits that are beyond our imagining. There are higher and higher realms far above our own, which far surpass anything that we could express in words. This endless continuum of evolution describes the reality of cosmic human beings.

Even in phenomenal manifestations, the mind of the parental God exceeds the far reaches of our imagination. The range of our perception depends on the degree of our evolution. It is a great mistake to think that what we perceive as God's love is the parental God's love in its entirety. Such misunderstandings occur when human beings lose sight of their true identity. The love of the great God manifests itself to meet the vibrational amplitude of the world which we inhabit. In the world where you live, you can better serve the great God or manifest divine love by living according to your own life's mission and maintaining the highest vibrations possible.

The vibrational amplitude of a planet is in proportion to the degree of its evolution. There is not even one planet with vibrations that are identical to those of another. It is humanity's destiny to continue to transcend these worlds progressively from one to the next. However, this explains the reality of our phenomenal side only. True humanity is a radiant body of light that shines like a great river of life. It is the radiant light emitting from the great God out into the universe. That light continues to expand even now to the infinite bounds of the great universe. Shining like the sun, shining like a river of life, humanity casts its light out into the world. Each individual within humanity is a body of light that progresses along the path of evolution so that it can manifest more and more of its shining divinity like the sun.

In accordance with our evolution, our embodiments of light grow and become stronger. Gradually increasing in size, they at last return to and are united with the great parental God. However, this is not something our words or vibrations can express at present. Perhaps it is best said that we are a stream of light without beginning or end.

The governor concluded his speech with these words and seemed to enter a meditative state with his eyes closed.

Seven Fundamental Waves

We also closed our eyes like the governor and commenced meditation. I could clearly perceive the telepathic communication exchanged by the governor and the people at the construction site. One particular exchange was with the person in charge of Central Site No. 6, the place that could be called the nerve center of the artificial base. The person in charge was asking for common values on the wave separation indicator. The governor instructed that 2, 3, 4, and 5 were the same and that 7 was equivalent to 1. He instructed him to take the middle of 5 and 7 for 6. Following this exchange, the governor continued to communicate with the other people who contacted him one after another. I could not understand how he could teach me so many important things in such a quiet manner in the midst of such exacting work. I felt extremely sorry to have bothered him.

Rest assured, speaking like this with you never interferes with my work. This construction will be completed within about two months. After that, we will move on to the construction of an even larger base, said the governor.

Where is the Central Site No. 6 with which you were communicating through telepathy?

The innumerable vibrations existing in the great universe are roughly classified into seven basic waves. Everything from molecules and electrons to galaxies that contain billions of clusters of stars is composed of intersections of these seven basic waves. This base is no exception to this universal law. As you see, there are six arrival stations for space vessels. The remaining one is to be located on the hill that is now under construction. This base also has seven different sections and each section differs from the others in its interior facilities and equipment. Mother ships are docked inside sections 3, 4 and 5. Sections 1 and 7 are linked together via automatic road belts. Between the space vessel arrival stations and on the ridges are dome-shaped hangars that house space vessels of various sizes. The inner structures of the hangars also differ from sec-

tion to section. The sections are separated by shutters composed of heavy gases. The entire base is designed to maintain a slightly higher air pressure than that outside.

How do you intercept the seven basic waves? Also, could you give me an overall idea of the combination and separation of extracted waves used as energy?

We have a wave receiver for use at the base. It is actually a combination wave receiver and separator. This machine is based on the same theory as that of the cosmic wave receiver at the top of a space vessel. Just by dialing, we can easily intercept necessary waves from the waves emitted from the center, or source, of the great universe. These waves have various shapes and characteristics after having gone through numerous intersections. The machine operates on principles similar to those of the radios that you have on the Earth, whereby specific radio waves are intercepted. The methods of wave separation and their applications alone number in the thousands. I will explain more about this later in the laboratory. We also dedicate a fairly large space to a facility with extremely complex machines; you may call this the largest factory on base. It is an airtight chamber located at the center of the base, that is, in the first sphere of the fourth section. This can be compared to the breathing organs of a human body. If you think of the wave receiver and the separators as the head, the airtight chamber would be the lungs. This airtight chamber cannot be fully understood at a glance. It is something like an advanced chemical factory on Earth.

Would it be okay to ask for a tour inside the base?

We cannot show you all of the base since it still is under construction. It is sometimes dangerous because we use extremely potent waves. Such places are off limits. However, you can see the places where the structural work is complete anytime you wish.

191

Before you do, I will show you the grand hall and other rooms on the upper floors of this tower.

Upon saying this, the governor looked back at us and smiled. Mr. M immediately replied, *It is very kind of you.*

A Tour of the Grand Hall

The governor gave a slight nod as he began to walk toward the door. We followed him into the same corridor we had walked along before. When we arrived at the elevator, there was a woman already waiting there. As she greeted us with a nod, the lights on the display board began to flash and the elevator door opened. The governor boarded first, followed by Mr. M, myself, and the woman. As soon as the door closed, the elevator descended to its next stop. When the door opened again, the governor, Mr. M and I got off and the elevator continued its descent. Across the corridor were two fairly large doors that were the entrance to the grand hall. These opened silently the moment we arrived in front of them. Inside was a large hall that could seat 2500 to 3000 people. The aisles of the hall extended radially from the semicircular stage at the center. The seats were automatically adjustable by pushing buttons.

This hall is designed as a venue for receiving cosmic people from other planets. On such occasions, many people living on the base gather here to receive the visitors and have discussions. The visitors from other planets come onto the stage one by one and relate their various experiences to the people living on the base. As they do, music is played in tune with the vibrations of their speech.

As he spoke, the governor glanced up at the ceiling.

From the central point of the ceiling of the grand hall, thin, transparent tubes extend radially. Overlapping these tubes are a series of concentric circles extending from the center of the ceiling to the edges, where they meet the walls. The speakers' words and music go from the stage to the center of the ceiling where they are then diffused equally throughout the entire hall.

The upper part of this tower is divided into four sections. The top two sections are the rooms where the tower staff work. These rooms are equipped with various kinds of sophisticated equipment that assist them in their work.

The next two sections are the fourth and fifth floors. On these are a variety of rooms ranging from grand halls to private rooms; however, except for the caretakers' rooms these are not used for accommodation. Accommodation facilities are in the building below the tower.

Each hall is fan-shaped with a stage at the center and is designed for its own specific purpose. Since every room is furnished with equipment for the diffusion of waves, you can hear everything clearly wherever you are, as if you were standing right next to the speaker. When lectures on various studies are held, special projectors are used to project images on numerous screens simultaneously so that developments and changes discussed in the lecture can be understood at a glance. Questions are conveyed to the lecturer through the display board.

The base also has its own social structures and organizations quite similar to those in the Earthly world, from the production and consumption of clothing and food to housing, education, religion, art, science, civil engineering and construction. However, what is fundamentally different here from society on Earth is that here all people work together in the spirit of harmony and oneness with the Great Life of the universe. This is the basis of our society and everything we do originates from this principle. All people have the freedom to choose the way they will fulfill their own mission within

193

their given environment and situation in life. People's work is evaluated not by its quantity but its quality. The purity or selflessness of one's vibrations or attitude while fulfilling one's work determines the depth and significance of that person's service. The things necessary for fulfilling the work of the cosmic people are provided naturally as needed. This is the fundamental way in which the social systems of this base and those of advanced planets operate.

As I listened to the governor speak, I thought of what is frequently the case in the Earthly world, where far too often there is an enormous gap between people's words and actions. It worried me to think about the rampant hypocrisy in our society. I wondered what the consequences would be for such behavior, remembering the adage, 'One lie leads to another.' The governor, who seemed to have perceived my apprehension, continued by saying:

There is not even one person among the inhabitants of this base who would try to deceive another. If a person should speak words that were untrue to the vibrations of his or her heart, we would be able to perceive it. Yet, we would never look down upon that person or condemn him or her as having an inferior soul or existing in a lower realm. On the contrary, we would communicate with the person in an affectionate way, suited to his or her personality and way of thinking. As a result, the distorted behavior would naturally disappear. So, in our society, we never have to deal with contradictions between words and actions or the problem of one untruth leading to another.

Music and Concerts in the Base

Listening to the governor speak, I became curious about the kind of concerts that were held here at the base. Although I am basically tone deaf and know nothing about music, I could not help but wonder how a concert would be given here. I wanted to know, for example, what kind of instruments the musicians played and what their musical scores looked like.

Why don't we take a look at the grand hall where concerts are held, suggested the governor as he went out of the hall. We walked along the corridor and down a staircase that shone like marble. Covering the center of the stairs was a runner of thick, dark green carpet. The corridor walls were painted a cream color. Following the governor, I saw one hall after another, but I was not at all sure what each of them was used for. Illuminated insignias that looked like neon signs were conspicuous above the door of each hall. The insignias varied widely, with no two being alike. One was in the shape of a plum blossom while another looked like an intricately shaped chrysanthemum. Another insignia was in the shape of waves and another of grass. The colors, shades and progression from one symbol to the next were all varied and intriguing. Although I could not tell what the marks signified, I had the feeling that they might have had something to do with the nature or purpose of each hall.

After walking past a number of doors along the corridor, we finally stopped at one. The insignia above this door was of waves and a cross that had a spiral extending from its center. This hall, I intuitively felt, was definitely a grand hall for concerts.

The door opened and we went inside. My estimate would be that the hall could hold an audience of 2,000 to 3,000. The seats and stage were arranged in a manner no different from that of a large auditorium on Earth. The only noticeable difference was the depth of the stage. The moment I entered it, I felt an overpowering sense of solemnity and grandeur emanating from the room. The governor began to speak in a soft voice:

One notable characteristic of this hall is that it is completely soundproof. It has been designed using the latest scientific technology to ensure that waves can be heard equally from every seat. The wave dispersion guide installed in the ceiling here is far more precise than what you will find in other halls. Here, we sometimes listen to music while watching the performance directly; at other times, we watch it through a special curtain made of a kind of gas that is charged with electromagnetic waves. This can be used when there is only one performer or a group of performers on stage. The curtain enables us to observe the flow of sound waves as they are converted into light waves. As they flow through the curtain, the waves of the melody are transformed into a kaleidoscopic show of light. The visual waves observed by the listeners and the waves perceived audiosensually join together to become one and flow into our essential being.

Musical instruments here are, on the whole, similar to those on Earth with the exception of a few minor differences. Pianos, for example, come in a number of different styles. For example, we have not only solo pianos but also round and oval ones that are played by several pianists at the same time. In our musical scores, the pitch of high and low notes is expressed by horizontal lines while the amplitude of the waves is expressed by colors. In the musical score these appear on two to three lines.

Hearing this somehow made me feel as if I were in a dream. The governor went on to say, *The music on marvelously advanced planets can express the waves of a person's sublime thoughts as melodies.* Incredible as it sounded, I somehow felt that I could understand what he was saying.

As we visited one hall after another, I realized that the very best of advanced scientific technology was gathered here. It was obvious that attention had been paid to every small detail, keeping in mind the particular purpose of each hall.

When we went out of the last hall, I noticed a young cosmic man waiting for us in the corridor. He nodded and approached us. At that time the governor turned to us and said, *I must leave now so I have arranged for this young man to be your guide. He will take you around the artificial base.*

I thanked both the governor and the young man politely. The governor accompanied us as far as the elevator, bidding us farewell as the elevator doors closed.

The image of the slim, tall governor dressed in a deep indigo space suit remained with me. He had very fair skin and black hair and his facial features were distinct and dignified. When I looked at him, I could not help but be deeply impressed by the warmhearted, loving thought waves flowing continuously from his eyes beneath his thick eyebrows.

Boarding the Automatic Transfer Vehicle

Although the distance from the top of the tower to the ground seemed to be substantial, the elevator we had boarded descended what seemed to be only the space of six or seven floors. Alighting from the elevator, we arrived at what looked like the main entrance of the control tower. The ceiling was high and there was a wide, arch-shaped entrance. On the dome-shaped ceiling were lights that gave the impression of being suspended. The centers of the lights looked as if they were floating in the air somewhat below the ceiling and they gave off a soft yellowish white light. There were a large number of automatic transfer vehicles parked in a line ready for boarding. I could see more than ten cosmic people looking after the vehicles that arrived and departed one after another.

The young man who was with us jumped out of the elevator the moment the door opened and proceeded to prepare one of the vehicles, which the three of us then boarded. From among the countless number of intricate road circuits inside the tower building, our vehicle was able to discern the appropriate one and put us on the right track. Mr. M and I sat side by side while the young man sat opposite us, taking control of the steering lever. The vehicle looked somewhat like an open car without a top and ran smoothly as if it were gliding along the road. There were several other vehicles that had departed shortly before us but, unless there was a certain distance between the vehicles, they would not move.

It was my guess that these automatic vehicles constantly emitted special waves both at the front and rear to maintain a fixed distance from other vehicles or objects on the road. Should the waves come into contact with an obstacle, they would be repelled. The waves would then be picked up by a sensor that transmits a signal to stop the attraction/repulsion motion of the automatic road vehicle. I realized that this was the reason why collisions never occurred. I also recalled how neatly arranged the road belts were when seen from the sky.

Our car went half way around the roundabout that surrounded the control tower building, entered the fourth section and headed in the direction of the ridge. The road belt was now flanked by an orchard on both sides and was probably heading towards the center of the artificial base. In a short time, we came to the foot of the base's hill. We came to another road belt on the border between a farm and a hill. Going straight through the intersection, we commenced our ascent of the hill. Part way up, there was a fork in the road. We took the road branching to the left. Deviating somewhat from the straight road, we began to run along flat land. Soon the automatic road vehicle stopped and we found ourselves at an entrance in the hill which led into the artificial base.

The Underground Artificial Base

The entrance was somewhat larger than I had imagined and was not in the shape of a horseshoe. There were two road belt tracks leading inside, and they looked as if they were being drawn into the cylindrical opening of the entrance. Several signal lights on the display board beside the entrance were flashing continuously. I turned to the young man who was driving our transfer vehicle to ask if he would tell me how the entrance to the base operated.

With a smile, he nodded to me and, pointing at the display board, willingly replied: *Do you see that round switch-like object? Various waves that cover a fairly long distance are continuously emitted from it. When they come into contact with an automatic vehicle, are intercepted and then transmitted back, a barrier is created. The light rustling sound like rainfall that you hear is actually the sound of a heavy gas curtain that constantly seals off the entrance. The density of the gas increases when an automatic vehicle comes through here. It is as if the vehicle were passing through a thick waterfall of heavy gas. Before it passes through this gas curtain, we completely seal the vehicle by placing a cover on it, and it then proceeds through the area slowly. The gas itself is harmless to humans and animals but it has a tendency to cause people to cough when they come into contact with it. To prevent this from happening, we seal our cars completely before going through the passageway.*

199

Mr. M then began to speak: *That's similar to what is done when a steam engine is going through a tunnel. The windows are shut to prevent the steam from going inside.*

Why is this barrier necessary?

The way the base is designed, the atmospheric pressure inside must always remain slightly higher than that outside. There are a number of reasons for this, but one of them is to keep the base free from outside influences so that it can maintain the independence of its own environment. As you tour the base, you will understand how precise the facilities and equipment are. When you realize how sensitive these devices are, you will easily understand the importance of the constant and stable environment in which they must be kept.

The Interior of the Base—A World of its Own

A somewhat large green light came on, and the automatic vehicle passed smoothly through the barrier. After traveling through the tunnel for a short time, we came to a large hall-like room. The walls here too were painted a cream color. There were wide corridors with several road belts running through them. In spite of its spaciousness, there were very few supporting pillars in the room. Although I could detect no light source, the inside was as bright as outdoors at high noon. Nowhere was there a hint of the darkness or dampness that one would expect in an underground area. The place was an entirely different world. The temperature was slightly higher than outside, and I could not help but feel that the people here were fortunate to be in this pleasant environment. We proceeded straight ahead until we came to a road belt roundabout that seemed to be at the center of the base. It was in a fairly large square. We got out of the vehicle and began to walk.

No matter which direction we walked in, there were no visible supporting beams to be seen. It was as if we were going through a series of large connecting rooms rather than passing through a long corridor. Wherever I looked, various kinds of machines and devices seemed to have been installed. The corridors extended to the right and left in a cross shape, at the ends of which were four identical rooms. At the entrance to each room was a display board and several lights. Here again, each entrance had its own particular insignia which shone in relief like a fluorescent light. The room the young man now guided us to a displayed symbol that looked somewhat like an Egyptian hieroglyph.

The Underground Scientific Factory

The moment the button at the entrance to the room was pressed, the lights on the display board began to flash and the door opened. The young man entered first and we followed. Stepping into the room, I felt overwhelmed by what I saw.

It was a fairly large room, filled with a vast array of instruments and other complex equipment. Because the equipment obstructed my vision, I was not able to see to the other end of the room. Two thick chimney-like structures extended down from the ceiling at what appeared to be the center of the room. Surrounding the thick pipes were several radiation plates from which stemmed several other pipes. Some of these were surrounded by several winding plates from which also stemmed several pipes. Some of these pipes were linked directly to nearby machines while others disappeared into the floor. It reminded me of some kind of scientific factory on Earth. Everything I saw was beyond my reckoning, with changing colors on meters, twinkling lights and swinging pendulums here and there. I lacked the vocabulary to express what I was witnessing in either speech or writing.

One thing that particularly mystified me was the quality of the light in the room. Its interior was several times brighter than the corridor and there was an absence of shadows or poorly lit areas.

The young man began to speak: *I would like to tell you about the facilities in this room in as much detail as possible. First of all, the thick chimney-like structures at the center of the room are pipes for the cosmic waves that are intercepted above the base. The frequencies of the waves have already been considerably reduced by the time they are guided to those pipes after passing through two separators. This processing is to facilitate use of the waves for various purposes. Here, the fine light waves are transformed into electromagnetic waves. Basically, what is most important in the separation and combining of waves lies in the mediums and the methods used. On Earth a medium would generally be considered a solid body. However, here at the base presolid and preliquid waves, that is, particular substances with certain frequencies, play this kind of role to a great extent. Because this is new knowledge to you, it might be hard for you to fully grasp a detailed explanation of each of these numerous, complex machines. So, I will instead give you a brief overview of the fundamental principles at work.*

The facility to amplify, alter, or assign characteristics to the electromagnetic waves serves two functions: supplying electromagnetic waves for use inside this section and supplying waves for use in other sections of the base. Before these waves can be used as energy, certain common conditions must be met throughout the entire process. This is automatically calculated by each section and is indicated at the required stages in the process. When an instruction is given, the necessary calculations and indications are performed.

As you are aware, this base is divided into seven sections, each differing in the quantity and quality of original waves that are intercepted. In addition, each particular section has its own particular role to fulfill.

Does each section have facilities like these?

Yes, it does. Not only that, there are also various laboratories and research rooms in each section. Now let's pass through this room to the next one.

With the young man in front of us, Mr. M and I proceeded to the next room. It was outfitted with a variety of machines made of a transparent material that looked like glass. Some machines stood alone, while others were lined up in a row. A number of cosmic persons were at work, intently monitoring the machines. I looked at both sides in an attempt to gain as much knowledge as possible, but it was simply impossible to find out about everything that I wanted to know. How I regretted my limitations. I was overcome with a feeling of frustration. Suddenly, however, I heard a voice coming from somewhere:

There is no need to feel regret. The knowledge of all space science phenomena actually already exists within you and is at your disposal whenever you need it. You may have thought that all of these wonderful technological achievements exist only at bases in distant space but that is a great misunderstanding. It is essential that you understand this if you want to learn more about the science that you observe at the base.

The voice captured my full attention as I walked.

But how can I understand it? You must tell me the way.

Very well. If you think of seasons in the Earthly world, you know that there are spring, summer, autumn and winter. Who do you think created those seasons? In autumn, leaves turn red with-

203

out being told to do so by anybody. Even without your effort, sea-sons change naturally according to the divine Mind that governs great nature. Just as nature shifts naturally according to the divine Mind, the time will surely come when your questions will be answered.

Somehow, the words made me feel as if I had suddenly come to realize how wonderful our true human nature is.

Yes, it's true! I have been guided to the base to learn this. Thank you, God, and thank you, Goi Sensei. Feelings of deep apprecia-tion rose from the bottom of my heart and I could not hold back the tears of gratitude that had gathered in my eyes. We were now guided to the next laboratory.

Cosmic Waves and Insulation Belts Surrounding the Planets

This room was also filled with various kinds of machines and equipment. They were all so fascinating that I wanted to find out as much as I could about each of them. Unlike my insatiable thirst for knowledge of a moment ago, however, I now felt liberated from my insistence on knowing every small detail. As we were walking around, we came across a large hanging scroll on the wall. As we stood in front of it, the young man turned around and told us: *This diagram has been created to help us understand how the waves originating from the great God work.*

The illustration that he pointed to showed the Earth's solar system among a seemingly infinite number of stars and plan-ets scattered throughout the great universe. The planets in our solar system were located in the center of the illustration. Waves originating from the realm above the parental sun that controls our solar system were also shown in the illustration.

Each time a change occurs in the waves in this stratum, it affects each layer of the insulation belt surrounding a planet. To enable the observer to understand the changes at a glance, they were indicated in the illustration through color gradations. Next, the young man pressed a nearby button. Suddenly, each of the stars and planets looked as if it were floating in the air. It reminded me of the astronomical map that I had been shown previously when I was aboard the space vessel. The two maps were very similar. Cosmic waves originating from the source of the universe repeatedly intersect until they reach the parental sun of our solar system. This phenomenon of repeated intersections was also clearly visible on the diagram.

This illustration attempts to convey to us how complex waves are.

As he spoke these words, the young man pushed another switch. This time the light originating from the parental sun was transformed into waves of seven colors. With each shift in color, the insulation layers surrounding the planets reacted by changing color. I was told that the waves could be roughly classified into two types: those that reach planets directly and those that reach the planets after undergoing repeated transformations. These two types of waves travel in a parallel path until they reach the surface of a planet.

On Earth, the sun has always been thought of as a scorching fireball that burns at immeasurably high temperatures. I was told, however, that this is not an accurate perception. It is actually a verdant planet overflowing with peace and harmony, and a homeland to highly evolved cosmic people. In accordance with its heavenly mission, the sun radiates special waves that are transformed into great waves of light when they reach one of the layers of insulation surrounding a planet. Planets receiving these special waves perceive them as radiant light itself. If the light were emitted to Earth directly from the sun, the gross difference in temperatures between the equator and the north and south poles could not be explained; it is just too great. Within our own solar system, there are planets that are scorching hot as well as those that are freezing cold. Venus, Mars and other advanced planets, on the other hand, do not experience extremes of heat and cold. How is it that such a situation exists? I was wholly absorbed in studying the continuously evolving conditions and changes on the planetary map as if it were a living thing. Suddenly a puzzling question sprang to my mind: *How in the world did these insulation layers surrounding the stars and planets come into being?*

They are combinations of those existing from the very beginning and those created later.

Is this planet that looks gray Earth?

Yes. The color represents the planetary status of Earth.

Oh, my! It is enveloped in numerous insulation layers of gray, dark brown and many other colors.

That is because of the karmic thoughts produced by Earthly humanity. Those thought waves have accumulated gradually over time, covering the Earth in thick and heavy layers of waves. You can understand that the Earthly world, whose evolution is supported by various kinds of waves that travel to it through these contaminated layers, is an extremely backward planet where truths are intermingled with karmic thoughts.

The young man began to walk as he provided these comments. Passing through several areas outfitted with equipment for experiments, we stopped in front of a relatively large structure that was shaped like a horseshoe and resembled an electric furnace. Heat was being generated from inside the furnace, then traveled out through conductors in the right and left arms that extended from the furnace. The conductors were divided into several sections, each radiating its own discrete waves. The furnace was designed to catch the colors generated by the waves radiating from each of these sections.

About Heat

The purpose of these waves is to facilitate an understanding of the relation between light waves and heat and to provide fundamental knowledge about heat and light. When two or more heavy waves running counter to each other collide inside the furnace or when strong waves pass through specific mediums, a change occurs. This change results in what is known on Earth as heat and it is used in various ways. When this heat travels through a certain conductor, it emits light. When special waves are radiated on this light, they trigger various changes. Although there are differences in their amplitude, both the heat and light generated through these processes result from the intersection and integration of waves with common natures or affinities. The meters here automatically record all these changes with the utmost precision.

At that moment, I began to have my doubts about our definition of heat on Earth. I wondered what cosmic people thought of molecular movement or radiation.

Presumably perceiving my thoughts, the young man resumed his discourse on heat: *The concept of heat on Earth is lacking in one very important respect. Prior to the manifestation of heat, there is another kind of wave that is emitted from the source of the great universe. Only with the presence of this wave can heat occur. The changes in waves that are currently recognized on Earth as heat account only for a very small part of all of the changes that*

207

take place. What is not known on Earth is that prior to and after the manifestation of heat, there are additional changes in waves that we refer to as 'large heat.' Due to a lack of understanding of this factor, scientists on Earth have a hard time dealing with the enormous amount of heat that is necessary for nuclear fusion. However, this problem can be easily solved through the adjustment of the unknown kind of wave mentioned earlier together with the radiation of a further type of wave that has an affinity with the frequency of the heat conducting body. Based on such principles, concepts beyond what you can imagine are commonly applied here.

When he finished speaking, he started walking again.

As I followed after him, I continued to contemplate what he had said about waves. It seemed logical to me that, just like electric waves on Earth, there would be waves composed of several different frequencies. For instance, if we took a certain range of waves with consistent common characteristics from maximum to minimum and numbered them starting with 1-1, we would find that there would be a countless number of wave systems such as 1-2, 1-3, 1-4 and so on. These systems would expand vertically and horizontally in patterns such as 2-1, 3-1, 4-1 and so on. Considering the various characteristics of distortion, deviation, and affinity, I realized that the world of waves must have unfathomable depth and breadth.

The Spirit of the Stars, the Spirit of Human Beings

I recalled what I had learned earlier, that is, that the unity of the waves' amplitude and number was expressed through color.

A number of fundamental realizations came to me one after the other. For example, wasn't the yellowish white light of the sun that shines its light on our planet a harmonious blend of a nearly infinite number of different waves? And at the very core, where the light shines white, do not all of the nearly infinite number of waves, each with its own characteristics, come together in perfect harmony, blending perfectly into one?

Yes, the point of unity shining white, the great emptiness. A nearly infinite number of waves and, at the same time, the returning point of these infinite waves, the point of oneness. When the rays of white light sent from the great universal God repeatedly intersect and return to the one, a star is born. The core of the star is white light and is emptiness. Do not all of the trillions upon trillions of stars scattered throughout the great universe and all the human populations of the universe living on these stars have their own heavenly missions, having at their core this white light and emptiness? Do they not each go about fulfilling their heavenly missions in the movement of great nature? Yes, a star that shines high in the heavens and a human being are one and the same.

It seems only natural that the spirit of a human being, whose core is filled with bright white light and emptiness, has an affinity and can communicate with the spirit of the stars. Could it not be that the stars have characteristics similar to humans: stars that speak, stars that beckon, stars that happily extend a helping hand? And like humans, are the stars not either male or female, and are they not separated into stages of development such as infancy, youth, middle and old age?

Do not the stars, that shine with the brilliance of life itself, and humans beings both give expression to the spirit of the great God? The thought ran through my mind that the life bestowed by God on stars and on human beings is exactly the same. The hearts of human beings and the hearts of the stars come together and become one within the infinite world of *Kuu*,[11] becoming a white light which gives birth to a star's waves and its science. As this realization dawned upon me, I felt that my entire past, like the white clouds in the sky, had vanished and I was being enveloped in a shining body of light which was in oneness with the mind of Goi Sensei. As this happened, I keenly sensed that I was walking steadily forward along the road of my own heavenly mission.

All things great and small are part of the flow of the one great life. This is true for the grass growing along the roadside that goes unnoticed by human beings. It is also true for the life of a solitary tree that takes root deep in the mountains or valleys. It is true for human beings, and it is true for the stars that twinkle brightly in the evening sky. When I experienced this feeling, my soul returned to oneness with God and my heart merged with the lives of the grass, the trees, and the stars. Their spirits became one with me and they communicated and interacted with me.

A Drink to Cure Exhaustion

I followed in the steps of the young man but was oblivious to where we were going and how we would get there. My present mental and physical state had put me out of tune with my present surroundings.

Next, we will view the hangar of the mother ship, said a voice that came from somewhere beyond my consciousness. However, my earlier irrepressible curiosity and enthusiasm were not to be found. I just plodded on automatically. My mind was filled with feelings of homesickness and a longing for Earth. A strong feeling of nostalgia swept over me like a wave. At that moment, the young man stopped walking.

You look very tired. Why don't we take a rest?

Even before he finished speaking, the words, *Oh, that would be great!* had escaped my lips.

Walking on a bit further, we came to the door of another room. The insignia above the door was of a sun just appearing over some mountains and a bright light cascading downwards. The young man pushed a button and the door opened without the slightest sound.

It was a splendid reception room done completely in white. In the center was a round table, six chairs that looked very comfortable, a cupboard, various stands, and a number of other items. Here and there were a number of spheres of different sizes that emitted beams of light around the room. The young man indicated for me to take a seat in one of the chairs, so I did so. He then pushed a button on the wall and in a very short time an angelic figure, a cosmic woman, entered the room carrying two cups on a tray.

Upon her entrance, I looked up, startled, and our eyes happened to meet. She seemed like a bright and lively person. She appeared to be somewhere around twenty years of age, with a warm smile, pure white skin, and eyes like deep black pools that shone with intelligence. With a big, unaffected smile she approached our table and said, *Please enjoy your drinks*, placing the cups on the table. With that, she left the room.

The young man said, *This is a beverage that we drink here when we feel a bit tired. It's a kind of tea made from the essence of fruit. If you drink it, you will regain your energy.*

I drank it down quickly, noticing that it had a rather thick consistency. It had the taste of a normal fruit juice but was far more delicious. As I swallowed the liquid and it passed down

211

my throat, it seemed as if I could actually feel it being absorbed into my body.

As Mr. M, the young man and I sat comfortably sipping our beverages in that splendid relaxation room at the base headquarters, I became aware that, even then, Mr. M and the young man were in constant telepathic contact with the governor in the control tower. Realizing this made me reflect upon the kindness the governor had shown to me. He had given me such a valuable opportunity to experience life and reality at the base, and had guided me through many complicated concepts and ideas. Feelings of appreciation welled up from the bottom of my heart. Perhaps the young man sensed my feelings for it seemed that he glanced over to Mr. M for a moment and then turned my way. He started speaking to me in a quiet voice:

As you seemed extremely tired a little while ago, I communicated with the governor to ask if we should go back to the control tower. The answer from the governor was that we should take a rest in the relaxation room and then resume the tour. I have also been advised to slow the pace down so that you don't wear yourself out.

Next, I want to give you an opportunity to see just how a mother ship is docked. Before that, you can relax while I talk about the basic principles behind a mother ship and how it is docked. When we have finished talking here, we can go see the real thing. Since we have an extremely detailed diagram showing its layout and construction, I will outline the main principles involved as we are looking at it.

Thank you, I replied. *You have been extremely kind. I can find no words to express my appreciation. I will be very happy to have things explained in the order you suggest. I think it will be easy to understand that way.*

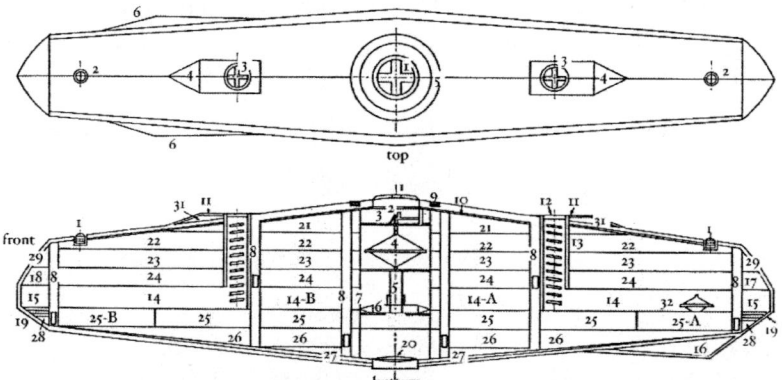

Figure 11. Blueprint of a small mother ship. Upper Plane: (1) cosmic wave receiver, (2) backwards cosmic wave receiver, (3) vessel adsorption plate, (4) communication apparatus, (5) location of corridor, and (6) Special electromagnetic emission device and stabilizer. Side View: (1) cosmic wave receiver, (2) expanding and contracting tubes, (3) mother ship control room, (4) gyrocompass, (5) electromagnetic pole, (6) regeneration and rectifying tank, (7) passageway device and stabilizer, (8) elevator, (9) exterior, (10) electromagnetic cylinder, (11) landing platform, (12) cross-shaped adsorption platform, (13) spiral descending conveyor belt, (14) hangar for space vessels, (14A) research rooms, (14B) communications, liaison and measurement instruments rooms, (15) emission room, (16) automatic gravity adjuster, (17) backwards observation room, (18) backwards observation room, (19) magnetic plate for space vessel emissions, (20) observation telescope, (21) individual rooms, (22) individual and shared rooms, (23) individual and shared rooms, (24) main hall, conference rooms and communication rooms, (25) store rooms for food, clothing and materials, (25A and B) storage rooms for various equipment, (26) fresh fruit, vegetables and store rooms, (27) automatic gravity distributor and observation instruments, (28) wave movement reduction device, (29) room for automatic measuring instruments, (30) micro light waves, storage room, (31) communications equipment, and (32) space vessel.

Blueprints of the Mother Ship

All right, then, the young man said as he stood and walked over to the cupboard behind him. It seemed that he had barely touched it when it opened to reveal the interior. I don't know how the door of the cupboard actually opened but the inside was divided into a number of shelves made of what appeared to be thin, transparent plates of glass. I could see that the pane of glass on each shelf had markings of various colored symbols on it. In the middle were what appeared to be scrolled blueprints that had been rolled up. The young man casually took one out. On the end of the scroll, about twenty characters consisting of dots and lines very similar to Morse code were visible in various colors. The paper of the scrolls themselves seemed to have been made of a transparent material resembling vinyl.

The young man appeared to be about to open the scroll when he suddenly looked at both Mr. M and me. As if he had suddenly thought of something else, he laid the scroll back on the table and started speaking. I somehow felt that at that instant the thoughts of Mr. M and the governor had been transmitted to him telepathically and a brief exchange of ideas had taken place. They were words without words, unvoiced vibrations transcending time and space. This was, in effect, the communication of cosmic humans. This sudden realization came to me like a flash of lightning.

This blueprint of the mother ship is completely unlike the various kinds of blueprints used on Earth. The information contained on one page of the design is equivalent to scores of pages of diagrams on Earth. While it may seem somewhat difficult to understand, the principle is extremely simple. Once the blueprint is drawn up, vibrations are copied onto it. This is the same principle as printing a number of photographs from a single negative the way you do on Earth. For us, it is something we take for granted; we do it on an every day basis without even thinking. One sheet of the design can be separated into dozens of copies showing the diagram from a number of perspectives as needed: a plane diagram, a complex diagram, a combined plane and complex diagram or a three dimen-

sional diagram. This is the unique aspect of this type of blueprint. Please take a look and you can see for yourself.

When he finished saying this, he took out a rather thick board that looked like a drawing board. On top of it was a frame that resembled a picture frame. After taking the board out, he set it on top of the desk.

A Blueprint with Unique Features

The surface of the board was milky white and as smooth as glass. The scroll-like blueprint, made of a transparent vinyl-like material, was unrolled and spread out on top of the board. Rectangular in shape, it measured 1 x 1.5 meters. A very basic outline of the mother ship was shown on the drawing, traced in lines of deep sky blue. I found it hard to believe that such a crude drawing could be a blueprint. However, as I looked at it closely, the young man placed a series of thin, transparent, glass-like plates on top of it. Placing one, then another on top of the drawing, he continued until he had placed a total of seven plates on the board. After he had done this, the frame on the board seemed to clasp onto the transparent plates and secure them to the board. The board was plugged into an out-let and electromagnetic waves flowed into it. The frame-like area around the board became illuminated like an electric light. (In the same way as electric power through cables was available throughout the base, different frequencies of electric-ity were also available.) The young man then proceeded to press a number of buttons, as if he were conducting a series of tests.

Suddenly the outline of the mother ship rose in bold relief from the blueprint as if it were floating above the board, revealing a wholly different perspective of what we had seen

215

earlier. The exterior surface of the ship had a particular coating over it. The layer beneath the surface contained a network of pipes that emitted electromagnetic waves. Between this layer and the next was a margin of empty space that ran consistently throughout the ship. The view we were observing was that of the mother ship from the side. Next the view shifted from the exterior layers to the interior. Even without the young man's explanatory remarks, just by looking at the plan I intuitively grasped that the mother ship operated on the same principle as other spacecraft. The only difference was the uppermost cabin where the captain worked. Surrounded by a series of outer layers, this cabin formed the core of the mother ship. This alone set it apart from other vessels. The operational design of the cosmic wave receiver which could be raised or lowered was the same as in other vessels. While the cosmic wave receiver of a space vessel is set in the center of a ship, in small to medium mother ships additional booster receivers are placed at the front and rear of the ship. With waves from the front and rear receivers passing to the center through a kind of guiding mechanism, a total of three receivers provide the ship with its energy supply. The waves then pass through the captain's body before flowing onto an amplifying gyrocompass that revolves constantly.

With the exception of the outer round three-layered section, the ship looked no different from a submarine. The launching tubes of the space vessel also looked like torpedo tubes. Just like an independent spaceship, the central core of the mother ship was completely outfitted with all vital equipment and machines. The mother ship was divided into nine different levels. Of these, the hangar which stored various vessels occupied the most space.

Descending from the core of the ship, this level was the sixth floor. On the fifth, fourth and third levels were various rooms for cosmic people. Both the front and the rear sections were designed in the same way. The seventh and eighth levels served as storage areas for equipment, food supplies, and other apparatus. I was completely absorbed in this magnificent three-dimensional plan, fully taking in and digesting each one of the changes on the board as it occurred. As I continued to follow the plan, a diagram which I did not understand appeared. It was of a device that looked like a stabilizing board that might be used on the underside of a boat that skims over the surface of the water on Earth. I was at a loss as to what it was. Up until this point I had continuously followed the progression of the moving three-dimensional blueprint and had become completely absorbed in the precise diagram of the mother ship. This had made me feel that I was grasping the essentials of space science. Now, faced with this difficult problem now, I returned my attention to Mr. M and the young man who were standing in front of me.

Space Vessels also Follow a Set Course

Mr. M and the young man were smiling at me with expressions of empathy and kindness. Perhaps sensing my feelings of confusion and frustration, the young man began to speak: *Space vessels and mother ships have the ability to freely move up, down, forward, backward, straight ahead or diagonally. Regardless of the direction they are moving in, they always move on a fixed course in space. And the part of the ship facing the direction it is moving in is considered the front.*

I think you understand the overall function of the mother ship. People on Earth might be of the understanding that in outer space there is no left or right, no fore or aft, no up or down. Or they might be of the opinion that even if such directions did exist, there would be no particular standard or object that would serve as the basis for establishing directions in space. However, this is a gross misunderstanding. First of all, I will give you an example of a situation on Earth that may help you to better understand what I am trying to say. Supposing that a ship is to navigate on the open sea. If it has no means of determining which way to go and simply sails haphazardly, will it reach its destination? The answer is obviously no. The ship can be sure of reaching its destination only after confirming its position and speed. It does this in various ways using instruments like the compass, sextant and sea charts. In the same way, all space vessels and mother ships navigating the great universe establish their position using various methods. All of these use the center of the universe as a standard.

However, one cannot help but wonder how a crew that is navigating through space and other passengers on board can carry on a normal life in zero gravity conditions. The answer, however, is quite simple. As human beings, we are created in such a way that we are always drawn to the center of the universe. When we lose the ability to be drawn to it, we are no longer able to function as true human beings. Similarly, if space vessels or mother ships flying through space at zero gravity possessed their own gravity sometimes and did not at other times, the principles of space science would not hold true. The device that you were wondering about just now is the control mechanism of the ship that continually provides the gravity inside it, maintains it at a consistent level, and, like a rudder, steadily guides it on a forward course.

Determining a Space Vessel's Correct Position

Now I understand.

You said a space vessel can use various methods to determine its correct position when navigating in space. If you don't mind, would you tell me about these?

As I believe you are aware, the universe is comprised of seven kinds of waves radiating from the origin of the universe. The most powerful are those coming directly from the center of this great source. The space vessel intercepts these waves to take its bearing, with the vessel always facing the origin of the universe. The waves, possessing tremendous energy, form belt-like layers divided by their position in the heavens. When a spaceship enters a wave belt, it immediately receives information via its wave separator, allowing it to ascertain its position in space. The crew can also transmit special waves to nearby stars to establish its position or use the vessel's automatic recording meter. This device continuously tracks the vessel's position on astronomical charts as it travels through space.

Would you mind also giving me a simple explanation of wave belts?

The young man did not answer my question immediately. Instead, he seemed to be taking his time pondering something. As usual, Mr. M stood calmly by, looking on with a smile. If I did not have a basic explanation of what seemed very complex, I felt I would not be able to understand what I needed to know. The young man's expression became increasingly serious. With a solemn look he finally answered:

When you study science on earth, you investigate matter by looking at molecules, atoms, electrons, and the fundamental materialization of things. You learn that electrons on different axes and facing the same nucleus rotate at different speeds. Matter appears in a number of forms, its characteristics depending on the number of

219

electrons it possesses. These facts are considered to be the basis of physics by those who study it. However, this constitutes only a very small part of a whole that people fail to grasp. There are protons, neutrons, mesons, and forms preceding mesons that are not yet known on earth. Scientists there believe them to be equivalent to light waves. No matter how we look at it, the breadth and depth of this world is beyond our reckoning. Essentially, it is a world of waves. This is the realm of cosmic science.

I will outline for you the most essential points of cosmic science. When certain waves come into contact with a medium that is in tune with their nature, they cause certain changes to take place and are transferred to the world of rough waves. These are what we call mesons and electrons.

How should I regard such mediums?

Well, we could think of them as waves that are reflected directly from the center of the universe or from stars that lead other stars. There are those waves that intersect repeatedly and, in doing so, bring about changes; there are other waves that work simply from their vibrations from the moment of inception. Mediums that are created in this way are, for the most part, mediums formed from strong, direct waves. While we simply call them waves, they are in themselves as complex as heaven and earth to understand. I suggest that we talk about them more at a later time.

Secrets of Space Routes

I would like to tell you two or three more fundamental things about wave belts. I think you are well aware that the stars that are scattered throughout the vast universe—from the largest galaxy to the smallest atom that is like a miniature sun—all face one sole center as they continue to ceaselessly rotate. You are also aware that there are a large number of complex waves that are not perceived by the five senses and, therefore, remain unknown. While people are aware that electrons rotate on a fixed axis around a single nucleus in a very regulated manner, they are not aware that activity of a different kind is unfolding around the outside of the core, where layers of waves in the shape of whorls are spreading outwards. This is the same both for an electron and for a star. As a separate entity with a single core that holds energy in proportion to the circular waves coming from it, it continues to emanate infinite waves, all the time controlled by one great center. These circular waves are just like the waves that wash up on the shore of a beach, ebbing and flowing in great whorls through the great universe. This is what I meant when I spoke to you of wave belts. I just wanted to make sure that you understood what I meant by 'wave belts.'

When a space vessel or mother ship enters a wave belt, it takes on the same energy as that of the wave belt itself. (It adjusts its waves, uniting with the wave belt.) To explain this in simple terms, it is like placing something on the waves of the sea. It gently floats there without resistance and moves at the same speed as the wave. We could say that this is basically what happens.

Within the great universe, an almost infinite number of wave belt intersections occur over and over again, generating movement proportionate to the energy of each wave belt. A discussion of wave belts can become very complex so let us take this up again on another occasion when I can describe them to you as we look at the charts.

As I listened to the young man's discourse, I felt that the door to the mysteries of universal science was suddenly starting to opening. I felt as if I had departed for some distant place. Again new questions sprang up in my mind.

Docking and Launching the Spaceship

What happens to the mother ship's emission of electromagnetic waves when it is in space flight?

It is the same as with any other spaceship. With the exception of the waves at the wave receiver, the landing pad, the rear gravity stabilizer and the entrances, all waves are converted into electromagnetic waves and emitted through the wave projecting cylinder. As you noticed when you looked at the cross-section of the mother ship, it is elliptical rather than round in shape. Emissions from the ship are more frequent from the right and left sides than from the top and bottom. If we rated the level of emissions from the left and right of the ship as 5, the emissions from the top and bottom would correspond to a level of 3 by the same standards. To measure the electromagnetic waves, we take the greatest common divisor of the points of intersection after they are mapped out as points and lines. Based on these, the waves are labeled Wave 1, Wave 2, Wave 3 and so on, and are judged on their functions and the quantity of electromagnetic waves they emit.

Would you be able to give me a simple explanation of the way a spaceship is docked and the way it gives off emissions?

When a mother ship is docking one of its own space vessels or when it is docking a vessel from another mother ship, the vessel preparing to be docked first hovers at a certain locale. The vessel receives continuous signals emitted from the mother ship and in this way keeps in constant, close contact with the mother ship during its approach. At the top of the mother ship is a landing platform where the vessel lands. The moment the vessel makes contact with the mother ship, the landing takes place so rapidly that the vessel actually looks as if it has been sucked into the mother ship. Once the vessel makes contact with the landing platform, the adsorption plate automatically begins a rotating motion as the spaceship descends into the interior of the mother ship. This is a very smooth, gentle process. When the ship can no longer be seen on the landing platform, the door automatically closes and the mother ship returns to its normal state. As the space vessel that has landed rotates in a spiral-like motion passing through a series of curtain-like layers of heavy gas and undergoing wave adjustment procedures, it is carried to the hangar on the sixth floor. Space vessels docking inside the mother ship do not operate on their own power. This is also the case when vessels are docking at mother ships on the artificial base.

On the other hand, when space vessels are ready to be launched, they are transported to the launching room located in the fore and aft of the mother ship. There they undergo inspection. The vessels are then launched by electromagnetic waves radiated from both the launching room and the vessels themselves. They depart so rapidly that they almost look like missiles shot from the mother ship. When a large number of vessels is involved, the launchings are executed in a very fast procedure with one vessel following another in quick succession.

How many people can this mother ship hold?

This mother ship is a small one so its normal capacity is about 1500. However, when there is a need, it can easily accommodate up to 5000 people.

You say 1500 or 5000—how could there be such an enormous range in capacity? How on earth can you make arrangements for sleeping or dining?

It is understandable that you should ask such a question. However, we are equipped with enough beds to accommodate more than 5000 people when the need arises. The beds just need to be assembled. Dining arrangements can be made in the same way. On both the fourth and fifth floors, we have a total of four venues for eating and another four for sleeping. On the fifth floor there are many rooms, including the grand hall, conference room, and com-munications room. In addition to these, there are rooms allocated for certain people to do their research and hold discussions. On the fourth floor there are also several rooms for academic research and music studies. The third and second floors are divided into individual rooms as well as rooms that can accommodate four to five people.

At this time I started to lose concentration and felt that I could absorb no further information. My state of mind did not escape the attention of Mr. M or the young man.

That's enough for the moment. We can talk about the principles and design of the mother ship at another time. Let's take a break and have some refreshments.

I had hardly grasped these words when I realized that the young man had pressed a button close by.

The Necessary Wisdom will be Provided When It is Needed.

I felt like closing my eyes for a moment to say a prayer for world peace. As I did so, a white light suddenly began to shine brilliantly before my eyes, gradually turning into a large ring of light. At the center of the light, the dignified image of the mother ship took shape. All the various types of machinery and equipment that I had learned about appeared one after the other as if I were watching a movie. About then I began to wonder whether I would be able to grasp everything I needed to know about the complicated equipment and how it was set out so that I could relate this knowledge accurately to people on Earth. Just thinking about how I should attempt to explain the advanced science of the base—a science that had developed from a fundamentally different foundation—would leave me, I feared, at my wit's end. These thoughts passed briefly through my mind.

Next, I found myself overcome with doubt as I contemplated what to say. More specifically, I questioned how I could correctly interpret the reality of this world. Little by little I went into a slump, overwhelmed by these thoughts. All this took place in the space of an instant. I snapped out of it when I heard a voice from someone behind me.

Your tendency to worry unduly about things is shared by most people on Earth. If you attempt to understand things on the basis of your own knowledge alone, you will not succeed. If, on the other hand, you leave everything to God, you will find the answers and knowledge that you require. Like water from a fountain, the necessary knowledge and words will flow continuously to you at the time and place when you need them. And they will be transformed into actions. The necessary mathematics and theory will be brought down and communicated not as an ultimate truth, but as concepts that people in that world will readily understand. Before you know it, those vibrations will be relayed to the people on Earth.

I see. Yes, now I understand. It was very wrong of me to think that I could come to terms with everything on the strength of my own knowledge. I am sorry, God. I humbly ask your forgiveness.

Popuna and Seri, Fruits of the Stars

At that moment, I sensed that somebody had entered the room so I stopped praying and opened my eyes. The young woman whom we had encountered earlier had come into the room carrying a large tray-like bowl of fruit. Bowing to Mr. M and the young man, she placed the fruit on the table and, after bowing slightly to me, left the room again. She was wearing neat, white clothing made of a light, airy material. She was very beautiful. An indescribable warmth and wisdom of tremendous depth and breadth seemed to be radiating from her clear black eyes.

Please help yourself, urged the young man.

Mr. M added: *This fruit is very similar to the apples you have on Earth. It comes from Venus and is known as popuna. The tree it grows on also resembles an apple tree. However, the leaves are larger and the tree itself is somewhat taller. As we were coming down from the artificial base on our way to the control tower in the transfer vehicle, you may have noticed some trees growing on the plain. They were popuna trees. Although they do not grow quite as large as the trees on Venus, they still grow to a good size and produce very fine fruit. They do not have any of the sourness that some apples have. If you cut the fruit into four pieces and remove the core, you can eat the entire fruit without peeling it.*

After listening to Mr. M's kind words, I joined him and the young man, cutting the fruit into four pieces. I ate one piece and then another. It was so good that before I knew it, I had eaten all four pieces. The fruit had a fragrance similar to bananas while its taste was similar to the 'Delicious' variety of apples. They were also a bit larger than Delicious apples and a bit more yellow. After having one of them, I felt quite full. Mr. M then reached for a different kind of fruit. It looked very much like a large plum but was more reddish purple and about the size of a mandarin orange.

This fruit is known on the base as seri. The seri trees grow quite large here. The fruit begins to ripen at the beginning of summer and continues until the beginning of autumn.

Earlier you mentioned that there are no harmful insects that attack the fruit trees. Could you tell me a bit more about what it is like when the fruit is being harvested? Also, when the trees bear an overabundance of fruit, do you follow a selection method whereby you leave only the best fruit on the tree? What methods do you use to prune and rejuvenate the trees and preserve cuttings?

Mr. M and the young man looked at each other for a moment. I got the feeling that they found my meaning difficult to comprehend.

It is inconceivable for us to think that because a tree should produce an abundance of fruit, people would practice a process of selection, choosing some in favor of others. Because the fruit is life given to us by God, we let it live as such. We do not see its life as being different from that of a person. Though their nature and shape may be different, the grass, trees, fruits and vegetables are lives issuing from God and gifts for which we show our love and appreciation. That is why we could never choose one fruit that grows in preference over another. We regard that as the work of the divinities who protect the plants that grow; it is outside the bounds of the work that we as human beings are asked to do. That is why in our judgment there is never an overabundance of fruit, or branches on a tree that have grown too long. In fact, we have never even contemplated such things. All fruit that grows will definitely grow large. If we study the fruits carefully, we notice that no two are alike. None grows too large and none grows poorly. Just thinking of this we can understand the depth and breadth of God's love.

I felt somehow awkward and embarrassed, bewildered at the realization of the enormous gap between the perceptions of people on Earth and of cosmic people. I no longer felt like pursuing this topic so I asked another question: *A moment ago you mentioned seasons. Does Venus have four seasons like Earth?*

Both Mr. M and the young man burst into spontaneous laughter. I also got caught up in the mirth of the moment and began to laugh too. Attempting to stifle his laughter, Mr. M answered, *Yes, they do have the four seasons of spring, summer, autumn and winter but these are completely different from the seasons on Earth. There are no extremes of hot or cold and the seasons pass from one to another with a climate that is like spring on Earth.*

Although I was now offered some seri fruit, I was too full to eat any more and politely refused. Although there were two other kinds of fruit in the bowl, I did not learn their names.

The Mother Ship's Arrival at the Base

At that time I wanted to inquire about what it was like when a mother ship landed at the base. Just as I was about to ask the young man this question, he began to reply to it as if he had read my mind:

Just before a mother ship approaches the base, the communication facilities inside the ship stay in continuous contact with the base. This is handled by the control tower. As the mother ship approaches, the tower advises the mother ship of the course it should take, where it should hover, and its position for landing. This is very much like an air traffic control tower on Earth.

How different are a vessel's speed when navigating through space and when approaching the mother ship to land?

The basic principle is for the mother ship or space vessel to intercept waves from among the myriad waves of varying amplitudes that are unceasingly radiating from the origin of the great universe, from parental suns, and from the infinite number of stars scattered through the heavens. From among this infinite number of waves, the mother ship intercepts only those waves which suit its purposes. These waves then filter through the spirit of the captain, where they undergo further separation. From among the separated waves, only those that are needed are amplified before passing through a number of devices where they are transformed into rough waves. These waves finally radiate from the four directions of the space vessel or mother ship, very much resembling the activity of a star. Having a place that is filled with radiating electromagnetic waves is the first condition which must be met. Next, the electromagnetic waves in this place must be capable of changing their amplitude. This is the second condition which must be met.

These waves of differing amplitudes, which are almost limitless in number in the universe, place the space vessel or mother ship inside the appropriate wave belt, where they continuously repeat the same, expanding motions which correspond to the amplitude of the waves. Once inside the belt (though this may be somewhat difficult for you to follow) the electromagnetic waves of the space vessel or mother ship are transformed, corresponding to speed of the amplitude of the wave belt. When this happens, the vessel takes on the same movement as the wave belt. In other words, it adopts the speed of the wave belt as it navigates through space. This is the same principle as what occurs when on Earth when you send a balloon up in the sky and it flies to distant places on the prevailing air current. Thus, the speed of a space vessel or mother ship is equivalent to the motion of the wave belt that it is in.

Going forward, backward, vertically, horizontally, left, right, parallel, or hovering—a space ship navigates in a variety of ways. Would you tell me how I should conceive of the ways in which it moves?

I think you now understand that a space vessel flies on wave belts the way a hot air balloon on Earth flies on an air current. The difference between the two, however, is that the hot air balloon exists in one fixed place whereas the space vessel can be in an enormous number of places, far more than are conceivable to people on Earth. In other words, it can change its place at will. Even from what appears to be a single point in space in the great universe,

229

numerous wave belts having waves of different lengths are endless-
ly flowing out from angles of 360 degrees in the direction of the
motion of their waves. From amongst these various wave belts, a
space vessel or mother ship skillfully selects the wave belt that suits
its purposes and utilizes it. This means that it can navigate as it
wishes, and at a speed of its own choosing, whether it is hovering,
going slow, fast, ultra fast, or ultra, ultra fast.

Now I understand. The fundamental function, or mission, of a
space vessel or a mother ship is to separate, select, transform, and
adjust waves, isn't it?

That's correct. That is exactly what its function is: not to navi-
gate on its own power. The challenge facing it is how to switch over
and make the transition in moving from one wave belt to another.
To say it in everyday language, it is how to control and adjust speed.
To be more specific, it means being able to fly in the space of a sec-
ond to places more distant than any human could imagine. I may
be repeating myself, but transforming waves into rough waves and
decelerating the speed of a space vessel are actually operations more
difficult than flying. It is extremely difficult to get a space vessel to
decrease its speed or to hover in space. This is quite the opposite of
what people on Earth might imagine.

From the Landing of the Mother Ship to the Docking

Could you please tell me what happens from the time the moth-
er ship gets ready to land and makes its approach to its docking at
the artificial base?

I mentioned to you earlier that as it approaches the landing
point, the mother ship maintains close contact with the base's con-
trol tower. When the order is given to proceed to the entrance of the
hangar, the mother ship descends vertically from its hovering posi-
tion, adjusts its orientation and moves slowly forward toward the

docking entrance. During this entire period, the control tower main-
tains close communication with the mother ship. As the ship con-
tinues its approach, the first door opens automatically. At the same
time, the wave adjustment gas curtains Nos. 1, 2 and 3 are activat-
ed. The mother ship goes through the docking entrance on its own
power. However, as it passes through gas curtains Nos. 1-3, all elec-
tromagnetic wave functions cease upon contact with the curtains of
gas. At that time a special transfer vehicle stands waiting for the
mother ship. This large-size transfer vehicle guides the nose of the
ship as it is gradually docked in the hangar. When the mother ship
is completely inside the hangar, all electromagnetic activity stops
and the ship is moved to its resting place in the hangar.

As the ship travels through space, how are crew and passengers,
as well as supplies and necessary materials, brought on board?
Could you outline the ways in which this is done?

You have already seen that there are various places where regu-
lar space vessels land, and you also have seen their internal organ-
ization and functions so you are somewhat familiar with them.
However, we have not yet talked much about mother ships. I would
like to give you an overview of them now, then later I can show you
the things I have described.

Like other space vessels, mother ships have landing places
which are reserved especially for them. Structurally, this kind of
landing place is very similar to a dock on Earth. Usually, a space
vessel is held in a stable position by cross-shaped adsorption plates
to which it adheres. Mother ships, on the other hand, have two sep-
arate cross-shaped plates, one fore and one aft. These are joined
together by a connecting plate. Together, these three function as a
single adsorption plate. There are differences in the heights of the
various levels of the mother ship; however these are more or less
standard and in the docking room there is a rather large, rectangu-

lar-shaped building, the design of which takes into account the heights of the mother ship's levels. The inside of the building is equipped with various facilities. What I have related just now refers to stationary structures. In addition to these, scaffold-like structures are assembled and this scaffolding is, to some extent, moveable. This naturally depends on the mother ship's size. So that both large and small mother ships can land with ease, one side of the scaffolding is adjustable. This adsorption plates can also move to some extent.

When a long space voyage comes to an end and the ship is returning, the entire landing area is filled with people who come out to greet the ship. When the mother ship adheres to the adsorption plates and is firmly secured, the emission of electromagnetic waves ceases. At the same time, almost as if they had been eagerly awaiting this moment, the passageway bridges swiftly extend from every level of the landing place toward the mother ship's exits and connect with the ship. After that procedure is complete, the cosmic people who have been waiting on board begin to disembark. With families and friends reuniting and the anticipation of returning home, the atmosphere is tense with excitement and joy, much like a big festival. Wave adjustment, for the most part, is done on board. Once you have seen the landing place, I think you will understand what I mean.

When I first entered this room I did not notice anything in particular, but on the opposite wall there were a number of signal lights. While small, they were of several different kinds and were blinking on and off. I had no inkling as to what they meant, but the young man started speaking the moment he seemed to take note of them: *Quite a long time has passed. If you feel all right now, we could head for the control tower and see the mother ship hangar. How do you feel?*

Thank you kindly for all the trouble you have taken on my behalf. I have fully recovered and would appreciate the opportunity to go look at the mother ship hangar.

Why don't we have a cup of tea first?

The moment the young man finished speaking, the young woman who had served us fruit earlier entered the room with a tray-like bowl containing three cups. Smiling, she placed the cups on the table and then, bowing her head slightly, left the room again. The drink had a fragrance and consistency somewhat denser than tea. It seemed to me like pureed fruit. It was very delicious and I drank it all in one go. I realized that it was probably somewhat rude to gulp it down so quickly, but I felt relieved when I saw that Mr. M and the young man had done the same.

Thank you very much, I said, expressing my gratitude.

Let's go, said the young man, standing up first and leaving the rest area of the artificial base. Outside the room was a fairly wide corridor which took us in the direction of the large hangar.

Visiting the Large Hangar

The ceiling was high and its color was milky white. While I believed that it was painted, it also gave the impression of being made of marble. I now wondered about the texture of the materials I was looking at. No matter what room I entered, I found it strange that there was no source of light to be found. It also seemed strange to me that nothing in the rooms cast shadows either. With thoughts like these running through my mind, we walked for what seemed to be about three or four minutes and then came to a door. Looking up, I saw an illuminated insignia above the door. In the middle of a circle was a cross, inside of which was a long, elliptical light-brown mother ship. On both ends of the ship were symbols that resembled Morse Code. The moment I saw this insignia above the door, I felt that this must be the entrance to the mother ship hangar. When the young man pressed a button, large doors opened to the right and left. Looking down at my feet, I noticed a road belt leading to the interior of the hangar. It occurred to me that a certain portion of the supplies used at the base might be brought in at this hangar.

The interior of the hangar was truly an amazing sight to behold. I do not have suitable words to describe what I saw. Was there any structure on Earth comparable to this in size? The very high ceiling was not rounded into an arc but conveyed the impression of having straight lines. Painted white, the room was like a great hollow expanse of heaven and Earth. Within this expansive space, the magnificent form of the mother ship stood quietly at rest. Cosmic people could be seen in twos and threes in various places. In stark contrast to the enormous mother ship, the people appeared to be no larger than small peas. The entire sight defied all description.

Again, I could not help but wonder how this great hollow space could be brighter than the daylight outside. This question now absorbed my full attention. Whether the youth was following my thoughts or not, I do not know. However, he took this opportunity to speak:

You are probably wondering how light is provided in this hangar. From an Earthly point of view, the interior of the hangar should not be bright since there is no apparent source of light. However, it is not that there is no light; it is just that the light source is not understood. It is not visible. In fact, in cosmic science, there are various devices that can measure the type of light waves found here. If we used these devices, the source of light would become clear. The principles, therefore, are simple. When special waves which are radiated parallel to the hollow of the ceiling function, 1824/46 waves flow through this room as they do now. When these waves and the special waves collide and create a constant affinity, they produce light in proportion to the quantity of special waves. The light source at that time can be perceived through gauges, but it cannot be discerned by our eyes.

Time and Space on the Moon Base
Are Faster than On Earth

On Earth, we have calculated that it takes seven minutes and 20 seconds for light from the sun to reach our planet. Accordingly, we make the speed at which the light of this sun travels the general standard for measuring the speed of light. But is the speed of light travelling from the sun to this base on the moon where we are now also the same? It is my belief that it is not the same but I am not sure why. Also, how is the frequency of the light waves illuminating this great hollow different? Could you please tell me?

Earlier, you will remember that I talked about time and space being different from star to star or planet to planet. Depending on the heavenly position of a star in the sky, its own waves and the waves of the people living on it join together to create that star's unique vibrations. I said that the star's position in the heavens was determined by how different its waves were from those of the parental God, emanating from the center of the universe. The more a star develops, the more time and space are reduced. Therefore, there are no stars which share the same standard of time or space, which is to say, the same speed. As you have noticed, the speed of time and space here on the moon base are faster than on Earth. Let's *take a look at the fundamental principles behind this from the per-spective of cosmic science.*

The stars scattered throughout the universe each have their own position in the cosmos according to the law of the heavens. The core of each individual star is surrounded by thick layers of waves. These are broadly divided into four layers. The function of each of these layers is fixed to a great extent. In addition, the thought waves of the people who live on that star (or planet) surround the star in over-lapping layers. Light waves passing through this heavy, rough wave belt are inevitably affected by it. As you can imagine, the original nature of these light waves becomes distorted as they pass through the numerous, heavy layers.

People on Earth are familiar with the phenomenon of light refraction that occurs when light passes through an object. The phe-nomenon of light wave distortion in the law of cosmic physics and the refraction of light are fundamentally different phenomena but they have certain aspects in common. When human beings on Earth observe the world around them, the see it through a series of thick layers. When we look at the world through tinted glasses, we get the impression that the world is actually that color. However, when we remove the glasses, it is as if we are seeing the real world for the first time. For hundreds of millions of years, people have been clouding the glasses through which they look at the world, so to speak. What people on Earth believe to be the speed of light is strikingly different from the speed of light on the moon base. In the same way, the reckoning of time is also different.

Let me explain in simple terms the fundamental ways in which time is different. On Earth, there are expressions describing units of time such as seconds, minutes, hours and days. Each of these has its own corresponding amount of time. For example, one sixtieth of a minute is one second, and so on. In a phenomenal world where waves have the very slow frequency found on Earth, under ordinary circumstances when people count aloud, they are usually able to count only up to one, or perhaps just slightly more, in the span of a second.

Let's just reflect for a moment on what is contained in this second of time. Suppose that on an advanced star or planet, or the moon, where the frequency of waves is much more rapid than that of Earth, a person could count up to 30 or even 60 in that span of time. In essence, that would mean that one month on Earth would be equal to one or two days on the moon or Venus. Now, if we assume that what takes place within one month on Earth is equal to what takes place in a single day on a planet like Venus, we would not see units of time as simple chronological measurements marking the space from one point to the next. Rather, we would see them as units indicating an equal frequency of waves. This frequency expresses what is contained or transpires between one point of time and the next.

We might take it for granted that a second on Venus is the same as a second on Earth, but that is a mistake. Time is an expression of what transpires within a given unit both in terms of quantity and quality. Standard units are derived from measurements of equal quality and quantity. Furthermore, time and space are in fact derived from a common place. The common place is the greatest common denominator of the wave frequencies, the frequencies of the infinite number of waves of a star. The point where the vertical and horizontal lines intersect is the point of emptiness, marking the point of departure of the science of the stars.

If we establish as the standard point of departure the place where two perpendicular lines intersect, that is to say the point of emptiness, what appears within that area is the time of that star. What appears outside of it is the space of that star. At the center of *the great universe, time and space blend into one and shine. Until that stage is reached, however, time and space are different for all of the stars.*

The science of advanced stars cannot be judged on the basis of the time and space of the less advanced ones. When the science of an advanced star is transferred to a less advanced one, the celestial position of the advanced star takes the lead. The wave frequency of the less-advanced star undergoes a change, becoming equalized with that of the advanced one, albeit only partially. Working from the place where the wave frequencies are equal, the science of the advanced star continues to be transferred to the less advanced star in a gradual process.

A Visit to the Impressive Mother Ship Hangar

Rather than say that the mother ship hangar was enormous, it would be more appropriate to say that it was on a scale so grand that it defied description. Both sides of it, at first glance, seemed to stretch out in a straight line. More careful inspection, however, showed that they bent in a gradual curve and, in fact, continued on in a gradual circular shape. The enormous mother ships were housed inside, each mounted on four specially designed transfer vehicles which were strategically and carefully positioned to maintain a huge ship in perfect balance.

On Earth, the same ship would have been securely fastened to a stabilizing platform. In the hangar here, however, one got the impression of mother ships resting in a tranquil sleep. Here they did not seem so enormous. This was due to the gargantuan size of the hangar, which put the ships in a wholly new perspective. Nevertheless, if you took a look at the cosmic people working in the hangar alongside these grand ships, you would be reminded of their grand scale. Counting the ships one by one, I got up to 14 but could not see any further from where I was. It was hard to believe that these ships, utilizing the enormous energy of wave bands, could fly close to or faster than the speed of light in a single instant. Although I understood the concept of how these ships operated, actually coming into contact with them made me doubt my own eyes. I questioned my state of mind, not ruling out the possibility that I was dreaming all of this. On the other hand, I also questioned my doubts at this moment, thinking that perhaps they were just the thoughts and feelings accumulated over long years on Earth, trying to keep me tightly boxed into an Earth person's narrow way of thinking.

I became keenly aware of how easily I could talk of undergoing 'a change of 180 degrees,' but when it really came down to it, I experienced great difficulty with the challenge of change. I was completely absorbed in this self-realization as the three of us walked around the end of the hangar. Suddenly turning around to see where Mr. M and the young man were, I noticed that they were both smiling, almost as if they had done it on cue. I suddenly realized what was at the bottom of their mirth. *Oh, blast it!* I thought to myself as I realized I had been caught off guard. They had fully grasped the progression of my thoughts, second by second and minute by minute, and knew absolutely everything that had transpired in my mind.

Feeling a bit awkward, I turned my eyes downwards toward my feet. As I looked at the ground, I noticed that the surface was not hard like concrete but more like an asphalt-paved road.

It was not, however, the normal black color of asphalt; it was more of a gray. As I walked along the inside of the large hangar, I noticed that a number of different colored lines had been drawn on the surface of the ground. Rather than being straight, they were gently curved and ran parallel to each other. They continued on down the hangar further than my line of vision could follow them. I had the impression that they most likely continued around the entire hangar.

Could you tell me what these lines are for?

Oh, you mean the different colored lines drawn on the ground? They aid in positioning the mother ship into its proper place in the hangar. The ship is mounted on the four special transfer vehicles which carefully maneuver it into its place in a sequence of movements until it arrives at its special spot. The same process takes place when it is moving out of the hangar. Electromagnetic waves at work above the lines dictate the direction in which the transfer vehicles will move. This makes it possible for one cosmic person to move the ship single-handedly.

Lighting in the Hangar

As I walked through the spacious hangar, I felt as if the artificial light inside were no different from the natural light of the sun. If there was any difference, I wanted to know what it was. As if reading my thoughts, the young man began to speak about light waves:

Perhaps one of the first things you noticed when you visited a space vessel or a base was the absence of any visible source of light. This is what I was talking about earlier. People cannot help but wonder what the difference is between the artificial lighting here and normal sunlight. Although I say 'lighting' here, I wish to emphasize that light is one facet of the way in which waves appear. While there are certain aspects of waves that we can perceive through our five senses, there are an incredible number of phenom-

ena in waves that we cannot discern because the waves move so fast. The number of these phenomena is beyond our comprehension. Likewise, the nature and characteristics of these waves vary. Before going into an explanation of them, however, I would first like to talk about us cosmic people and our fundamental thinking on light and waves.

Amongst the myriad stars scattered throughout the universe, certain ones have reached a highly evolved state. Without exception, each of these is guided by one Being who is a personification of absolute love and wisdom. Coming after this one Being are a number of other leaders. Some stars have systems that operate on the principle of an even number of leaders numbering 2, 4, 8 or 16, and others have systems based on an odd number of leaders numbering 3, 7 or 9. In addition, there are systems using compounds of even and odd numbers, or multisystems with combinations of even and odd numbers. While the systems may differ depending on the stars' evolution or position in the heavens, each of them is wholly governed by its one, central Being. The will, thoughts, and absolute love of this one Being are directly felt by each individual member of the population regardless of their position or the kind of work they do. This is why life goes on smoothly without the slightest gap in communication. We could perhaps compare each of these stars to a human being in whom all cells work together in perfect harmony.

Each member of society knows that he or she is respected. No two people are alike, and the role each plays is different. There is no one who is useless. With this understanding, we each carry out our own work in the settings which have been prepared for us. In this way, from those in leadership positions down to the average citizen, we work together. This is how the societies of cosmic people on advanced stars work.

241

If we were to depict the shining form of this large number of unified people as an embodiment of light, it would possess a brightness and clarity like the light of the sun. It would be a light composed of an almost infinite number of rays. Although its intensity might be only 1/100th or 1/1000th of that of the sun, to the naked eye it would look just like the sun because it is made up of the same light and brightness as the fantastic light of the sun. Each unit that forms the society of a star projects a brightness very similar to that of the sun.

At this point I inquired: *The light and brightness of the sun, as well as its warmth, is actually not what we humans understand it to be, is it? It seems that rather than the simple body we take it for on Earth, it is actually an intriguingly complex whole made up of an almost infinite number of separate bodies.*

That is correct, the young man replied. *And that is why, in the great scheme of nature and in the great flow of life where many things come into being, we are able to advance our evolution along a straight path in accordance with the divine will.*

The Signal Above the Door

We somehow arrived at the staircase which was the passageway to the floor above. Though the staircase looked very much like an escalator, the stairs showed no sign of movement. However, once a person placed both feet on it, it immediately glided into motion, operating on the same principle as the self-operated transfer vehicles described earlier. With alternating forces of attraction and repulsion, it moved along in the most natural way, enabling us to make a smooth transition to the floor above.

Both on the floor above and the floor below, six passageways stood one next to the other. We came out into the passageways and, after walking a short way along the corridor, came to the entrance of a room. As usual, there was a light over the door which blinked off and on continuously in long and short flashes much like a Morse code type signal. It was now sending out what seemed to be quite a long message. Before we entered the room, Mr. M and the young man observed the message it was communicating. At the entrance there were buttons for opening and closing the door. When one of the buttons was pressed, the signals above the door changed color, blinking animatedly from left to right.

From the signal above the door, we are able to tell at a glance what is stored inside the room. This is the room where instruments related mainly to electromagnetic waves are kept. All kinds of devices for measuring, observing, transmitting and gauging waves are stored here. Above the hangar there are three floors, and directly below the landing pad various types of equipment, such as wave separators and wave amplifiers, are kept. The hangar is organized in an integrated, three-dimensional system where all the equipment can remain closely interrelated.

The equipment is categorized and stored in separate rooms according to its use, such as communications, observation, and so on. This is the room where replacements are stored for equipment that becomes damaged or simply worn out. These symbols show by category what kinds of equipment are presently in stock. We can tell what the room contains without even going inside.

The Role of the 'Caretakers'

Is it possible for us to have a look at some of the equipment stored here?

Sure, whenever you like. Why don't we just step inside now and have a look.

As he spoke these words, the young man pressed a nearby button and the doors on the right and left silently opened. It seemed as if there were no cosmic people in attendance in this room. Lined up on both sides just inside the entrance were a number of powerbox-like devices measuring about one meter in width and two meters in height. Numerous attachments, signal lights, small light bulbs and other devices that might convey codes covered the surface of these boxes.

What function do these machines serve?

Basic Numbers	Basic Colors
1	white
2	yellow
3	orange
4	vermilion
5	red
6	dark red
7	purple
8	blue
9	green
0	brown

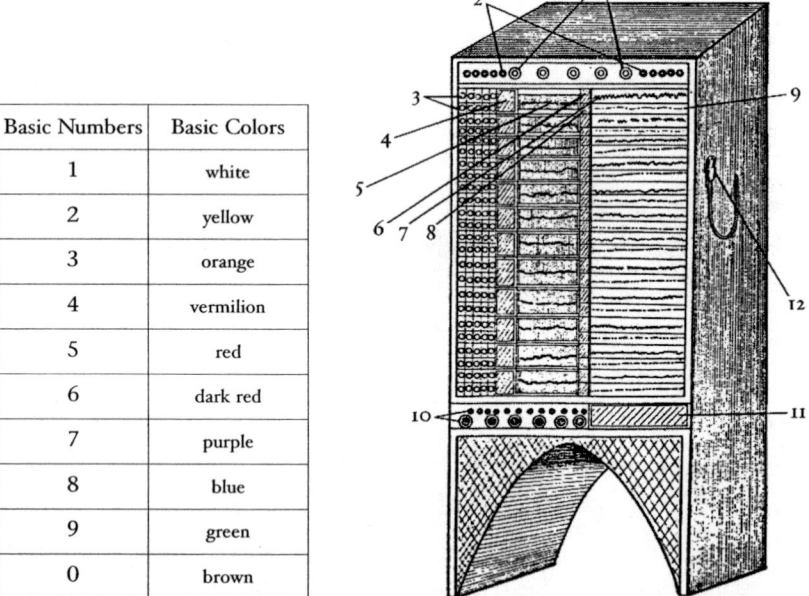

Figure 12. Caretaker machine. Parts: (1) machine name, (2) contents, (3) machine model, (4) symbol, (5) classification by type, (6) content indicator symbol, (7) capacity indicator sign, (8) location indicator, (9) weight, capacity and classification, (10) switches, and (11) vocalizer. Functioning: (1, 2, 3) signal colors indicate changes, (5, 7) interpretation via wave shape, (9) Morse code with color flow through changes in dots and lines, and (4, 7, 8) symbols indicate changes.

At the press of a button, they provide us with all sorts of information, such as current reports on the inventory of the equipment room, the place where each piece of equipment is stored, its function, and any other relevant information. They are called 'caretakers.' Let's try one out.

Before he even finished saying these words, the young man placed his hand on a button and as he did so the topmost signal light on the 'caretaker' lit up. The lights on the next row also lit up, changing to various colors. At the same time, the voice of a person, the source of which I did not know, could be heard. Upon pressing another button, the next row of lights below became active. Watching the movement of the lights, I realized that they moved in synchrony with the sound of the voice.

The voice that you hear is giving information about the inventory of equipment used at various stages in making corrections and adjustments to heavy gaseous bodies, in the process prior to reducing their original waves to electromagnetic ones. This varies according to the compounds in the heavy gaseous bodies. The information the 'caretaker' is giving right now pertains to an inventory of one million to three million units. It is reporting on the size of the inventory and categorizing the contents according to performance. The information provided here only pertains to what is used at this particular base. Equipment used for experiments and other purposes is kept in the underground warehouse of this artificial base. There is no one in this room, but this machine does the work of a faithful caretaker. This is why is has been given the name of 'caretaker.'

Is it possible to communicate with this caretaker through ordinary speech?

Just here on the side of the box is a type of microphone. If you take it off the hook and voice your request into it, it will give you

245

vocal information and signals communicated via changes in the colors of the lights.

How does it keep track of the inventory as it enters and leaves the warehouse?

Without the permission of this caretaker, no article or piece of equipment can enter or leave the warehouse. All details, including the volume of inventory being issued from or being placed in the warehouse, must be entered via the microphone. A calculation is made and the result is the balance of the inventory.

This is the first time I have come into contact with these machines called caretakers. Are there any other places where they are used?

In our society, there is probably no other device so widely used. There are a variety of types of caretakers, each with its own function. Regulating the inventory and providing information on the nature and function of various devices in stock are basically quantitative functions. However, caretakers are used for a multitude of purposes beyond these, including the categorizing of waves and the gathering of accurate data on waves at work in compound bodies and in light. The results are used for diverse purposes, from comprehending every type of wave emitted by human beings to measuring the distance of stars.

In addition, caretakers are used to distribute food, clothing and living supplies as needed in our society. However, please do not get the wrong impression. Hearing how these caretakers attend to the needs of people in our society, people with only scant knowledge of them might jump to the conclusion that human beings here are treated like machines. This is not the case. The fundamental principle underlying everything in our society is the immense love of God for each human being. This rules out any possibility of human life not being respected. It must be understood that these machines are used within a society that is motivated by love and respect for human life.

Now I really understand. I was just about to inquire about that point, but you have cleared all doubt from my mind. It only stands to reason that within such a wonderful social system as you have on the base here, the likelihood of people being treated like machines is nil. My problem is that I tend to think in terms of society on Earth and what could happen there with the use of similar devices.

This being said, we continued our inspection of the store-rooms.

At a glance, we can see what equipment is stored here.

Passing by a number of caretakers poised attentively on either side of the entrance, we came to a large number of metal cabinets standing about two meters high and one meter deep.

As we passed in front of the cabinets, the small lights on them flashed vigorously as if they were greeting us. After walking a bit further, the young man turned to me and said,

Here we are. These are the caretakers that measure electromagnetic waves. We can open the door and have a look inside.

Saying this, he pressed a button and the door at the front opened. The interior was divided into four levels. One, two, or three devices about the size of table clocks could be found on each level. The area above these was covered with a semicircular piece of translucent material that looked like rice paper. This seemed to have been placed over what appeared to be a rubber-like covering about 5 millimeters thick.

It would seem that this depository is for storing valuables.

The main part of this type of device is a very sensitive light sensor board. The utmost care is taken in positioning the warehouses of the base to avoid their coming into contact with rough waves. Also, the areas around the warehouses are outfitted with wave pre-

vention devices. Each individual device on the shelves is also outfit-ted with a cover that suits its particular needs.

If possible, I would like to know more about these sensor boards which seem to be the life's blood of these devices.

They are very thin boards made of materials very similar to the silicon and sulfur that you have on Earth, but that have undergone a number of processes. Being positioned on a single axis, several of these boards are layered one upon the other but with a certain amount of space between them. Two of these sensor boards paired together make up one device. A very mild current of electric waves is passed through the positively charged portion of the device. This enables it to pick up changes in the other sensor board. You have grasped the process up to this point. However, to understand any-thing beyond this point will require that you acquire a basic knowl-edge of waves as well as an understanding of the various laws at work on the base. Let's continue our discussion at a later time.

Chapter 6

THE WISDOM OF SPACE

Returning to the Control Tower

It was at about this time that things began to click in my mind. Since coming to the base, I had had a number of matters explained to me and had also been given the opportunity to observe things firsthand. I had learned a considerable amount about waves and believed that I had a fair understanding of them on the whole. However, it now became clear that any knowledge I might have had was negligible at best. I also came to the realization that my understanding of the laws governing the base was non-existent. This caused me to question whether I even had the right to talk about the social structure or the science of the base.

As these thoughts passed through my mind, the words came to me, *Accept things as they appear to you.* The moment I acknowledged the meaning of these words, an illuminating light flashed through my mind accompanied by the thought, *Be thankful for the teachings of the parental God. Trust in the wisdom of your own body and soul and all will go well.* At that moment, I felt a pervasive sense of gratitude toward my guardian spirits and Goi Sensei, whom I believed were guiding me.

Standing attentively nearby, the young man said:

I have just received a communication from the governor. Since the inspection of the interior of the base is just about over, we are to return to the control tower to dine with him. We may end our tour here and proceed to the tower.

Is it possible to go to the top level of the base from here? I would like to go there to see the landing pad.

That is one way of getting to the control tower. It won't take very long so we can take that way.

Leaving the warehouse, we walked along the corridor for two or three minutes before arriving at an escalator. Going up the escalator to the next level, the young man told me about each of the rooms: there was a room for adjusting waves, a room for separating them, one for recycling them and one for reinforcing them. There was also a room for observation and communications. Directly underneath the landing pad there was also an integration room for six of the twelve base districts.

We ascended the staircase. Coming to the landing pad, we headed for the exit. I was overcome with a sense of light-headedness. However, this lasted for only a moment. Coming into contact with the fresh air outside, I felt an indescribable sense that all this was familiar to me.

The three of us boarded the transfer vehicle that would take us to the control tower. As we descended the mountain ridge, I was filled with an inexpressible feeling of joy and eagerly looked forward to reaching the control tower.

After a short time, the transfer vehicle we were on arrived at the lift to the control tower. As usual, there were a considerable number of cosmic people coming and going. Alighting from our transfer vehicle, we boarded the elevator. Once the young man, Mr. M and I had gotten on the elevator, the door closed and the elevator shot upward at tremendous speed. It stopped in the passageway leading to the uppermost chamber, where the governor was. Coming into the corridor, the slight fatigue I had felt until now disappeared completely. The air we breathed from the control tower rising high into the sky had a wonderful lightness about it.

The signal control beacon above the door of the governor's quarters shone as always with a dazzling beauty. I had barely caught a glimpse of it when the door closed. The young man walked straight ahead. Not to be left behind, Mr. M and I followed him. Dressed in navy blue space wear, the lean governor appeared to be studying something very carefully. As we approached, he immediately raised his head and smiled. He addressed the young man first:

Welcome back. I realize that you were in the middle of your tour, but we have visitors and I did not wish to keep them waiting too long. I am sorry to inconvenience you by making you come back so soon.

Next he spoke to Mr. M: *Thank you for all your trouble. The captain of the space vessel has come for you so please take a seat.*

The People of Earth have been Dreaming for a Long Time.

Bringing myself to attention, I suddenly gave expression to my feelings of gratitude:

I was given a tour of the artificial base under construction. It exceeded the limits of my imagination in so many ways that I was spellbound. The science of Earth and that of the base are worlds apart. The science of the base is so wondrous, like a prize that lies beyond reach. It is still beyond the grasp of Earthly humans. Just as animals living in water have no knowledge of things on land, people from Earth have no inkling of the truth and nature of the moon. Most humans from Earth would not think of it other than as a hostile place of extreme temperatures where no people or animals can survive. When will the time come when they will understand? When I reflect upon this situation, I somehow feel that Earthly humans have been dreaming for a very long time. I would very much like to hear the governor's comments on this point.

The governor responded:

The time you speak of has already arrived. Gradually a knowledge of the science of this base will be transferred to Earth. At present, some of the less complicated aspects are already in the process of being transferred. It might seem like an enormous task, but it is not one that will be achieved by the strength or intelligence of humans on Earth. When the divine will determines, it will be done gradually by the people who are destined to do it.

At that moment, a small box-like device on the governor's desk began speaking out energetically to him. (This was another type of caretaker. We had seen some of these earlier in the supply room at the base. I remember the young man telling us that there were several varieties of caretakers and they came in different shapes. He had also explained to us that many people depended on these caretakers.) The signal light blinked on and off repeatedly, emitting small wave patterns like an oscilloscope on Earth would. Watching the shapes of the waves, I could not help but think that they represented the words of someone speaking. At this point, the governor made the words pause for a moment and seemed to be responding to them. I felt that he was communicating by telepathy with the captain, who was waiting in another room. I also got the impression that the governor worked every day without a moment's leisure, communicating with and giving instructions to each section of the base, where large numbers of people were working. I could not help but reflect on the enjoyment that these people working in space must have felt as they went about their daily tasks, completely absorbed in their work. This was just a fleeting thought, however.

Meeting the Captain Again

The governor rose from his chair and said, *We are keeping our guests waiting. Shall we go down to the reception room and join the others?*

We all rose from our seats and followed the governor out of the room. Turning left into the corridor, we came to a passageway with staircases leading both up and down. Descending to the floor immediately below, we arrived at a corridor. This floor seemed to be largely divided into meeting rooms, communication rooms, and rooms for private use. Passing by a number of these, we came to a room where the tables were arranged in the shape of a horseshoe and where a number of round lamps emitted waves in circular patterns. A series of five circles came from each lamp, with the base of the waves illuminated and seeming to float. I immediately and intuitively knew that this was the reception room most suited to receiving small groups of people.

I have asked the captain to wait in this room.

As he spoke, the governor pressed a button and went into the room as soon as the door opened. Mr. M went in next, followed by me and then the young man. The door closed soundlessly behind us.

Excuse us for keeping you waiting. Everybody has arrived now.

As he spoke these words, the governor motioned for the captain, who had risen from her chair, to be seated, and the rest of us as well. The governor sat down first.

I was so delighted to see the captain that I forgot all else and immediately burst into conversation with her.

So much had happened in such a short period of time. After arriving in a space vessel that had traversed the great expanse of space, I had observed the activities of the base and seen self-propelled vehicles, sky taxis, construction sites, and the building of an artificial base. In the process, I had become totally absorbed in this new, heavenly world and had thoroughly become part of it, forgetting that I would ever return home. At one point, as I was resting in one of the ante rooms in the interior of the artificial base, the faces of all my friends on Earth had suddenly begun to float through my mind like figures projected from a revolving lantern. It was at that moment that I first became conscious of having come to this base from afar. A feeling of nostalgia for my home planet surged forth in me like an incoming tide. At the same time, I had a moment of uneasiness wondering how I would get back. However, the thought that Mr. M would be with me and would be sure to have a good plan quickly put my uncertainty to rest. Nevertheless, without realizing it, I had subconsciously continued to search for the captain. I felt that she would come for me sometime, somewhere.

Now, here in the control tower, this expectation suddenly met with reality. I emitted an exclamation of happy surprise, overcome with feelings of nostalgia.

You have come for me, haven't you? I said.

She smiled, reassuring me with her wise and gentle eyes.

That's right. It is almost time to go back.

A simple *Thank you* was all I could manage to say. The rest of my words seemed to be trapped at the back of my throat.

The captain had a somewhat round face and her eyes shone with intelligence. Coming from her was a constant flow of waves that seemed almost tangible. Her very existence was so pure and clear that it was almost like air. I had been so absorbed in following all the activities at the base that now, upon meeting the captain again, it seemed that we had not seen each other for a long time. I was unable to calculate how many days, months or years had elapsed. Any attempt at doing so would merely be a mechanical measurement of time based on the coarse waves of Earth; it would be pointless to try to evaluate the changes and various phenomena of a world with a clock from a different dimension.

I somehow feel as if I have not seen you for some time. How long would it be in terms of time on the base?

The spontaneous laughter of the captain suddenly dispelled the air of formality in the room. Taking a look at my confused expression, she could not restrain her mirth.

Well, you arrived just as the sun rose in the morning, didn't you? And since then, how many nights have you spent here? That's right. It is now evening. So what does that mean? You have been here from only morning to evening. Is that not correct?

Yes, I guess you are right. And yes, I must have known that only a half day has passed since I arrived.

But in your terms, this corresponds to the work of many years. Wouldn't you say so, governor?

The captain then turned the conversation over to the governor.

Time is a Measurement of Work

You may be aware that the base has its own particular reckoning of time. I see that you have had a look at your watch. The same time measured by your watch is used as a standard at the base. If there were no common standard of time, society at the base would not function efficiently. However, while this so-called time is a stan-

dard at the base, it does not an indicate the true nature of time here. It is a hypothetical standard used in the process of expressing the true nature of time. Time must be something which can express the amount of work done. That is why your half day on this base corresponds to a number of years. The depth and the breadth of the work that has been accomplished here is quite evident to us.

Using the time of a particular world as the sole standard to make conjectures as to the amount of work completed would be a mistake. It is only through an understanding of the amount of work done that we can perceive the true nature of time and see, know, and measure things.

A half day at the base must correspond to a number of lifetimes on Earth! I exclaimed.

On behalf of the people on Earth, I would like to express my heartfelt gratitude to you for taking the trouble to show me this fantastic base. I will take every opportunity to let people know the truth about the world that exists here.

The governor took in my words and continued to speak.

Memories Can Always be Recalled

Conveying to people on Earth what you have seen here at this base is the most important part of your work. I would like you to take every opportunity to reveal what you have learned.

Of course, it goes without saying that, in the short time you have spent here, it is next to impossible to understand all that you have seen. On the other hand, once something has been imprinted on your consciousness, it never disappears. While you might think it complex or believe that you have forgotten it, you will most certainly be able to recall it from memory when necessary. You will recall and understand not just the superficial appearances but also the theories, workings, and other factors that are the underpinnings of our society.

When you take the viewpoint of people on Earth, you might wish that you could take back an encyclopedia containing all the information you need from the moon base. However, in our world, we do not need the assistance of an enormous encyclopedia. Once something has been recorded on the waves of the spirit, it can be viewed at any time. Whenever you feel that you want to know the true form of some manifestation, please do not hesitate to call upon us. If you call upon us, we will come to wherever you are. I also want you to know that we will reply in tune with your waves, in a way that is easy to understand. This is why the half day spent at the base, which you could not reckon in terms of time, has such value. To look at the experience on only a superficial level would be no different from taking a trip to fairyland in a children's storybook. The difference is that this story is about something which will actually happen. Regardless of whether the people of Earth believe it or not, the time will come when it will have become a reality and every person will be able to experience it with their five senses.

The Pillar of Light Connecting God and Man

When will that time come?

After they are born on Earth, people pass through a number of stages, fulfilling their appointed tasks and then returning to the world of their origin. In the space of a lifetime, a number of situations develop. These can occur without a clear beginning or end, and some conditions may seem to continue unchanged.

While individual lives have birth and death, heaven has no beginning or end. The expansive oceans, the mountains, the rivers, the sun that shines its light on Earth without missing a day all year, the changing seasons and the unchanging moon continue to appear, without beginning or end. The moon we see when we are children and as old people seems the same, but what we see is not the true form of the moon. It is the moon reflected in the heart of the beholder, the moon as one imagines it. The true moon, when the beholder's clouds of doubt have cleared, appears to one's shining spirit like a perfect, polished mirror, unblemished by even a wisp of cloud. The deep spirit of the great God contained in a single ray of light becomes the moon, a person, the shining of the sun, the vast mountains, and the expansive sea. When a person has discovered this true form, he or she becomes one with God and radiates a dazzling, brilliant light.

In the shining place where God and a person become one, a pillar of light is formed between heaven and Earth, and the love and wisdom of God spontaneously well up, revealing the essential nature of a human being. Unfortunately, the people of Earth have lost sight of their original nature. Instead of beholding their inner light, they have been looking at fading shadows and taking them to be their true selves. Yet they need not worry. Divine forgiveness is flowing forth. The divine moment has come when Earthly human beings can find liberation from the mistaken ways they have perpetuated for thousands of years.

One way this is happening is through the movement for world peace, which is a direct expression of the will of the universal God and the divinities who guide and protect the Earth. When human beings feel this divine will surge up within them, and pray wholeheartedly for peace on Earth, a pillar of light forms between heaven and Earth. As a result, more and more people rediscover their essential nature, which transcends life and death. And, as the sites of prayer for world peace continue to spread out, the immense redeeming light being radiated to Earth will shine ever stronger and the advanced science of the stars and the base will come to this world. Without a doubt, it will come.

The sites of prayer for world peace will continue to grow in every country and region. The time will come when people everywhere, regardless of race or nationality, will join those praying for world peace. This, together with the change of the Earth's position in the heavens, will transform human beings' way of thinking beyond imagination. A wonderful, peaceful society will come about, just like those on Venus and the moon. It will be free of all conflict and guided by one central divine Being. In that new world, a new and fantastic science will contribute to society in a way that is beyond the dreams of people on Earth today.

Words like 'old age,' 'sickness,' 'poverty' and 'pain' will fall from use. Life and death, as a stage in the evolutionary process, will be truly understood as simply a process of shedding the physical clothing of one world and donning suitable apparel for the next.

There is not one among us here who does not pray for this heaven to be realized on Earth as soon as possible. That is why we are always working with you when you pray for world peace. Dear friends on Earth and kindred spirits in prayer for world peace, we want you to know that whoever calls upon us, we will go to them without fail and watch over them. There will be a time when we will definitely show ourselves to you. At that time, shouldn't we all join hands and unite our spirits for the evolution of the Earth and the building of a heaven on Earth? We ask that you relay this message to all kindred spirits.

As the governor spoke, his face shone with a radiance that made him look like a completely different person.

Vessels Powered by Vibrations from the Mind

I had learned from the governor that a space vessel or mother ship can be flown at will by the main person operating it. I had wanted to ask how these ships could be flown via such vibrations at a speed that is barely visible to the human eye. For some time I had wanted to ask a captain about the firsthand experience of being in charge of a ship's navigation. But now that I had the opportunity to do so, I realized I no longer had the desire to.

I heard what I needed to know and received instruction regarding facilities and equipment. I was very keen on taking this opportunity to learn about such things.

The captain nodded as she smiled and then began to speak:

The space vessel and the mother ship are individual, controlled bodies moving through space, like the planets Venus, Mars and Mercury. The movement of the cosmos can be understood as a type of law. In the midst of this great movement are single, central bodies that continually emit waves in expanding spirals. These are called stars. The Earth and the moon are also among these bodies. Rather than being separate, the stars and their satellites gravitate toward a center, and though they are controlled, each moves in accordance with its own divine role. In this way, these heavenly bodies are very similar to human beings.

Each planet is inhabited by hundreds of millions of people who have built a variety of social systems. Beyond their differences, all of these systems share a strong belief in brotherly love and dedication to serving others. It would not be a mistake to think of each of these planets as if it were a human body. The human body is composed of hundreds of millions of cells that work together in harmony, guided by the central functions of the brain. This is identical to the behavior of the planets and their satellites. Space vessels and mother ships are no exceptions. We can always think of them as human beings. A space vessel too can be thought of as if it were a single human body.

The brain can be thought of as the body's captain or the control room from which the captain maneuvers the craft.

It is not difficult if you think of it in this way. As I said earlier, in the vessel there is a control room from which waves are continually radiating and expanding outwards in spirals. This differs from a heavenly body surrounded by satellites in that the waves radiated from the center of the vessel can be changed at will. In other words, the central person has complete freedom to decide how to use them.

To explain our fundamental view in simple terms, there are an almost infinite variety of waves. Due to our limited knowledge of space science, there are still a vast number of waves which we do not comprehend. While we may understand them conceptually, we cannot truly grasp what they are like. Scientists on Earth, in turn, know only a minute fraction of what we understand. If people on Earth make the mistake of believing that they know everything, they will never be able to reach an understanding of cosmic science.

When Waves Are Different We Cannot See Them

In the control tower where we presently are, countless waves are passing back and forth and we have no idea how many different waves occupy the same place. You must be wondering how we can select and use these various diverse waves to position the space vessel and the mother ship in the path of the required waves.

The first thing you must know is that there are a large number of different vibrational areas, and for each of them there is a corresponding world. A pilot who knows a particular world can aviate in it, and the vibrations of the pilot's spirit can instantaneously attune themselves to the wave length of that world. This in no way requires any type of sophisticated technology. As soon as a thought flashes through the pilot's mind, the space vessel is in the world that corresponds to that thought.

Increasing or decreasing the speed is entirely up to the pilot. There are an endless number of space vessels continuously making their way around the Earth, but people on Earth cannot see them. However, if these vessels decrease their speed and fly at a relatively low velocity, they can be discerned by the naked eye. For the person operating the vessel this would not have any particular significance, but from the perspective of a person on Earth it would be an extraordinary occurrence.

Bullets shot from a gun move at a speed not visible to the human eye. However, there is nobody who would deny their existence just because they cannot be seen. However, what I would like to say here is that speed and velocity are not words used only to describe the way in which material objects move; they also refer to the movement of the waves which form an object.

Generally speaking, people confirm the existence of an object not conceptually but by seeing it with their eyes. Only then does that object find a place in their consciousness. To determine the existence of objects, the eyes are usually the sole basis for judgement. However, there are a number of real phenomena which do not enter a person's field of visibility. There are many people on Earth whose eyes discern only a small proportion of existing phenomena. This is closely related to the kind of mental waves a person emits. What is outside the range of his or her mental waves will not be visually discernible. What can be seen is only that to which the spirit is attuned, and whatever waves are emitted will determine one's field of vision. I think you now understand what I mean when I say that there are many stages of visibility. The power of vision corresponds with the power of the waves one emits.

While something may appear in the field of vision of one person, it may not appear in another's because the field of his or her waves is different.

How Can This be Understood by People on Earth?

I clearly understand what you are saying, but do you think it can be understood by many people on Earth? Isn't this very complex? I cannot help but feel that it is. Even if people can understand this conceptually, unless we can offer them specific ways to come to a thorough understanding of it on their own terms, it will remain a mere academic theory. Given the present conditions on Earth, I cannot help but worry that this may be the case.

The captain nodded as she listened to my each and every word.

That's right. I was going to say the same thing. People on Earth have long been in the habit of doing things on their own. When they make a decision to do something, they show a determination to struggle through on their own. Unless they do so, they do not feel as if they are really working. However, what we have been talking about is not something that can be achieved through straining and exerting oneself. It is not achieved by the hand, strength, or knowledge of materially-oriented human beings. When people emit waves similar to ours, or are in a place which is steeped in those waves, their own mental vibrations will naturally begin to flow in harmony with those of the people around them.

It was as if I was facing this knowledge for the first time. It suddenly made me feel light. In the early stages, one might strongly deny such knowledge and continue to doubt it. As time goes on, though, the person gradually sees its truth. Little by little, the thought takes hold and expands until it is finally confirmed at the conscious level. This expanded way of thinking then forms the foundation for similar ideas, which also expand and develop within the person.

The above is an example of what I learned from one cosmic person. Not everything I learned was presented to me in the same manner. It is merely a specific example of one method through which I learned.

The captain continued to speak:

The vessel appears where the pilot's waves are at work. For the people in space, the vessel moves entirely as their spirit directs. The spirit that moves a space vessel must surely be a realm of divine wisdom to which any human being can freely travel.

Would it be okay to think of this realm of wisdom as a lofty, deep world of enlightenment?

It is a world in which we exist without any trace of egoism or attachment. In that world, the vibrations of our individual self have wholly returned to the oneness of life and move freely and fluidly like a fish returned to water.

I realized that as I listened to the captain's serene and refreshing words I had lost all notion of time and place.

An Enjoyable Meal Together

As I glanced casually at the signal light rear me, I noticed that the colors were continually changing. The governor turned to the captain and said:

Breakfast is ready. Would you care to join us?

Breakfast with the governor? I would be honored. Thank you.

Her solemn response met with a burst of laughter from all those present. On this light note we all proceeded to the next room. The governor led the way, with the captain, the young man, Mr. M, and I following him into the corridor

We turned right and, after walking a short way, arrived at the entrance to a room. Above the door was a symbol composed of vertical and horizontal lines coming together to form a cross. At the center of this were circles of light that blended together in hues of orange and yellow. Underneath this were three wavy lines. Looking at this symbol, I proceeded to enter the room. The door closed smoothly behind us. We found ourselves in a long room about four by eight meters, its far end widening out in the shape of a fan. It was quite a luxurious room. At the center stood two rectangular tables with chairs around them. Decorative side tables which seemed to be of very fine quality also graced the room. In the center of the walls on both the right and left were three picture panels about 50 centimeters square, spaced at intervals of about 50 centimeters. The sound and transmission devices installed in the ceiling also caught my immediate attention. We all took our seats, the governor and the young man on the right and the captain and me on the left. The table shone beautifully like polished marble. Amidst the green of it was a pattern of scattered flowers both large and small. As I gazed at the flowers, I was drawn into the illusion of looking down into a garden. Drinks, fluffy white rice, vegetable dishes and dried fruit had already been set at each place.

I was sitting opposite the governor and the young man. Although I did not notice their entry, two young women dressed in white clothing appeared bearing drinks and fruit. They wore short-sleeved blouses with open collars that seemed to be without buttons, hooks or zippers of any sort. The cloth seemed to be as light as a feather and did not appear to be like vinyl or paper but rather a modern weave. The women's hair was cut short, along the line of their neck. They had a fresh, light appearance and looked to be about seventeen or eighteen. One of them had a roundish face while the other's was more oval, but they were both beautiful.

The table now fully set, we joined the governor in prayer. *We offer our deep gratitude to you, God, our Parent, who have given us this food. We ask that our lives may be spent in health dwelling in you.* As I repeated in my heart the words, *We ask that our lives may be spent in health dwelling in you,* I felt a deep sense of unity. With the governor's words of prayer, I felt a moment when we had all become one.

Thank you.

With these closing words from the governor, the prayer came to an end and each of us commenced eating.

The meal I shared with these cosmic people was truly enjoyable. It was a repast that satisfied not only our appetites but our souls. When we had all finished, the strains of a beautiful melody began to play.

Observing the Parent Star via Cosmic Television

Being tone deaf, I could not fully appreciate the beauty of this wonderful music. The governor, who had been watching me listen to the music intently, seemed to have switched on the screen on the wall facing us.

Let's take a moment to have a look at the cosmic television while we relax. You may have already seen this type of television on the space vessel. However, I would like to take a moment to explain the technology involved. Contrary to what you may think, what you see here are not images that have been photographed at close range and enlarged. The method used here is one in which special waves

of a certain amplitude are radiated onto an object and, after com-
ing into contact with it, are reflected back to go through a process of
separation, reproduction and amplification. This results in the
images you see. The amplification process is made possible through
waves consisting of very fine vibrations, thousands of times faster
than light or radio waves on Earth. If we did not use waves like this
for observing and communicating with distant stars, it would not
have been possible for us to understand the principles of proper evo-
lution, or even to maintain communication. What we are about to
look at is the parental sun that controls our solar system.

A single star no larger than a pea appeared in the center of
the large expansive screen. As we watched, this parental star
grew larger and larger on the screen. As it did, curtains of
transparent waves surrounding it also became noticeable.
There were layer upon layer of waves surrounding the star, and
all of them shone with a pale gold light that was truly capti-
vating.

I was absolutely awestruck by the band of waves captured
on the cosmic television screen. What exactly were these 'special waves' that the governor had talked about earlier? What I
was seeing triggered a number of questions in my mind. For
example, while we people on Earth observe the stars scattered
throughout the great universe, don't we also realize that there
are a huge number of stars that we cannot observe? The waves
that 'appear' or 'are visible' to us are within a certain range.
Observing the world that appears only within this limited
range, have we not made assumptions about the reality of the
universe at large—assumptions that are, in fact, untrue?
Haven't we also held on to these misunderstandings because,
like many things, their truth remains beyond our ken? These

thoughts flashed through the back of my mind and quickly vanished. The governor continued to speak:

The guiding star which you see on the screen here cannot be grasped with the technology you have on Earth. The existence of a guiding, parental star is not even known. But as you can see on this cosmic television screen, it maintains a close, essential relationship with our solar system and plays a significant role in the movement of the great universe. As this parental changes position, the positions of the child stars belonging to it also change.

Since you have been here, I believe you have learned that the position of the Earth in the universe is changing and that the time has come when humanity as a whole will be able to achieve a great sublime state. Now let's have a look at the special waves emitting from the guiding star, shown on another screen.

Taking a look at the image on the other TV as the governor suggested, I saw the same guiding star. Comparing both of them, I asked, *Isn't this one the same as the other?*

It's the same guiding star, but take a look at the waves being emitted.

A Window in the Heavens

The band of waves radiating from the single, ball-like star was not spreading out from the center in equal concentration. Though the waves were being emitted in a perfect circle, there seemed to be a strong resistance in one direction. The band of waves formed a ring that looked somewhat like those around Saturn. The waves continued to move and expand, particularly in the area of the ring. I was wholly captivated by the image on the screen. However, as I watched, the pattern of waves began to change. The star remained the same but the ring of a moment ago, which had been expanding in a horizontal direction, was now doing so vertically. After a while, diagonal rings also appeared. Multiple layers of rings were being emitted, and they were overlapping. I had absolutely no idea what to make of this phenomenon.

Sensing my perplexed state, the governor offered an explanation:

The emissions of waves from stars vary in type and behavior. Many emissions have a tendency to hold the direction of the waves. This tendency creates places where the waves come together and are most concentrated. In these places, the waves appear in the shape of a ring. There are just as many rings as there are differing waves. The movement of the rings caused by the star's own rotation and the rotation of the universe causes the rings to change further, making it hard to differentiate them. If you look at the television screen, you will understand what I mean.

A single star with numerous bands of waves could be seen. The rings were moving in accordance with the rotation of the star. Gradually they began to overlap until it was impossible to discern separate bands. All of a sudden, I could see a diagonal line of waves being emitted at a 15-degree angle. Again, I did not have the slightest idea of what these waves signified.

This is a special type of wave that the guiding star emits. In this instance, it is being emitted in a straight diagonal line and is quite potent. The stars that receive the emanation of this wave may receive it either wholly or only in the areas where it is needed. This wave is emitted through a window-like opening in the curtain of the other waves, which are several layers thick. Through this aperture only the necessary quantity of vibrations are emanated. This is known as the 'wave band window.' You are probably wondering how this wave band window opens and closes. It is done by the power of the divinity presiding over the star and is beyond the sphere of our conjecture.

If we think of each star as a person, the band of waves may be thought of as a sacred robe. Just as the robe may tell you what kind of person the wearer is, the waves and the color of the bands reveal the destiny of the star.

The governor continued his narrative.

The Earth is One Among Countless Worlds

Earlier you heard the captain explain that for each and every wave band a single world exists. When you heard the word 'single,' you may have imagined a finite world existing within a fixed frame. However, this is not the case, and these worlds are not so small or limited. To make it easier to understand, think of the world on Earth as being one universe. It was formed when coarse waves received emissions from certain other waves. These coarse waves determine the appearance of this universe known as Earth and what we can know about it.

Let's consider, for example, one factor that forms a standard for the waves of this world. In the world of forms, the speed of light is at the boundary line to the next world. There are things that travel faster than light but knowledge of these things is still beyond Earth people's reckoning. Therefore, the speed of light is the basis on which the distance and size of heavenly bodies is determined. However, when we observe stars that are far away, what we are observing is how they looked hundreds of millions of years ago. We are not looking at an accurate view of how they appear today. The brilliant light that we see now may have been radiated aeons ago. The life of that star may already be over, and it may have ceased shining. Without an understanding of the current state of these stars, it seems unnatural to include them with the advanced stars of the present.

Each world measures its breadth according to the amplitude of the vibrations that are the standard there. However, the speed of light is only one standard for understanding the breadth of the universe. Not realizing this, there are many people on Earth who maintain that no other world exists beyond their own. They hold to the mistaken belief that their world is the first and the last of its kind.

In the vibrational range between Earth and the Mind of the great universal God, an almost infinite number of worlds exist. Each of these is incomparably vaster and more advanced than Earth. In the midst of the coarse waves of Earth, people have been going about their daily lives and gaining experiences in accordance with their own divine missions. However, the present state of the Earth's people is that they have entrenched themselves in one range of waves as if in a whirlpool. Caught within this swirling mass of waves, they repeatedly go through cycles of birth and death. They have stayed at this level for a very long time.

Labor Pains of Giving Birth to the Age of the Universe

Most of the Earth's residents are completely unaware of the existence of the planet's guiding star that you see on this TV screen. In addition, apart from a small number of individuals, no one on Earth knows that other worlds exist or tries to discover their existence. Most go on as they have, without even entertaining the hope of rising to the next dimension.

One indication of the transition that is about to take place is a great elevation in the position of the Earth as a heavenly body. This occurs through changes in the parental star. A number of other changes will accompany this phenomenon. These will take place in the most natural way. If they occurred suddenly, it would cause one

third of humanity to perish. This would not benefit the many people who have been steadily uplifting themselves while living on
Earth.

As I said earlier, the precision of the great God's enormous plan
is hard for humans to even begin to comprehend. The science of
Earth is now progressing at a very rapid pace. Using a science based
on coarse waves, humans have created social systems made up of
individuals, groups of individuals, countries, and groups of countries, each pursuing its own advantages. These pursuits have deviated greatly from the original mission of science. The great God of
the universe is utilizing these deviant activities as a stepping stone
through which human beings may strive to discover their original
identity and purpose. There is no specific framework for carrying
this out. There is no fixed, absolute way in which each person gives
expression to their essential nature and mission; it is a very flexible
process. Each person works from what he or she knows.

Along with the progress in Earthly science, universal science of
a high dimension will appear unexpectedly, causing the thoughts
and feelings of Earthly human beings to turn in a 180-degree direction. The appearance of this universal science will be sudden and
will utterly defy all comparison.

It will be a surprise coming like a thunderbolt from the blue,
and it will result in very confused feelings. Human beings on Earth
will not know what to do; it will be the time prior to a great upward
transition, when people will be confused as to what course of action
they should take. Whether they like it or not, each and every one of
them will be indiscriminately swept up in a surging movement. It
will not be unlike the massive confusion and panic at the time of
the great flood, when only a very few could find refuge in Noah's
ark. The thoughts and feelings of all humanity will be caught up in
a maelstrom of chaos.

Humans on Earth will be wracked with pain similar to that experienced by a mother prior to a difficult childbirth. It is said that the larger the child, the greater the labor pains. Nevertheless, the pain of childbirth is followed by joy. The moment the mother lays her eyes on her newborn, the pain she experienced vanishes. She is filled with feelings of joy and hope for her child. The mother's eyes see far off into the future, when the child is grown, and her eyes shine with joy at the thought of it. This cosmic 'child' will be called the 'Age of the Universe,' and the period that follows will be the infancy of this new age.

After speaking uninterruptedly for some time, the governor picked up his cup and quenched his thirst. He remained silent for a time. I was thoroughly absorbed in each and every word he had spoken and could feel his words sinking into my body and soul. I held my breath in anticipation of what he would say next.

An End to Suffering

In the great flood, only those connected to God were saved. They were taken into Noah's ark while the vast majority of people were swallowed up by the rising waters, suffering a fate that was a far cry from God's merciful wish.

At that time, only a small number of 'good people' were rescued while the vast majority drowned in the great flood. However, this type of situation will absolutely not occur again. The majority of people on Earth will definitely be uplifted. Nevertheless, during the period of rapid upward transition, the Earth's people will have to modify their thought waves to those of gentleness, devotion, empathy and harmony, and this modification process may take time and be accompanied by pain. Furthermore, the pain will continue so long as each person's thought waves are out of harmony with the life flow of humanity as a whole. Bringing together the thoughts of each and every individual in humanity in a state of oneness and harmony is like the swift and steady flow of a great river born from the convergence of a multitude of individual streams. When we understand that these individual streams are not separate, the upward transition of humanity will progress that much faster.

The billions of people who live on Earth originally issued from one divine life, forming the world of humanity we see today. Life appears to consist of the separate existences of men and women, the old and the young, various nationalities, races, and social classes. If we go back to our beginning, however, we are all brothers and sisters. Forgetting this fundamental truth, humans have fought with each other and murdered their own kind time and time again. Isn't it a sad history that human beings on Earth carved out for themselves? This tragedy has come about because people have strayed from the spirit of oneness and have taken a twisted, arduous road. But they are now on the last leg of this sad journey, and the time has come for the suffering to end.

What then is the earnest wish of the divine Mind, which never blames humanity for attaching itself to an unreal world, a world of external appearances? It is, as I said earlier, for each person to inquire into their original nature and then understand that they, as individuals, are linked with the whole.

Prayer and People's Search for their True Nature

By nature, an individual human being can never exist as an isolated entity. Human beings came into existence through the divine will, so that the divine Mind could manifest itself through them. There is no individual who was born into this world through the will of his or her physical ego.

274

If the divine will had meant to confine human lives within a narrow framework, it would have created persons who were all of a fixed and standard type, sharing much the same character and way of thinking. Had this been the case, the creative activities of human beings would have reflected the unvaried ways of thinking of small-scale people of good will. As a result, the evolution of humanity would have been delayed considerably. Being well aware of this, the divine Mind chose instead to endow each individual human being with a unique mission within the flow of human evolution. Human beings were also given great breadth and freedom in fulfilling these missions. In this way, individuals and humanity merge into a single entity within the great divine spirit as a vibrant body of white light which will continue to shine forever like the sun. To understand these individual rays of light more easily, we can think of each of them as a single mission within the totality of human evolution. Each individual ray of light is an individual human being within the total population of Earth.

Having forgotten their original identity, and believing that their physical self is all there is, the billions of people on Earth are living as if they were scattered individuals. Although their true selves are shining rays of light that are continually working within the oneness of the universe, their physical consciousness has lost all memory of this. Reawakening this memory is the most important task that faces humanity.

If the people on Earth truly wish to be freed from their self-created attachments to pain and misery, and to rise above the never-ending cycles of rebirth in a world of suffering, what they must do is return their scattered thoughts and emotions to a state of oneness. In other words, they must unite their hearts in prayer for world peace. Every living thing on Earth longs for peace. Of the billions of people who form the population of the Earth, there is not one who does not wish for peace. No matter how malevolent their surface thoughts might seem to be, deep in their hearts all people long for peace. What greater relief could there be for human beings than to free their minds from doubt, hatred, struggle and anxiety? What greater happiness could there be than for large numbers of people to know that they can always live in peace in their neighborhoods, countries, and regions?

If there is anything that can reunite the hearts of the billions of people on Earth, it is praying for the peace of humanity. When people pray for world peace, their thoughts and feelings are returned to their divine consciousness, connecting them with all humanity. Even if initially there are only a small number of people praying, it affects all humanity. This is because each human being, as one ray of the same divine light and life, is connected with all others. A true prayer which resonates in tune with the will of this one great life resonates through the whole of humanity.

The prayer for world peace is a gift of divine love, given to humanity at this time when the Earth is to change its position in the cosmos. The words 'May Peace Prevail on Earth' are destined to resonate through the thoughts of each and every Earthly human being. Although it is not yet apparent on the physical plane, the thoughts, wishes, and prayers for world peace of all human beings have already merged into oneness within the divine Mind. Like the advanced stars of the universe, the Earth one day will be a wonderful world filled with harmony. However, this will not come about through the strained efforts of the physical consciousness. What the Earth's people need to do is to firmly believe that peace on Earth will definitely come about as part of a large-scale divine plan, and to continually pray for world peace while entrusting everything to the guidance of their divine and spiritual protectors.

Prayer Creates a Workplace for Cosmic Angels

It is important for all people to continue praying for world peace right where they are. Whatever their work, family situation, or circumstances, people who always pray for world peace transcend the world of karma to be on the same wave length as their divine and spiritual protectors. Wherever they are, their existence will serve as a workplace for the activities of cosmic angels, which will be carried out on a very large scale. Please believe firmly that the science of advanced stars will gradually come to Earth, and continue to pray for world peace.

We will definitely descend to the places where you pray and release the necessary waves. When a certain time comes, we will suddenly make the waves we emit coarse enough to be visible to the naked eye. People will be able to perceive them with their own eyes and ears. At the same time, we will call upon every type of space vessel and mother ship to appear for all to see. The basis for the thoughts and feelings of the people of Earth will be shaken. It will be as if they have awakened from a deep dream that lasted millions of years. It will be as if a thick fog were gradually clearing to reveal the truth. There will be no time in history to equal this great event when the waves of prayer for world peace will work their power, merging perfectly with us. The uplifting of Earthly humanity will proceed in this way, step by step, gradually producing more and more benefits for human beings.

Like the highly evolved stars, the Earth will be perfectly guided by one central Being. In particular, the economy and the political order will undergo a fundamental transformation. Accompanying this, the social structure will also undergo a dramatic change. It will be based on a social concept newly born, and will follow a system in line with the planet's new level of science. People will clearly experience and understand the joy of contributing to a unified goal and of helping and forgiving each other. A peace that shines with a pure radiance, a peace that can come about only through love and truth, will be born on Earth.

This wonderful, peaceful heaven and Earth already exists. It already exists in the divine plane, and it is a beautiful sight to behold. Please hold a firm belief that when the preparations of heaven are ready, this world will definitely appear on Earth. And please continue to pray for world peace with as many other people as possible.

Please do your best to convey this message to the people of Earth. It is in the places where you pray for world peace that you and we come together as one. I cannot overemphasize that this is how true peace on Earth will be established, and I pray with all my heart for well-being and prosperity of all my dear friends on Earth.

As I listened to the governor speak in his lucid, easy to understand manner, I wondered whether I would have another chance to hear him speak again.

A nearby signal lamp began to flicker. At that moment I felt that my friends and I had never before felt this happy. I was deeply moved and wished I could express even one-tenth of my joy and gratitude for the immense depth and breadth of Goi Sensei's work, and for the incredible good fortune of those of us who had come to be involved in it. The moment the governor finished speaking, I could feel Goi Sensei's presence, and each of us merged with him to form one shining light. In a sudden flash, the brightness of this shining light intensified and formed a pillar running through heaven and Earth.

Returning to the Space Vessel

The vessel is ready for boarding, the captain said quietly.

I could not hold back the tears that filled my eyes. The

governor stood up, followed by the others. He said nothing about meeting again, and I could not help but feel that we might not have another chance to speak like this. Although I did not express it in words, my heart was overflowing with gratitude. I felt as if a ray of light connected our two spirits and that there was a mutual exchange of feelings between us.

The governor accompanied us as far as the bottom of the control tower. Boarding an automatic transfer vehicle, we headed for the base landing pad.

On the way back to our awaiting space vessel, the captain did not say a word. Sitting opposite her, I could feel the vibrations of her spiritual waves flowing toward me like an electrical current. Her expression seemed like that of a concerned parent whose child had just taken an entrance exam for high school or university. I felt a tremendous warmth enveloping my whole being.

I said goodbye to the captain at the landing pad. Guided by Mr. M, we descended the mountain and went to look at the hangar. We flew over the great farming area and, at the roundabout, transferred to a vessel like a small air taxi. We reached the public works area where we were able to inspect the construction site. We then transferred to an even smaller vessel and flew to the artificial base. There we met with the leader of the control tower. He took the time to provide us with further details about the base. He told us about the enormous machinery inside the base, explaining how it was constructed and how it worked. Each piece of information he related passed through my mind in rapid succession.

As each new piece of information registered in my consciousness, it conjured up an image. The captain seemed to catch my every thought with her clear, deep eyes, understanding the steady stream of thoughts that were filtering through my mind. It was as if I were answering questions on an exam, making sure not to miss any of them or leave out any detail. I wondered what kind of grade I could expect to receive. I strove to control my feelings as I waited impatiently for the announcement of my results. I received the stern assessment through vibrations. My marks were not particularly high but, this being my first attempt, the outcome was not considered poor. I felt that my earnest desire to comprehend the truth was the one precious light that I could hold up as an achievement.

The joy of having been allowed to fulfill this great task overflowed from my heart. And the kind assistance I had received from others caused me to feel an even deeper, inexpressible sense of gratitude—toward them and toward my own divine and spiritual protectors. Steeped in the waves of these thoughts and feelings, I experienced a refreshing, sublime feeling. In that instant, I experienced an eternal sense of awe and mystery too multi-faceted to put into words.

We have arrived. You have done well today!

Upon hearing Mr. M's words, I instantly returned to my usual self. The captain smiled as if nothing at all had happened and, alighting from the vehicle first, she proceeded to walk to the vessel's landing pad. Mr. M and I walked five or six paces behind her. The entire sky was as clear as could be and the setting sun was a brilliant, burning red. There were no clouds in sight but a thin haze, like the gossamer of angels' robes, spread across the sky toward the setting sun, tingeing the sky pink.

Is it the spirit of the Gods I see in the sunset, reflected in the evening sky? These were the words that welled up from within me.

Chapter 7

RETURNING TO EARTH

Looking Down at the Moon Base from the Space Vessel

We ascended the stairs and entered the waiting room. There were a number of other cosmic people already there. They must have been waiting for the next vessel. Without stopping, we boarded our own vessel. I was aware that the door behind us had closed without a sound and that the captain and Mr. M had followed us into the room. The captain stopped and spoke to us:

I will go into the control room now. I suggest that you go to the telescope in the room over there. You can take a look at the moon base where you have just been. It will be very interesting to observe it from the sky.

The captain nodded in Mr. M's direction and went up the stairs.

For the first time, I became aware of the interior of the space vessel. It was a medium-size craft, a type that I was fondly familiar with. In comparison to the enormous mother ships, vessels of this size can look quite insignificant. Once aboard, however, I felt right at home and remembered how pleasant it was to travel in one of these craft.

We went down a narrow corridor and took the staircase instead of the elevator down to the lowermost room. This was the room with the large telescope. Mr. M motioned for me to take a chair. I sat down and took a look at the surface of the large lens. Mr. M was absorbed in adjusting it. All of a sudden, an image of the entire moon was visible on the screen in front of us. I realized that our vessel was already far away from the moon. I had no recollection of when or how we had taken off.

The vessel is already airborne, isn't it?

That's right. Because we were a bit late in arriving at the vessel, our delayed departure was holding up others. The captain was aware of this and arranged for us to take off as soon as possible.

We have now made a stop here in space. We are approximately 50,000 kilometers away from the moon. It is perhaps the most suitable distance for observing the moon base.

I was not at all sure why there was a suitable distance for observing the base. I had thought observations could be made at any distance. I wondered what Mr. M actually meant by this.

Space vessels and mother ships differ in their capacities. Just as they serve different purposes, there are vast differences in their equipment and performance. The equipment installed in each vessel depends on its particular function. The maximum distance this medium-size vessel can fly is the distance to the parent solar system controlling our own. It cannot fly any further than that.

On the outside, space vessels may all look quite similar but they differ from each other dramatically in terms of their makeup and performance. There are vessels that shuttle from base to base in a stepping stone fashion, like space taxis, and others with very sophisticated equipment that can travel extraordinary distances to link remote stars. Of course, the distance these various spacecraft can travel is in proportion to their capacity.

While he was delivering this explanation, Mr. M continued his efforts to adjust the telescope. The moon gradually came into focus, growing larger each second until it filled the entire lens. It then vanished in a flash. Next, a rich, green area gradually came into focus until we could actually see a close-up of objects on the ground.

That's the base!

The words just sprang from my mouth automatically.

It was a truly beautiful sight. There was no other way to describe it. Even viewing the construction site, I felt as if I were viewing a panoramic masterpiece. As I was studying the details projected on the screen, the image started to change. After passing over mountainous areas and plains, the lens suddenly shifted its focus, revealing an impressive, large base. Rather than a control tower positioned between the plains and mountains, there was a landing pad for a large vessel.

The Seven Grade-One Bases and the White Space Vessel

What exactly is the function of this enormous base?

On the moon there are seven bases of this sort. They are known as grade-one bases. The moon is divided into seven areas. All large and small bases for space vessels and mother ships in the seven areas come under the control of one of these bases. In addition, there is a central base from which all seven bases are, in turn, controlled and where main governing offices are concentrated.

The seven bases are like branch offices of the central control body. In the central office, there are departments or ministries for every function, and these are the highest governing bodies on the moon. There are also committee members sent from the parent star. Above these officials, there is a governing person who holds the highest position in the social structure on the moon.

From the viewpoint of the advanced stars, even the moon is still in its developmental infancy. Understanding this, the parent and more senior stars provide constant leadership, guidance, and advice. You once saw a space vessel emitting a very bright light. That was a high-ranking vessel that looked almost transparent and gave off a resplendent white light. That craft lands at the central landing pad of these seven bases. The light that appears on the moon's surface at that time has been observed by people on Earth, though they do not understand its cause.

I had neither seen nor heard of such an amazing craft. That white space vessel must be the source of what people on Earth refer to as 'the sun descending.' I had only seen it from afar.

This is how leaders from the advanced stars come to visit us. That white vessel has wondrous powers that far exceed our imagination.

Take a look at the band of roads that link the underground cities to each other. There are several automated road belts that carry self-operated transport vehicles, and there are large and small underground roads two and three levels deep. As you can see, on the surface they appear as a single groove.

Other than this image, which extended out radially, I was not able to clearly discern anything else about the underground city. However, it was clear from a number of geometric aspects that the roads were indeed artificially constructed. The image on the screen began to change. Mountainous areas first came into view and then the sea. The mountains were quite steep, dropping away sharply to cliffs at the coastline. The sea was beautiful, and its dark green color gave the impression that it had a fathomless depth. As I continued to watch, its image moved farther and farther away. There were a number of other places that I was eager to catch a glimpse of, but unfortunately Mr. M did not refocus the lens on any new images.

Dangers to Earth and the Earth's Future—
Images that Came to Me in a Dream

The vessel is heading straight for Earth.

Hearing these words, I abandoned hope of seeing any new images. Mr. M got up from his chair.

Let's take a rest in the lounge.

The two of us walked slowly from the room in a relaxed manner. We took the elevator in the corridor to the lounge on the second floor. The door opened. It was my third time in this room. The air inside was filled with a pleasant, familiar scent. Overcome by a sudden feeling of lethargy, I found that it took great effort just to make my way to the chair. I plopped into one of the easy chairs feeling the relief of someone who had just returned home after a long journey.

My mind was filled with the thought that getting home was all that remained for me now. I began to meditate quietly. The prayer for world peace welled up within me. Images of people began to appear in my mind. I saw Goi Sensei's moustache, then his entire face, filled with profound love and affection. Gradually, all of my friends and colleagues appeared one after another as distinct individual images, then vanished. Mountains began to appear. There was a border between two countries, and the armies of those two countries lined up in confrontation on either side of it. This must have been an event occurring on Earth.

Closer observation of the two armies showed that they were of the same ethnic heritage. Why would people of the same ethnic group or nation be at war with each other?

Looking down from the sky, at the rear of the two armies I could see great stockpiles of munitions that had been supplied by other countries. It was clear that preparations were in full swing for a large-scale war. Further in the rear, I could plainly see the frightening weapons of mass destruction that both armies were trying to hide from each other. What a horrifying sight it was! My whole body suddenly began to tremble.

This dreadful vision vanished, only to be replaced by another. What country could this be? From what I could see, it looked like a place with a hot climate. A large number of people were carrying guns and loudly yelling out words which I could not discern. They were downtrodden people who, for a long time, had been forced to work like slaves by another nation whose history was closely linked with theirs. Now, they had severed their bonds of subjugation. Yet before they could taste the joy of their liberation, they and their former oppressors were under siege from a third nation. Now, the people of the first two nations were calling loudly to each other, urging each other to take up arms against their mutual enemy. Looking behind this scene, I could see frightening, devil-like beings (souls), holding up weapons and dancing round the people, fanning the flames of their thirst for revenge.

How tragic it is when people who share the same blood feel the need to fight against each other! As I continued to observe the events unfolding below, I saw throngs of people pushing and shoving each other. No matter where I looked, I was unable to see one country building a peaceful, tranquil world.

In one port, arms were stacked up in piles as high as a mountain. These alone could have exterminated millions of people in the blink of an eye. But the scene did not end here. A large city came into view. It was a beautiful city, reflecting a relatively high standard of living. An eerie atmosphere pervaded it, however. Careful examination showed that it was divided into two sections, and a very heated, violent struggle was underway over the demarcation of the boundary. Looking carefully, I found that here, too, the people were actually descended from the same ethnic line. Does such a world actually exist, I wondered, where people from the same country fight each other with such hatred?

Continuing to observe what was happening, I noticed soldiers at the rear carrying a frightful supply of weapons of mass destruction. The repulsive smell of death rising from the city defied description. I shuddered at the thought of such a beautiful metropolis becoming 'a city of death.' In the blink of an eye, millions of people would vanish from the face of the Earth. At being shown so many horrifying scenes, I was at a loss what to think. I did not want to see any more. Although I tried to wake up, I was unable to.

Next, I saw a large planet turning gently around. *That is the Earth,* I thought. The beauty of its blue oceans and high mountains was enveloped in gray. It had lost all vitality and reeked of the same awful smell of decay as did the city of death. Every place on its surface showed signs of decomposition, and it was from all those places that the smell of death was emanating. Rotten remains were visible wherever I looked. Would such a horrific tragedy really take place? The pain emerging from the tightness in my chest spread to my entire body. What I was seeing was not, I hoped, the vision of a perished Earth. I was overcome with an indescribable, deep sadness and felt that I was falling into a very deep abyss. I do not know how many minutes or seconds had elapsed.

It seems that the captain is calling us.

I could vaguely hear a far off voice addressing me. It brought me back to my senses. It was his voice, the voice of

Mr. M, watching over me from the next chair. I felt relieved that he was at my side.

A Reunion with the Captain and Other Cosmic People

Let's go to the captain's room.

The signal lamp on the side kept flashing off and on. Mr. M stood up. Intending to follow him, I attempted to get up but felt a pain deep within my head and my throat was dry. I longed for a drink of water, but followed him towards the captain's room. Mr. M pressed a button and the door opened silently. To my astonishment, the room was filled with more than twenty cosmic persons. At the center was the captain. I had absolutely no idea when these individuals had boarded the vessel. I followed Mr. M into the room. The cosmic persons all rose from their seats and welcomed us with smiles. Warmhearted affection could be seen in the eyes of each and every one of them. I sat opposite the captain, and Mr. M took the seat next to me.

Seated in the chair the captain had motioned for me to take, I asked, *When will the vessel be landing on Earth?*

We have already landed.

The response was accompanied by a knowing smile. Without thinking, I tried to look out at the scenery from a window, but it was not possible. The captain added:

We have actually stopped in mid-air over the spot where we will land. We can touch down at any time. However, I thought it would be nice for all of us to have a meal together and spend some time in pleasant conversation before we say goodbye. That is why I invited everyone here.

I would like to express my deep appreciation for your kindness. I am truly grateful for what you have done, I said.

I am sure you have felt a number of things as you toured the moon base. I am wondering if you would care to say just a word about your impressions.

Oh, I do not know where to begin or how to describe what I saw. I am at a loss for words. There are many things I could say, though I do not know if they would be suitable. The moon base was wonderful beyond words. It was a world far more advanced than I could have imagined. It was like looking through a window at the Age of the Universe. From the bottom of my heart, I would like to thank everyone for making it possible for me to see such a wonderful world.

All sorts of dishes were being served but my heart was heavy. I could not shake my dark, foreboding feelings enough to join in the merriment around me. I had seen the sad demise of the Earth and how the planet would look in its final hours. Awed by what I had learned about the advanced stars, and amazed by the dazzling, impressive moon base, I was at the same time shocked by the knowledge of the Earth's fate. That sadness dominated the other feelings that were going through my heart. I could not help but pray with all my heart that the hand of merciful divine love would reach out to all those unfortunate people and save them. Yes, of course. that was it. The only hope was prayer for world peace.

Before we begin eating, let's pray.

Closing our eyes, we began to pray. What do you think were the prayer words offered by the captain in her clear voice? They were: 'May Peace Prevail on Earth.' The power of her prayer resonated through my entire being, making me quiver with joy. I had never felt such happiness. I could immediately feel myself entering a lofty, purified state. With the captain saying, *Thank you, everyone,* the prayer came to an end.

I could feel that my former spark had been restored. My eyes were shining brightly and I could sense with my whole being that the cosmic people were making efforts to rescue the Earth.

Please eat as much as you like. Don't hold back.

I drank all that was in the glass since I had been thirsty for some time. It tasted like a juice of some sort. Once my thirst was quenched, I began to feel a deep sense of gratitude. Perhaps when the cosmic people give their assistance to humanity, the people on Earth will be touched with the same feelings. This thought flashed through the back of my mind.

I was not aware of what I was eating. After all, how could I be thinking of anything other than the belief that humanity's only hope for the future was to pray for world peace? The last time I had parted with these cosmic people, I had felt an inexpressible sadness. However, I now felt a sense of urgency to return to Earth to do what I could for the development of world peace. I wanted to let as many people as possible know about the dangers that were threatening Earth.

As these thoughts were going through my head, the captain turned to me and asked a question.

Humanity's Only Hope

Earlier when you were meditating in the reception room, did you experience anything in particular?

I was shown the sad state of the Earth as it faced extinction, and I was overcome by an unbearable pain and sadness that gripped my chest. Will the Earth actually end in that way?

If things are left as they are, the Earth will surely meet such a fate. It will definitely write its own tragic end. The vast majority of people will perish. Of those remaining, many will suffer disabilities and there will be a shortage of food. Life will become an arduous road of pain and hardship. Yet one positive road remains open to them. That road is for people throughout the world to put all their efforts into rescuing the planet. People must pray, body and soul, for the peace of humanity. They must also get as many people as possible to join in this movement, understanding that every individual is needed. As these people join in prayer, they will gradually rewrite the fate that has already been determined.

The disasters which are to occur immediately will be delayed and, in that way, the fate of the Earth will be revised two or three times. As the number of people who pray grows, the harmonizing energy being emitted will also grow. At that time, people on Earth will understand our work better. The wisdom we possess will gradually be understood by many on Earth. The science of Earth, which has deviated from the mainstream of true science, was originally meant to manifest the universal divine will. As science begins to fulfill its true mission, it will show a wonderful new power.

Although people on Earth live in awe of it, the science of Earth is actually underdeveloped and not worth talking about. The more important issue for people to consider is whether the Earth can survive while they allow the existence of a science that fosters mass killing. When people know even the slightest bit about our science of the universe, they will no longer have any use for Earthly science as they have known it. People must understand that if they let things go on as they are, the Earth will certainly suffer the fate of extinction that you saw in your vision. In the sky above Earth, there are many space vessels with many cosmic people aboard, like us. For us, having a suitable place to work is of primary importance. And the places where you pray for world peace are also our workplaces. People who pray for world peace are our brothers and sisters. By cooperating with them and becoming one with them, we will bring about peace on Earth for the first time. We are confident beyond all doubt that there will come a time when all of our prayers will succeed in turning back the pending demise of Earth. That time will also be when each person awakens and becomes aware of how great and wonderful his or her mission in this world is. With happiness and joy, you will be able to find yourselves living in an uplifted state along with the other people of the world.

At the moment, we must do all we can to seek the cooperation of as many people as possible who will pray for world peace. I also implore you to relay this message to all of your prayer partners. The reason for your visit to the moon, and for our imparting knowledge to you about the science of the universe, was to let people on Earth know the truth about us and to ask for their cooperation. When many people pray for world peace, they will become united with us and Earth will definitely find harmony. Please believe this firmly and live wholly in the spirit of prayer for world peace.

I could feel her each and every word coursing through my soul. I could not hold back the tears that filled my eyes. A vision of Goi Sensei's face and the faces of my partners in prayer appeared before me. I felt a sudden surge of strength that enlivened all my five senses.

Landing at Holy Hill

We have arrived.

The voice sounded like Mr. M's. The captain rose from her seat, and the cosmic people in the room stood up at the same time.

The next time we meet will probably be at the place where you pray for world peace.

When do you think that will be?

We are coming very close to the time when the final stages of world karma will be dispelled, so I am sure that we will be meeting again soon.

I expressed my deep gratitude to Mr. M and the others and left the room. As always, he came to see me off. As I alighted from the vessel and stepped outside, the cold morning air felt refreshing on my cheeks. The two of us walked side by side. In back of us stood the superb medium-size space vessel, looking as if it were floating motionlessly just above the Earth. Mr. M came to a stop. I expressed my heartfelt thanks once more as best as I could, and wondered when we would meet again.

It's time to say good-bye.

When will we meet again?

If possible, I will come again with the captain.

I hope it will be soon.

While he said nothing, his expression held a powerful confidence that made me again feel buoyant with optimism. After taking two or three steps, I turned around. He was heading straight for the space vessel. At the door of the vessel, he raised his hand, promising to come again. The moment the door closed, the craft began to move. With a gentle lilting movement from left to right, its grand form lifted from the ground and disappeared.

High in the sky as the dawn was breaking, it appeared as a dot of light for a short time before vanishing from view.

293

APPENDIX

ABOUT THE *IN*

About fifteen years ago, I had the privilege of assisting Mr. Masao Murata, the author of this book, during a lecture series held here in Japan. One of my duties was to wait with him outside the entrance of the lecture hall and signal him when it was time to go in. As we sat there together, several times I had the opportunity of talking quite casually with him. On one such occasion, right out of the blue Mr. Murata suddenly asked me, *What do you think about the world's energy situation?* Since my mind was on the matters at hand I was a bit startled by the question and could not organize my thoughts quickly enough to respond. Unperturbed by this, Mr. Murata continued to speak:

Think about the energy sources that we are using. Where do they come from? Most of them come from the past, don't they? Petroleum, natural gas, coal... fuels like these came to us from living things that used to inhabit the Earth. But can we go on using them forever? If we continue to live this way, we may use up all the Earth's resources during the next half-century.

What can we do? Some suggest that we switch to nuclear energy, but that could be very dangerous and result in more pollution problems. Of course, solar power and power from the wind should be researched extensively, but there is something else we ought to think about. Now it is time for us to discover a new, advanced science—the science of cosmic beings.

By that time I had read several of Mr. Murata's books in Japanese, and had learned a bit about the culture and science of advanced planets. Knowing this, Mr. Murata proceeded to ask: *Think about the kind of energy cosmic beings are using. How do they operate their space vessels? The captain simply attunes his or her thoughts to the vibrations that flow through universal space. The space vessel's vibrations are so fine and delicate that as soon as a particular vibration resonates through the captain's body, the vessel instantly appears in that place.*

After that I sometimes reflected back on Mr. Murata's words and asked myself: How can we who live on Earth become more like those advanced beings? How can we learn their science? Like the ship's captain, how can we attune ourselves to the natural power and flow of the universe? I realized that there is only one way. We must develop our spirituality. Only then can we attune our minds and bodies to the guidance of the cosmic scientists who are striving to impart their advanced knowledge to the people on Earth.

Masao Murata was one of the original researchers in the study of cosmic science, and cosmic science is very much concerned with the development of spirituality. It was through cosmic science that two incredibly wonderful practices known as *In*[12] were recently conveyed to Earth.

An *In* (pronounced 'een' as in 'clean') is a way of attuning ourselves with the harmonizing energy and power of the universe. To form an *In*, we keep our minds and our breathing peaceful while forming various curves and angles with our arms, hands, and fingers. In the past, a variety of *In* were formed by saints and holy people to purify disharmony at certain times and places. The two new *In*, however, are not intended for a limited number of special people. They can be practiced by everyone who understands them and agrees with their purpose, which is to draw out and manifest the infinite divine qualities that are inherent in all human beings.

The first of these two new *In* is called the *In* of *Wa-re-so-ku-ka-mi-na-ri,* which means 'I am one with the universe' or 'I am a divine being.' It works for the development of the universal, divine Self. The second *In* is called the *In* of *Jin-rui-so-ku-ka-mi-na-ri,* which means 'Humanity is one with the universe' or 'Humanity is a divine being.' It works for the development of the divinity of everyone in humanity. In 1994, when the first of these *In* was conveyed to Earth,[13] I remembered my conversation with Mr. Murata and what he had said about the way the captain operates a space vessel. It seemed to me that, for many of us, this *In* might be an excellent way to attune ourselves with the harmony of the universe and exert whatever kind of energy the Earth needs.

In 1995, shortly before he passed away, I went to visit Mr. Murata and told him of our plan to publish this book in English. His face shone with delight, and I felt very encouraged to let this book serve as an opportunity for telling his readers about the *In.*

On the next several pages you will find illustrations of the two new *In.* On behalf of Mr. Murata, I invite you to learn and experience them for yourself. And if you would like more information about the *In* please visit the web site www.inproject.org.

It is my heartfelt wish that, through this book, the harmony of the universe will permeate the Earth and the big, beautiful spirit of Masao Murata will touch the lives of many people.

Yours sincerely,

Akira Kon
Editor-in-Chief, Byakko Press
August 1, 2002

HOW TO FORM THE
UNIVERSAL *IN* FOR THE SELF

◆**Before you start, say:** *Wa-re-so-ku-ka-mi-na-ri*

(I am one with the Universe)

1	Starting position: The *In* of Great Harmony

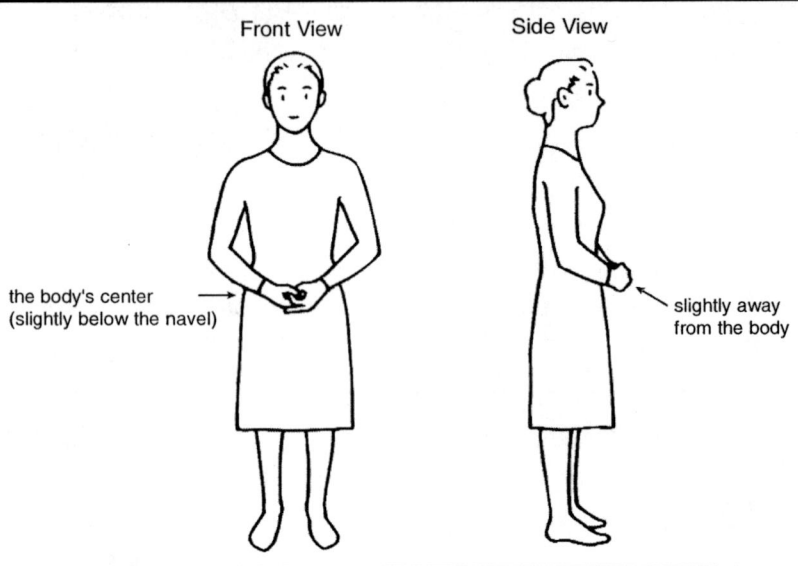

Front View   Side View

the body's center (slightly below the navel)

slightly away from the body

How to form the *In* of Great Harmony

1. Make circles by joining the tips of the forefingers and thumbs.

2. Link the circles together.

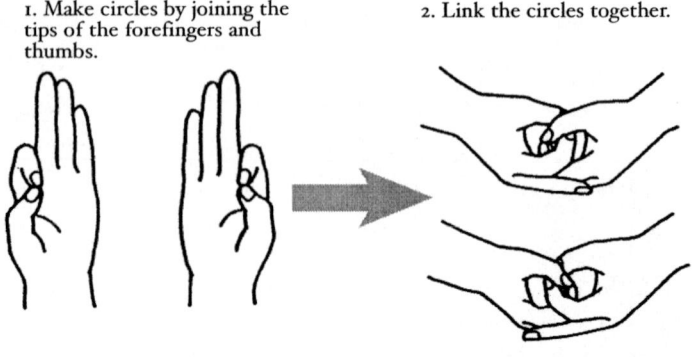

The palms face up. Either hand can be on top.

 With the hands in the starting position, begin to lift them from the body's center. While making the sound 'uu,' keep the circles linked and extend the remaining fingers. Lift the hands in a curving motion until they are level with the eyes.

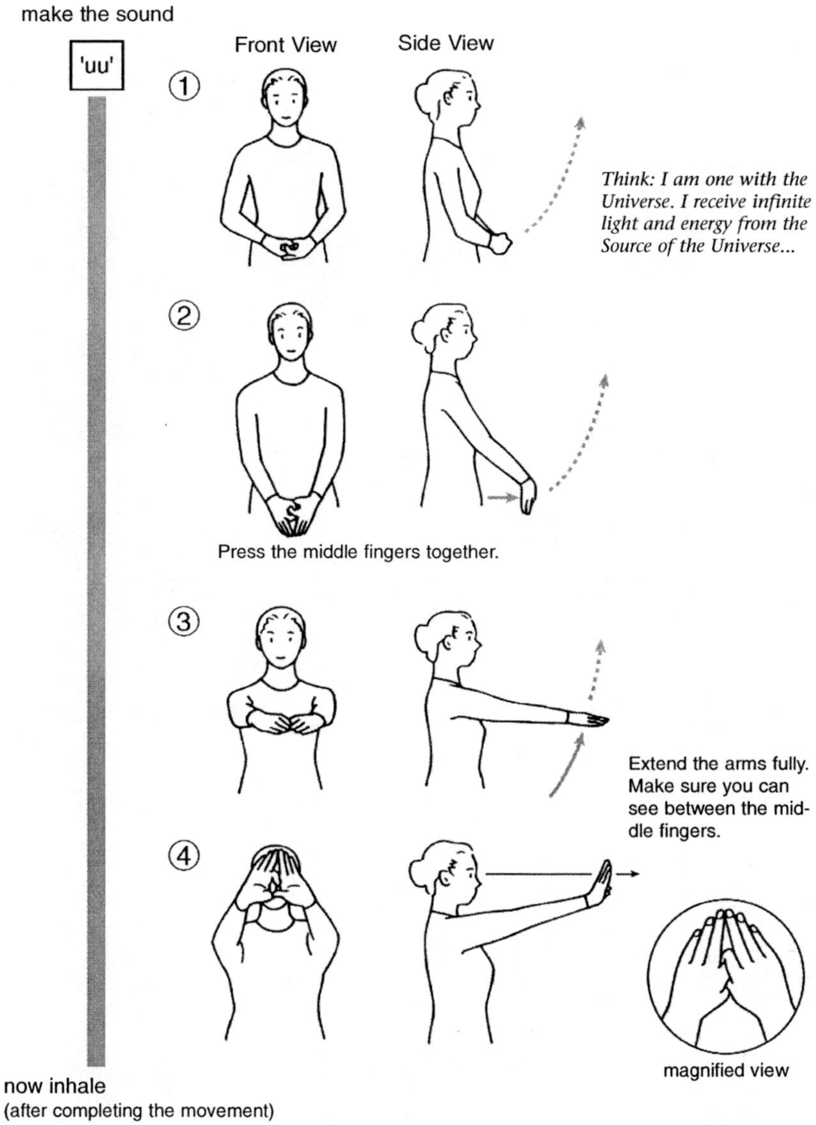

make the sound

'uu'

Front View   Side View

①

Think: I am one with the Universe. I receive infinite light and energy from the Source of the Universe...

②

Press the middle fingers together.

③

Extend the arms fully. Make sure you can see between the middle fingers.

④

magnified view

now inhale
(after completing the movement)

301

3

While making the sound 'uu,' gently bring the hands toward the face. While doing this, release the linked circles and cross the right hand fingers in front of the left hand fingers, the palms facing you. Touch the fingers to the forehead once, then extend them outward a little.

make the sound

'uu'

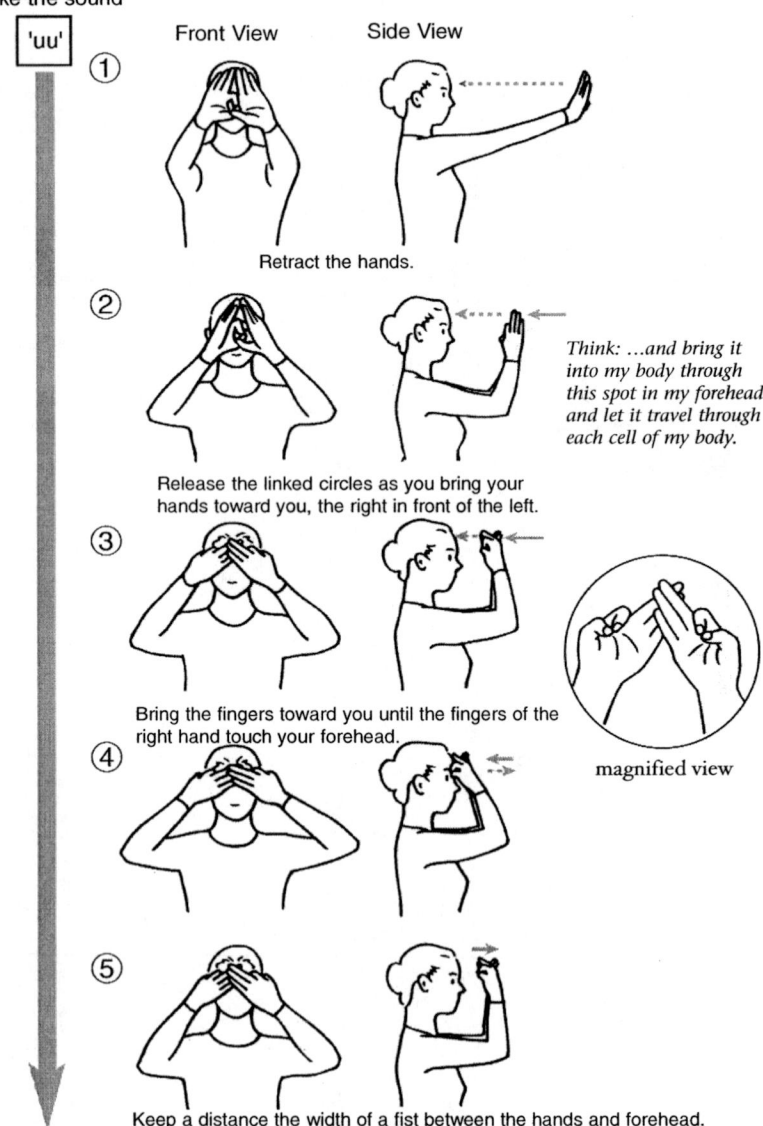

Front View Side View

① Retract the hands.

②

Think: ...and bring it into my body through this spot in my forehead and let it travel through each cell of my body.

Release the linked circles as you bring your hands toward you, the right in front of the left.

③

Bring the fingers toward you until the fingers of the right hand touch your forehead.

magnified view

④

⑤

Keep a distance the width of a fist between the hands and forehead.

now inhale
(after completing the movement)

302

 While making the sound 'wa,' bring the right hand down in a circular motion toward the left, moving round and returning full circle. (From your point of view the circle will be counterclockwise).

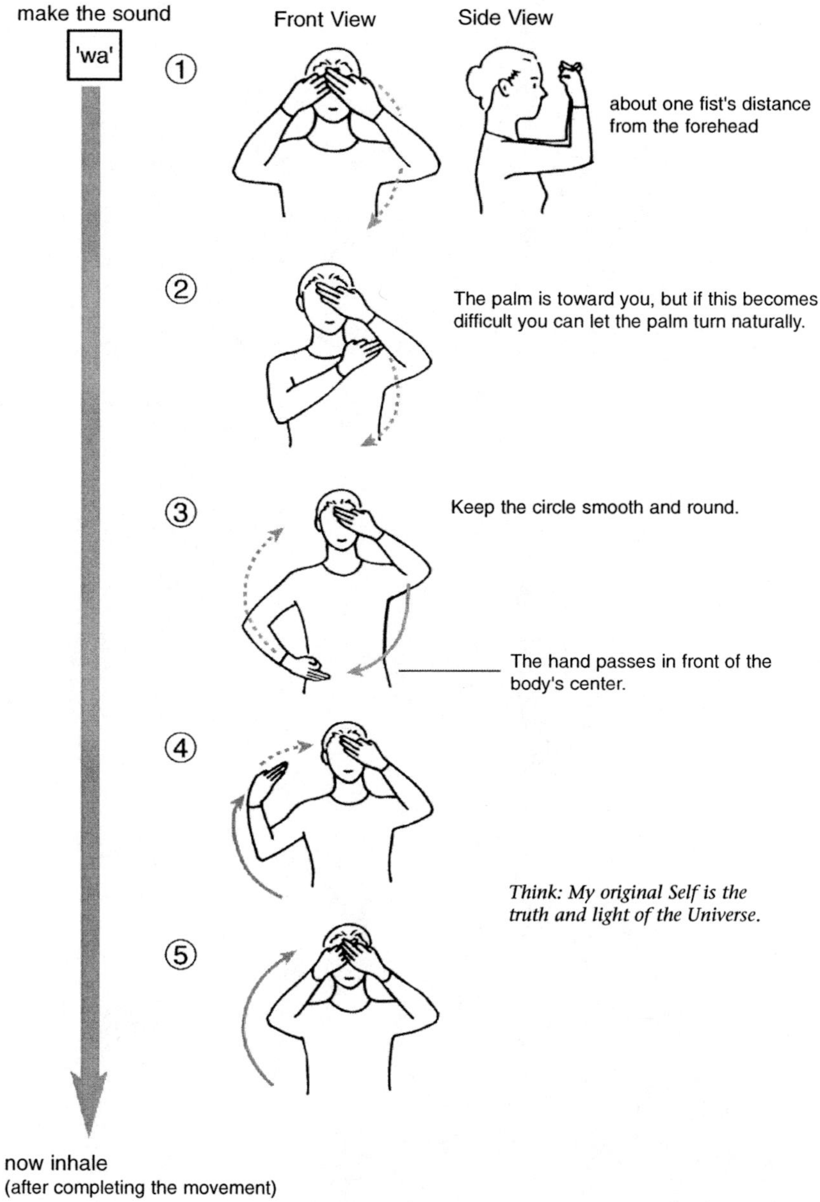

make the sound

'wa'

Front View   Side View

① about one fist's distance from the forehead

② The palm is toward you, but if this becomes difficult you can let the palm turn naturally.

③ Keep the circle smooth and round.

The hand passes in front of the body's center.

④

Think: My original Self is the truth and light of the Universe.

⑤

now inhale
(after completing the movement)

5 While again making the sound 'uu,' lower the hands, starting from in front of the forehead. While lowering the hands, again link the two circles formed by the forefingers and thumbs. Then stretch the hands out from the body's center and bring them back again.

make the sound
'uu'

Front View   Side View

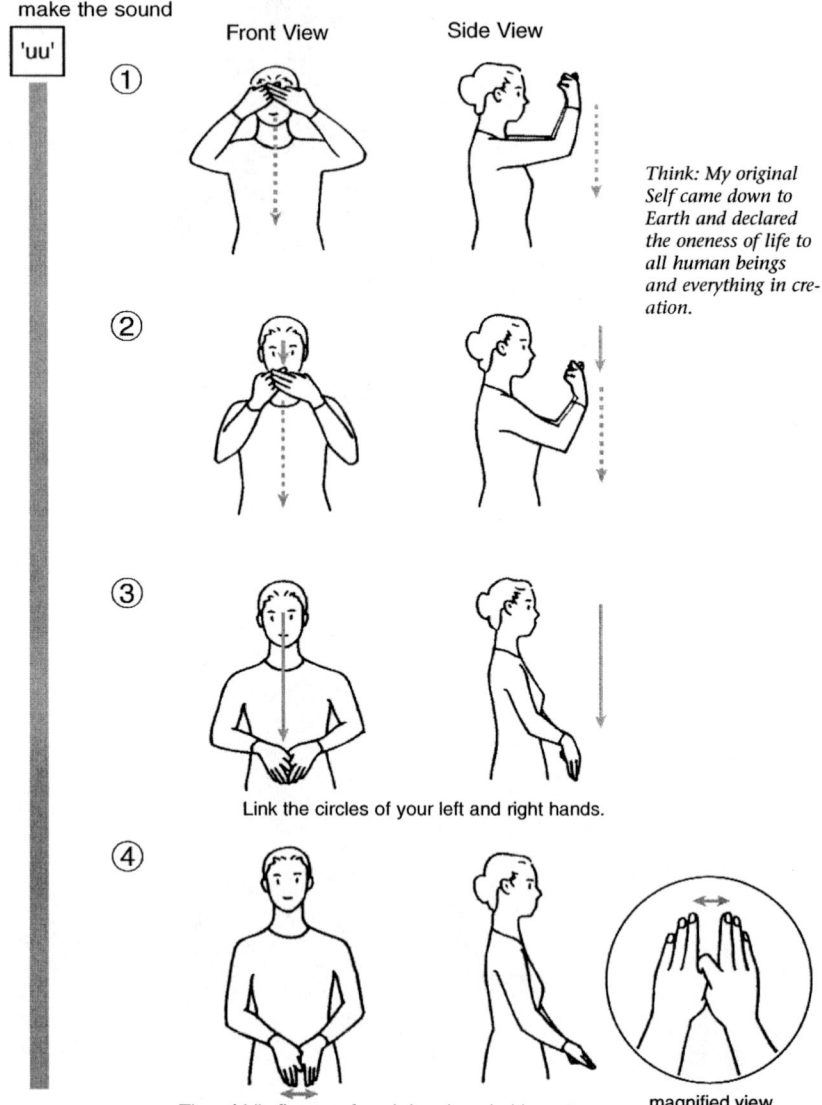

Think: My original Self came down to Earth and declared the oneness of life to all human beings and everything in creation.

③ Link the circles of your left and right hands.

④ The middle fingers of each hand are held apart.   magnified view

(continued on next page)

(continued from the previous page)

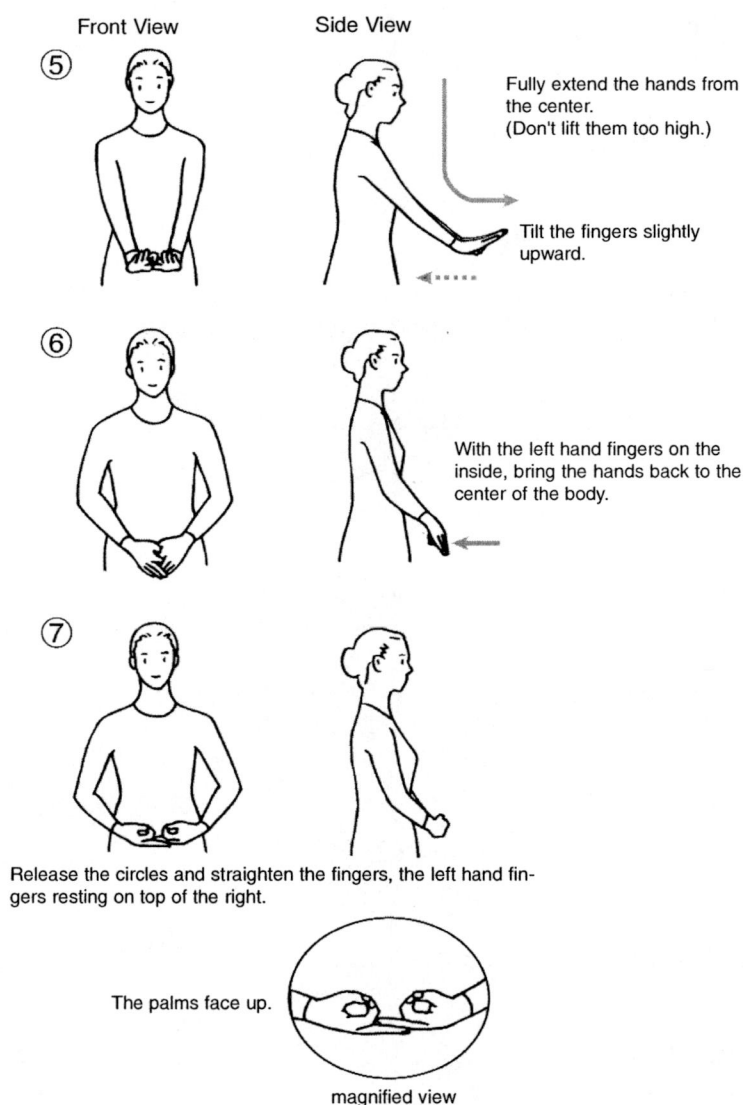

Front View   Side View

⑤ Fully extend the hands from the center.
(Don't lift them too high.)

Tilt the fingers slightly upward.

⑥ With the left hand fingers on the inside, bring the hands back to the center of the body.

⑦ Release the circles and straighten the fingers, the left hand fingers resting on top of the right.

The palms face up.

magnified view

now inhale
(after completing the movement)

305

While making the sound 're,' bring the left hand up to the right and around in a circular motion in front of the body. End the movement by touching the tips of the middle fingers together.

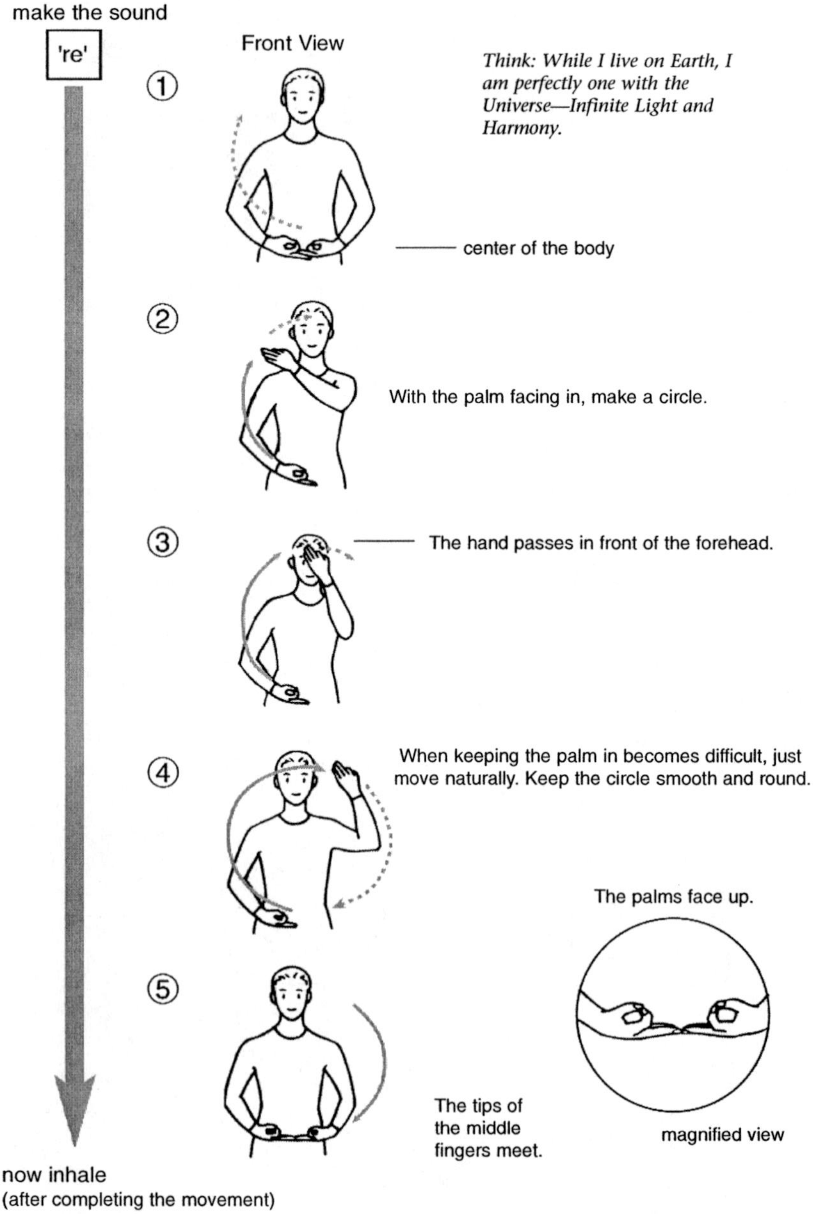

make the sound

're'

Front View

① *Think: While I live on Earth, I am perfectly one with the Universe—Infinite Light and Harmony.*

———— center of the body

② With the palm facing in, make a circle.

③ ———— The hand passes in front of the forehead.

④ When keeping the palm in becomes difficult, just move naturally. Keep the circle smooth and round.

The palms face up.

⑤ The tips of the middle fingers meet.

magnified view

now inhale
(after completing the movement)

While making the sound 'so,' extend the right hand upward to the left. Turn the upper body in that direction. Then bring the hand back and place it by the right hip.

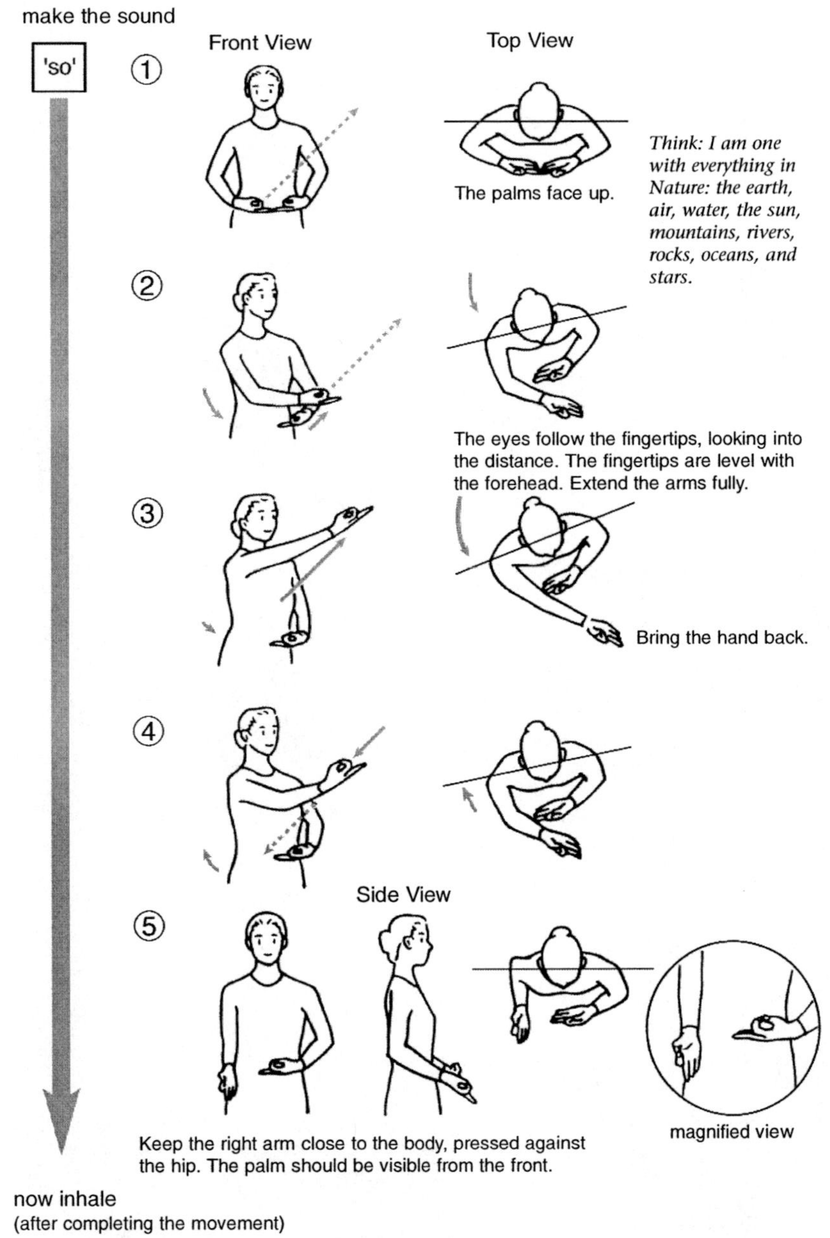

make the sound

'so'

① Front View   Top View

The palms face up.

Think: I am one with everything in Nature: the earth, air, water, the sun, mountains, rivers, rocks, oceans, and stars.

②

The eyes follow the fingertips, looking into the distance. The fingertips are level with the forehead. Extend the arms fully.

③

Bring the hand back.

④

Side View

⑤

Keep the right arm close to the body, pressed against the hip. The palm should be visible from the front.

magnified view

now inhale
(after completing the movement)

307

8 While making the sound 'ku,' extend the left hand upward to the right. Turn the body in that direction. Then bring the hand back and place it by the left hip.

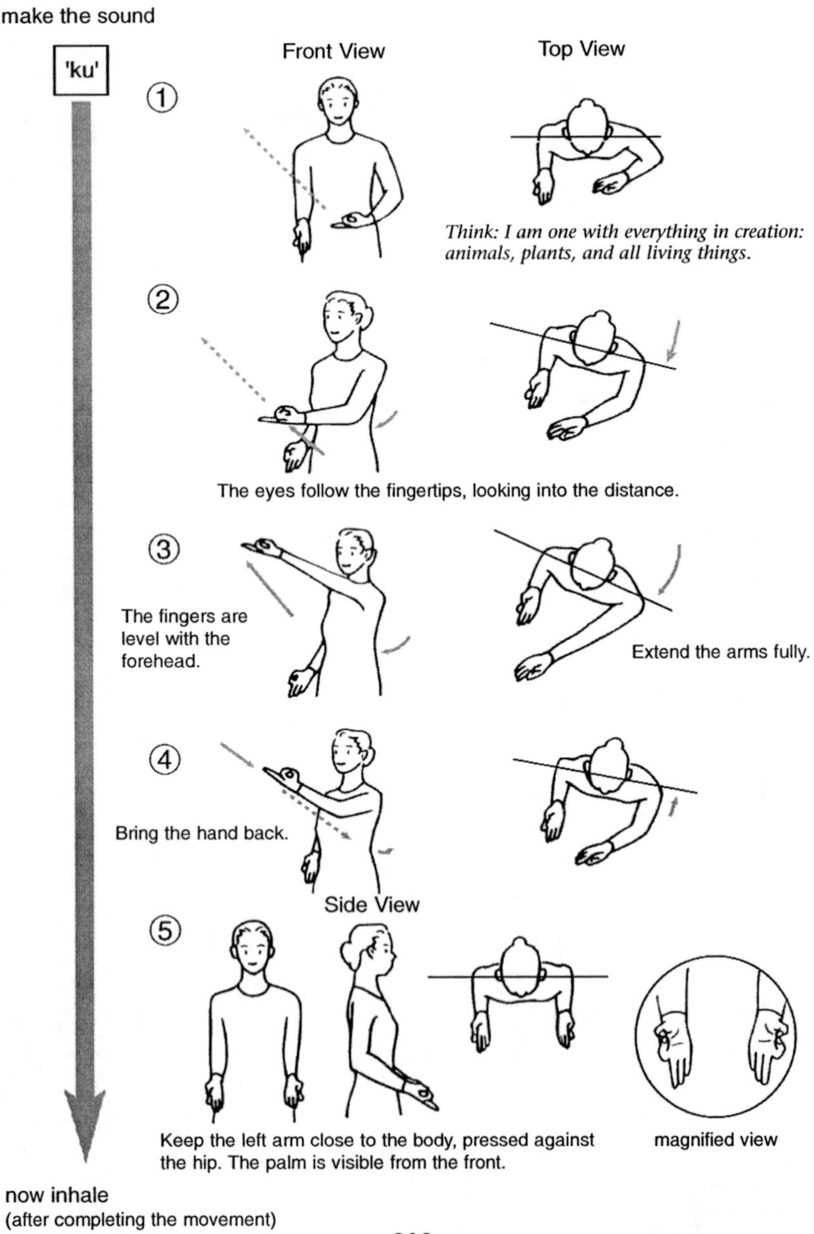

make the sound

'ku'

Front View   Top View

①

Think: I am one with everything in creation: animals, plants, and all living things.

②

The eyes follow the fingertips, looking into the distance.

③

The fingers are level with the forehead.

Extend the arms fully.

④

Bring the hand back.

Side View

⑤

Keep the left arm close to the body, pressed against the hip. The palm is visible from the front.

magnified view

now inhale
(after completing the movement)

308

9 While making the sound 'ka,' raise the right hand, fingers pointing up, palm to the front. At the same time, extend the left hand forward horizontally at the level of the chest.

make the sound

Front View   Side View

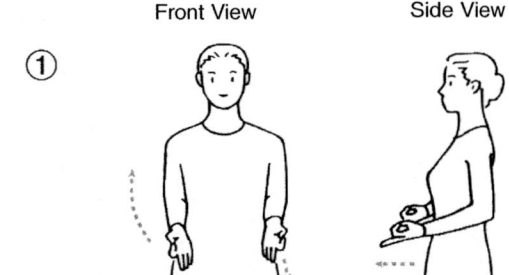

Think: I send infinite gratitude and blessings to everything in creation.

The fingers on both hands are extended.

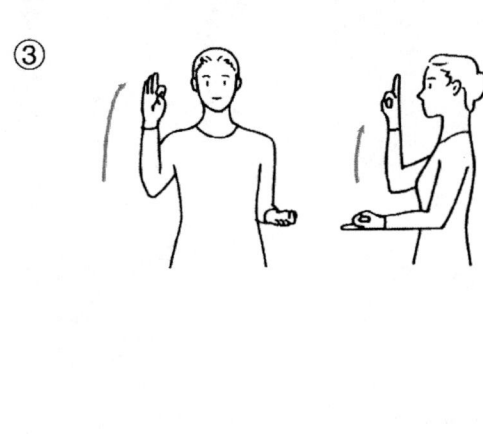

now inhale
(after completing the movement)

While making the sound 'mi,' reverse hand positions by bringing the left hand up and extending the right hand horizontally. Next, lower the left hand and bring the fingertips of both hands together in front of the body.

make the sound

'mi'

Front View   Side View

①

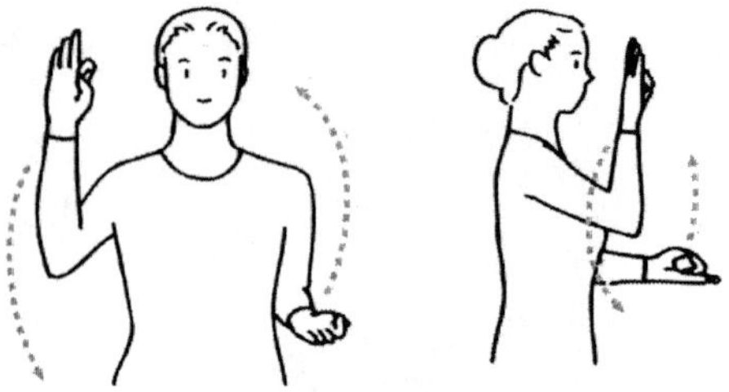

Think: I send infinite gratitude and blessings to everything in nature.

②

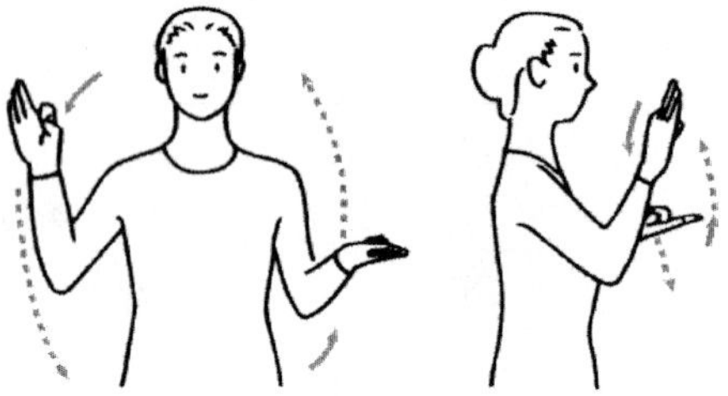

Extend the fingers on both hands.

③

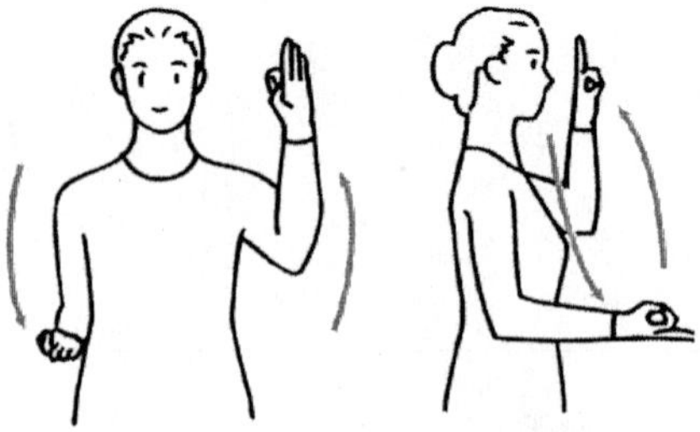

(continued on next page)   Don't inhale yet. Continue making the sound 'mi.'

(continued from the previous page)

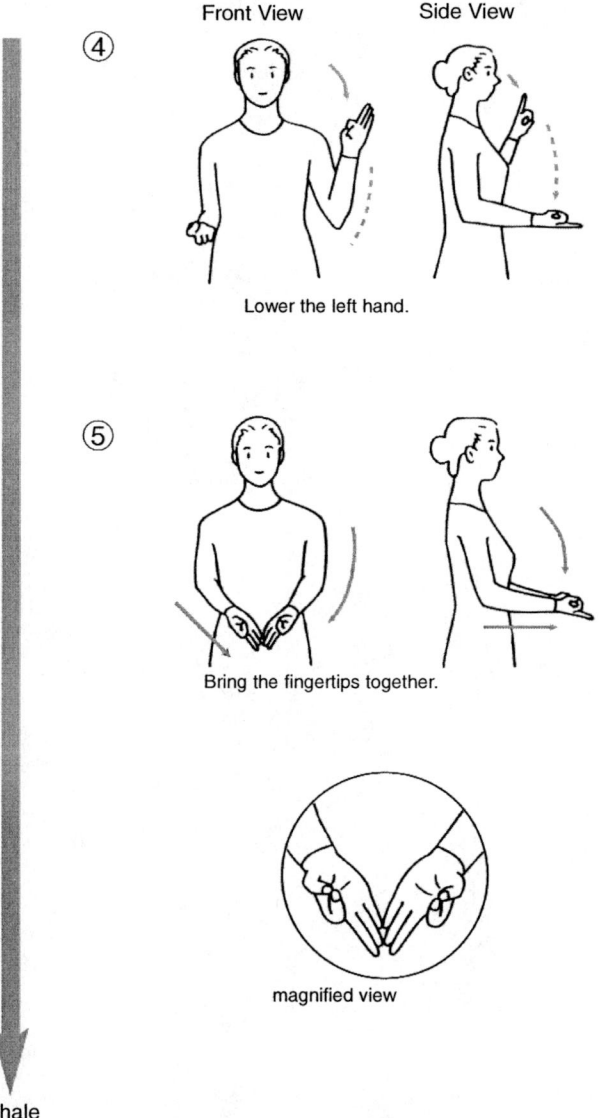

Front View   Side View

④

Lower the left hand.

⑤

Bring the fingertips together.

magnified view

now inhale
(after completing the movement)

11

While making the sound 'na,' raise both hands as if scooping something up. In front of the face, link the circles made by the forefingers and thumbs and press the palms and fingers together.

make the sound

'na'

Front View   Side View

①

Think: I embrace and uplift everything in nature and creation to heaven...

②

as if scooping something up

Think: ...while receiving infinite energy from the Universe...

③

magnified view

④

Link the circles and press the palms and fingers together.

Either the right or left thumb can be in front of the other. Press the palms together as much as possible.

now inhale
(after completing the movement)

312

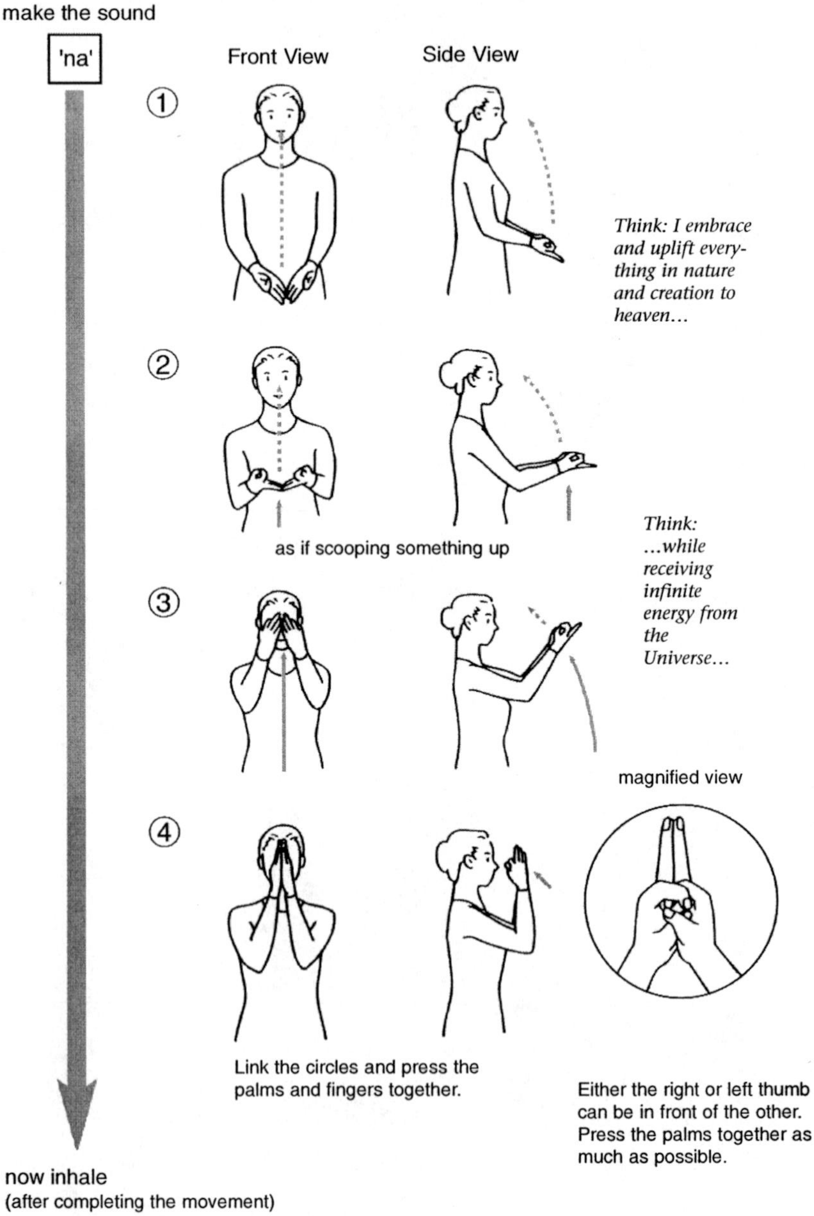

While making the sound 'ri,' separate the hands and lower them to hip level.

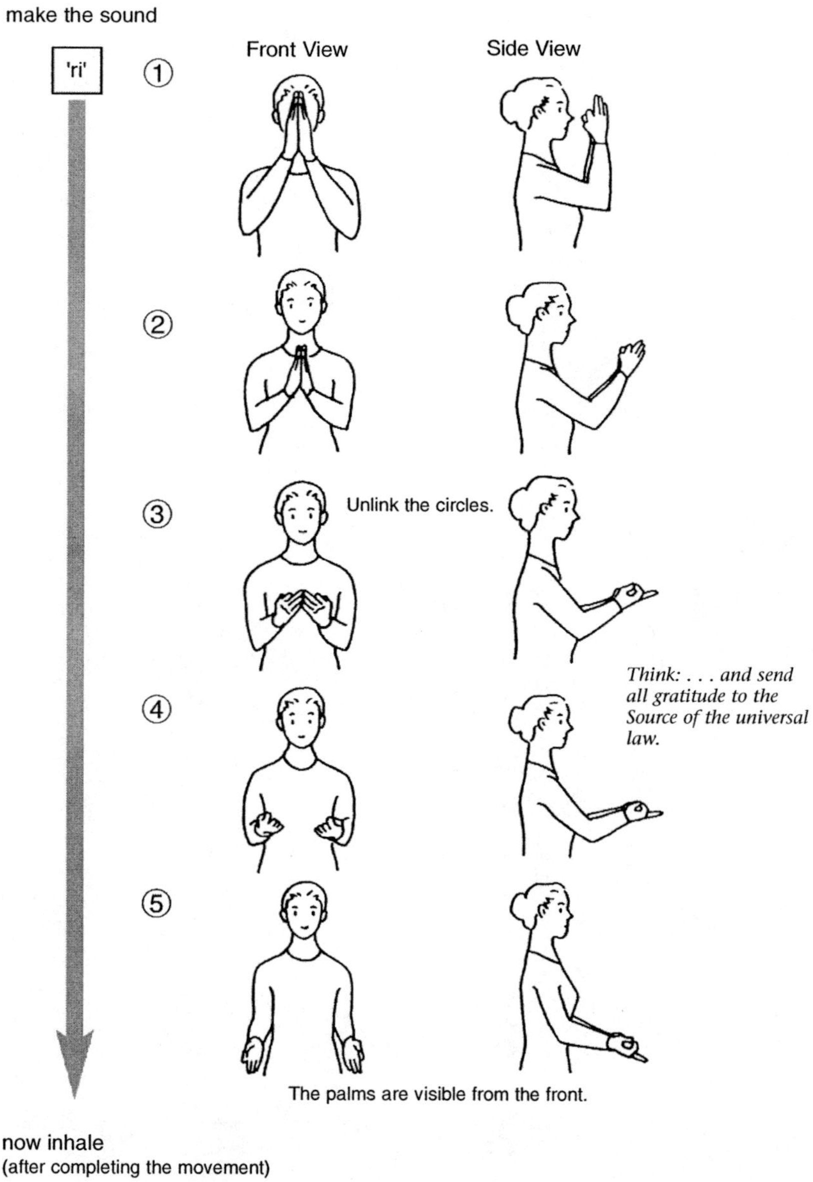

make the sound

'ri'   ①   **Front View**   **Side View**

②

③   Unlink the circles.

Think: . . . and send all gratitude to the Source of the universal law.

④

⑤

The palms are visible from the front.

now inhale
(after completing the movement)

13

Holding the breath and leaving the left hand as it is, extend the forefinger on the right hand. From the middle of the body, thrust the right finger straight down, and raise it until it is level with the forehead.

no sound
(hold your breath)

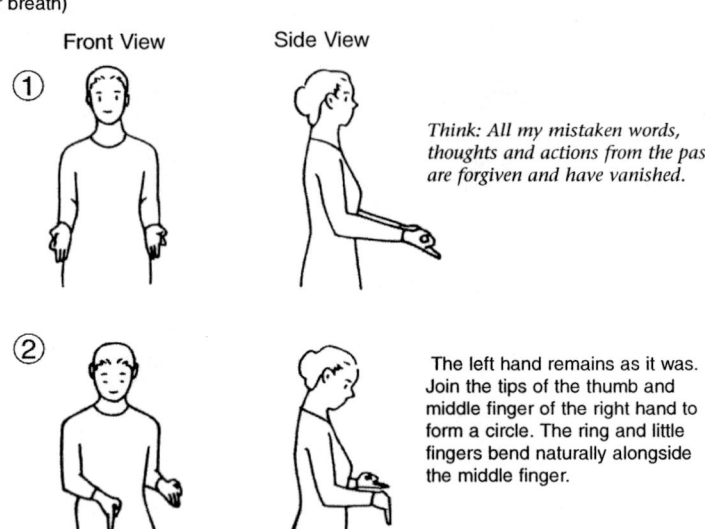

Front View   **Side View**

①

Think: All my mistaken words, thoughts and actions from the past are forgiven and have vanished.

②

The left hand remains as it was. Join the tips of the thumb and middle finger of the right hand to form a circle. The ring and little fingers bend naturally alongside the middle finger.

Point the index finger straight down from the middle of the body. The palm faces left.

magnified view

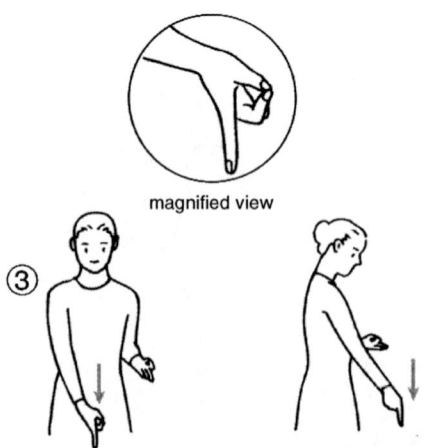

③

While making a silent shout in you mind and body, thrust your right hand straight down.

314

(continued from the previous page)

Front View   Side View

④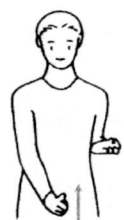

After thrusting the hand down, without relaxing concentration, turn the finger straight upwards. Lift the finger slowly.

⑤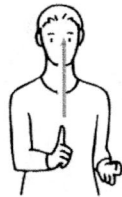

When the hand passes in front of the chest, thrust the finger upwards quickly. At the same time, again emit a silent shout in your mind and body.

Bring the hand down in front of the face and stop briefly.

⑥

Think: my infinite self has appeared.

Don't inhale yet.

14   Without losing concentration, lower the hands to the starting position and form the *In* of Great Harmony. Now release the breath.

Now inhale
(after completing the movement)

315

How to Form the Universal *In* for Humanity

◆**Before you start, say:** *Jin-rui-so-ku-ka-mi-na-ri*

(Humanity is one with the Universe)

| 1 | Starting position: The *In* of Great Harmony |

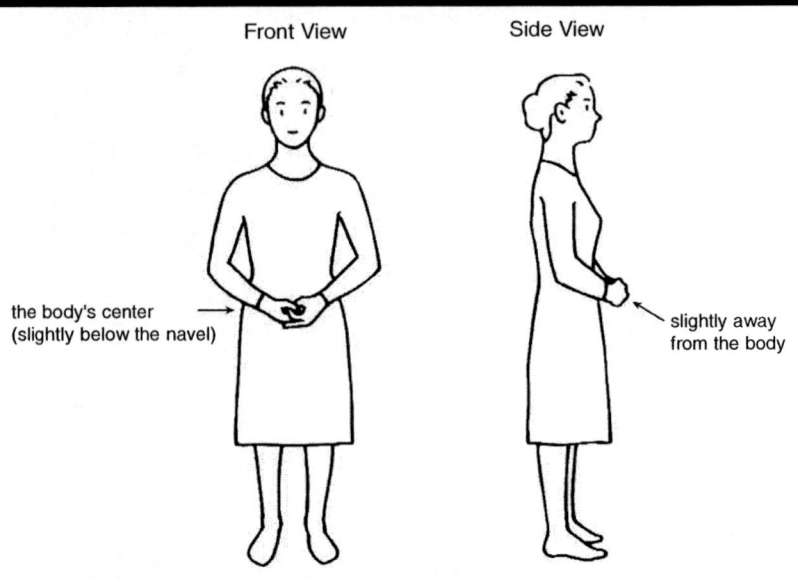

Front View   Side View

the body's center → (slightly below the navel)

slightly away from the body

How to form the *In* of Great Harmony

1. Make circles by joining the tips of the forefingers and thumbs.

2. Link the circles together.

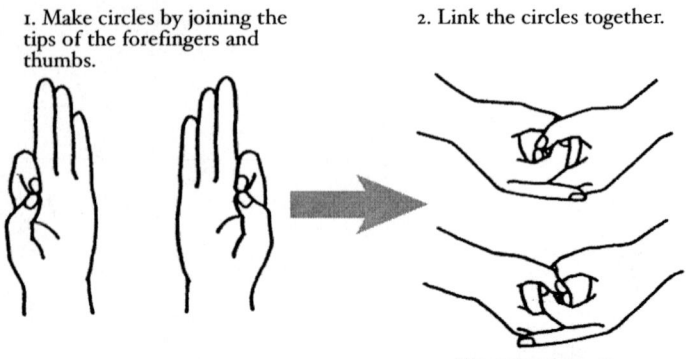

The palms face up.
Either hand can be on top.

After forming the *In* of Great Harmony, release the linked circles as you lift the hands upward towards heaven from the body's center. With the hands touching each other as in the magnified view, raise them upwards in a gentle, curving motion until they are slightly above eye level. Relax your elbows. Don't over extend your arms.

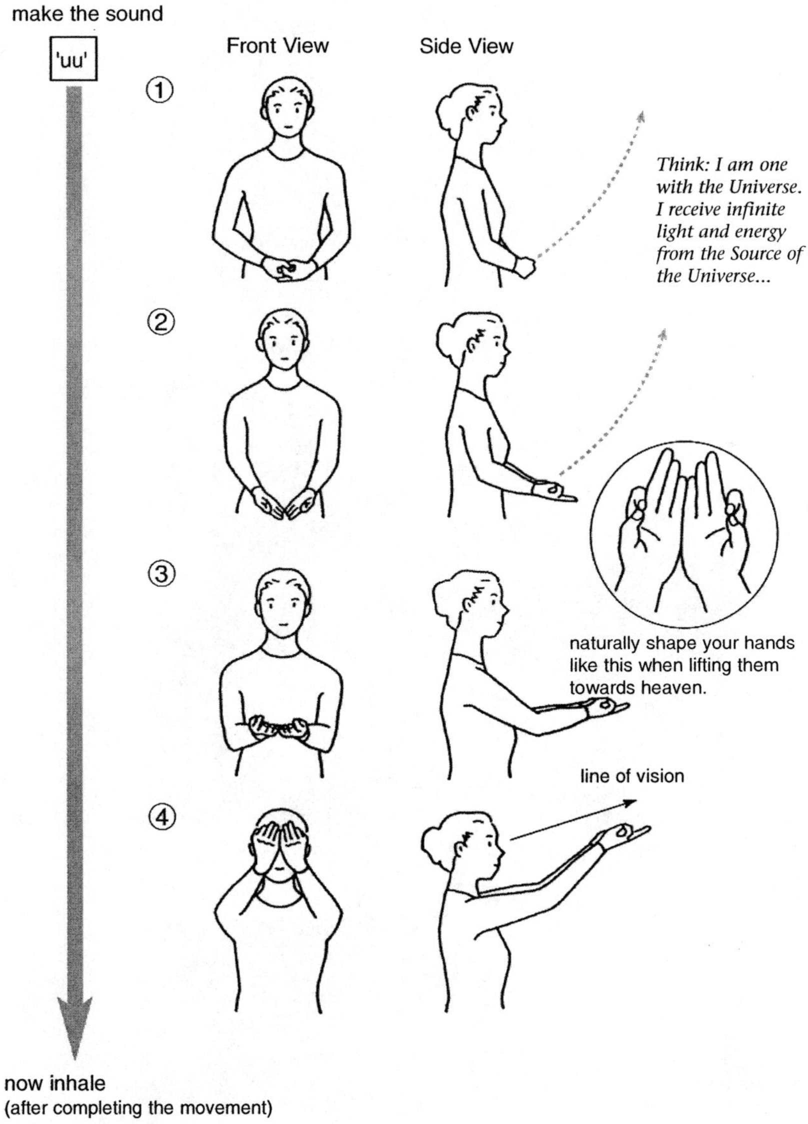

make the sound

'uu'

Front View   Side View

①

Think: I am one with the Universe. I receive infinite light and energy from the Source of the Universe...

②

③

naturally shape your hands like this when lifting them towards heaven.

line of vision

④

now inhale
(after completing the movement)

317

While making the sound 'uu,' and without moving your left hand, move your right hand upward to a vertical position. Make sure the wrists are constantly touching each other.

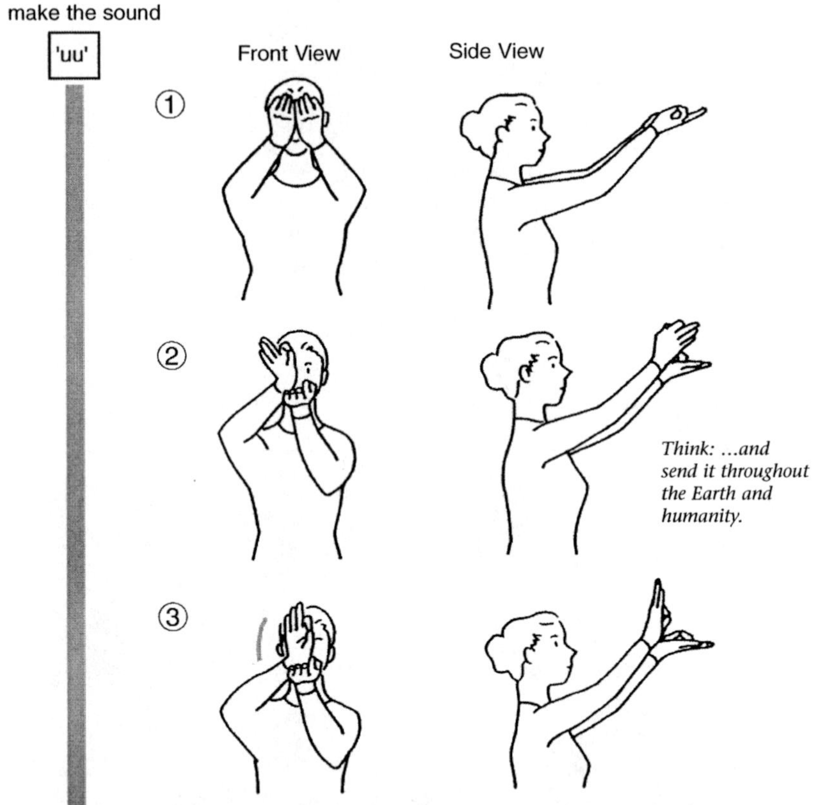

make the sound

'uu'

Front View   Side View

①

②

Think: ...and send it throughout the Earth and humanity.

③

Keep lifting your right hand until it points straight upward and is perpendicular to your left hand (with the wrists still touching each other).

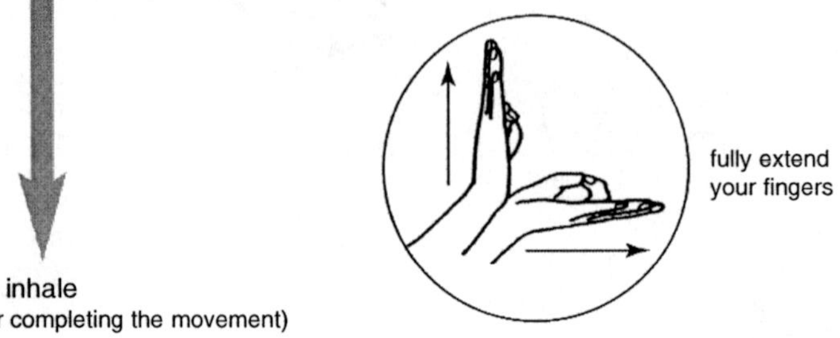

fully extend your fingers

now inhale
(after completing the movement)

 While making the sound 'ji,' and leaving your left hand as it is, bring the right hand up in a circular motion, forming a circle slightly larger than your face. The right hand moves clockwise and returns full circle.

make the sound	Front View	Side View

'ji'

① Image that you are drawing a circle.

Think: The body of humanity is infinite light itself—divinity itself.

② "body" (right hand)

③

While making the sound 'nn,' reverse the right and left hand positions by turning both hands with wrists touching.

'nn'

④ While turning your hands, make the sound 'nn.'

⑤ The left hand is perpendicular to the right hand.

now inhale
(after completing the movement)

Note: make the sound 'ji-nn' in one breath.

 While making the sound 'ru', keep your right hand as it is and make a circular motion with your left hand, forming a circle that is slightly larger than your face, and returning full circle. (From your point of view the circle will be counter-clockwise.)

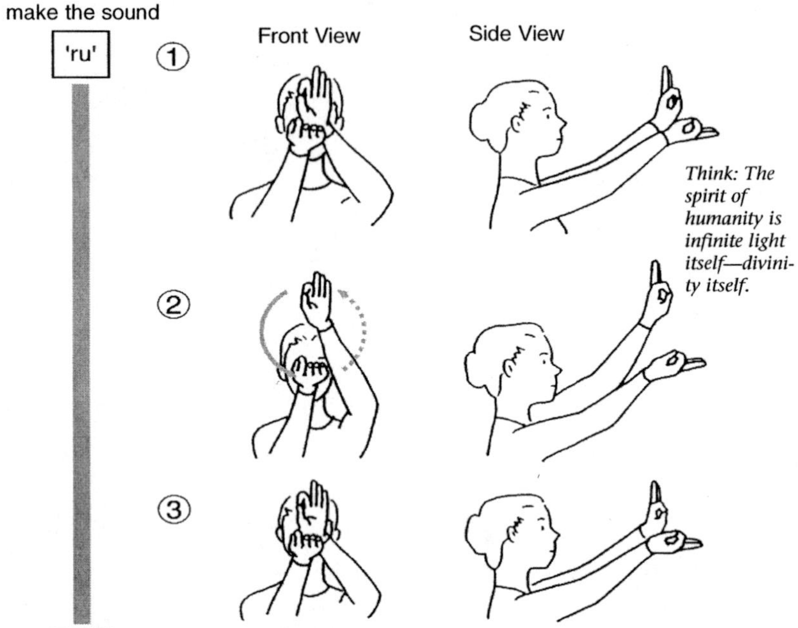

make the sound

'ru'

Front View   Side View

①

Think: The spirit of humanity is infinite light itself—divinity itself.

②

③

'ii' While making the sound 'ii,' keep your right hand as is and bring the left hand back into alignment with the right hand. When the motion has been completed the two hands will be touching each other.

④

⑤

now inhale
(after completing the movement)

Note: make the sound 'ru-ii' in one breath.

320

While making the sound 'uu,' bring the right hand towards the left side of the chest and the left hand towards the right side of the chest, and cross your hands in front of you. The fingers extend upward toward heaven and the palms face out.

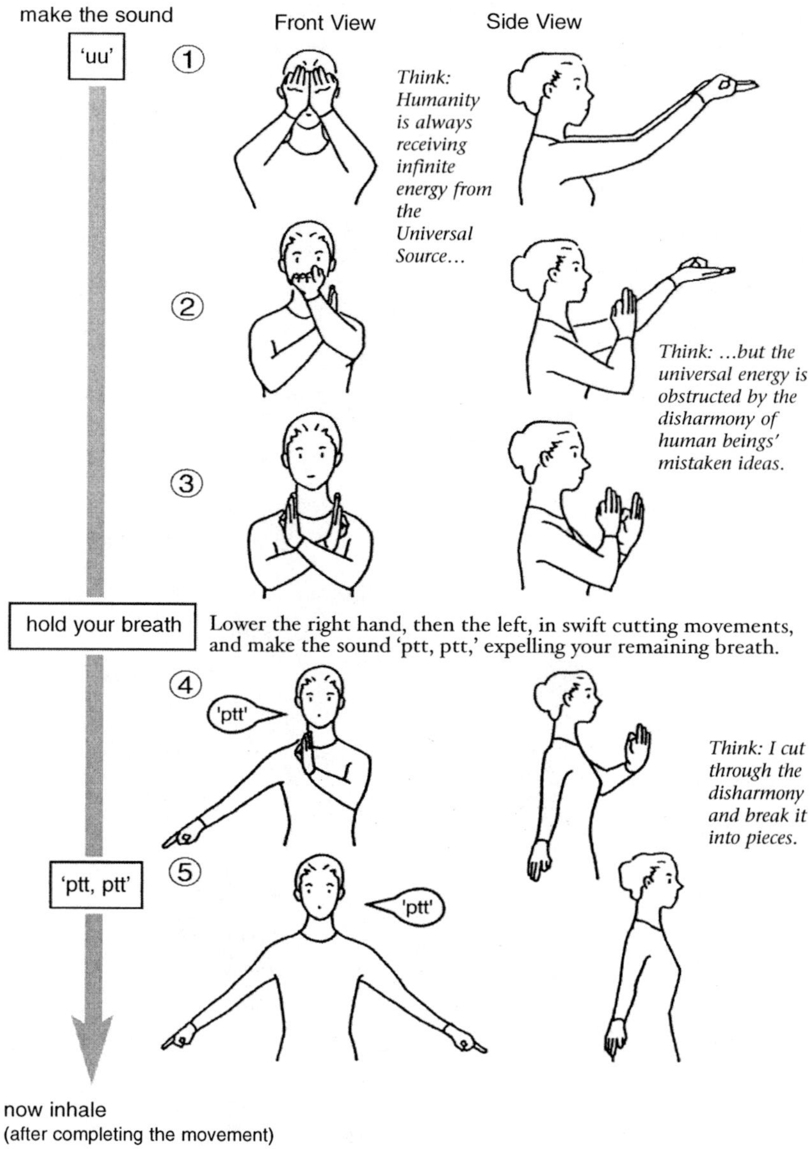

| make the sound | Front View | Side View |

'uu' ①

Think: Humanity is always receiving infinite energy from the Universal Source...

②

Think: ...but the universal energy is obstructed by the disharmony of human beings' mistaken ideas.

③

| hold your breath | Lower the right hand, then the left, in swift cutting movements, and make the sound 'ptt, ptt,' expelling your remaining breath. |

④ 'ptt'

Think: I cut through the disharmony and break it into pieces.

'ptt, ptt' ⑤ 'ptt'

now inhale
(after completing the movement)

 While making the sound 'so,' bring both arms up to shoulder level. Forming a wide arc, bring both hands in front of the chest. The tips of the middle fingers are touching. The palms face downward.

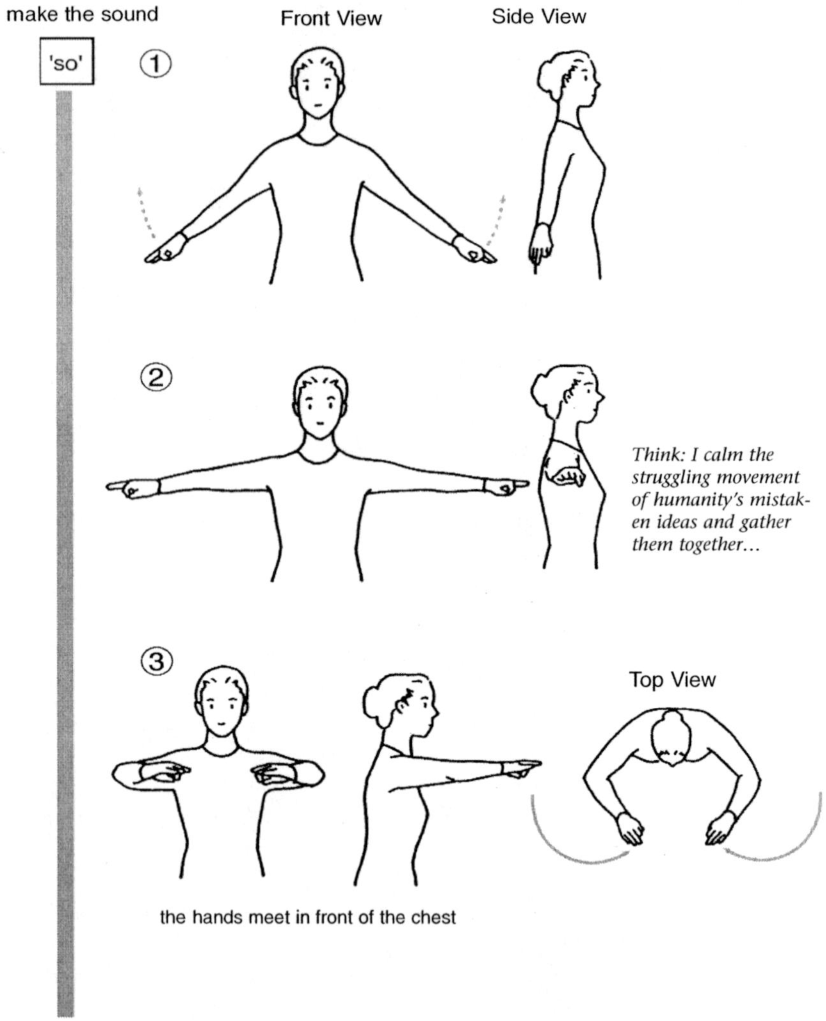

make the sound   Front View   Side View

'so'   ①

②

Think: I calm the struggling movement of humanity's mistaken ideas and gather them together...

③   Top View

the hands meet in front of the chest

(continued on next page)

(continued from the previous page)

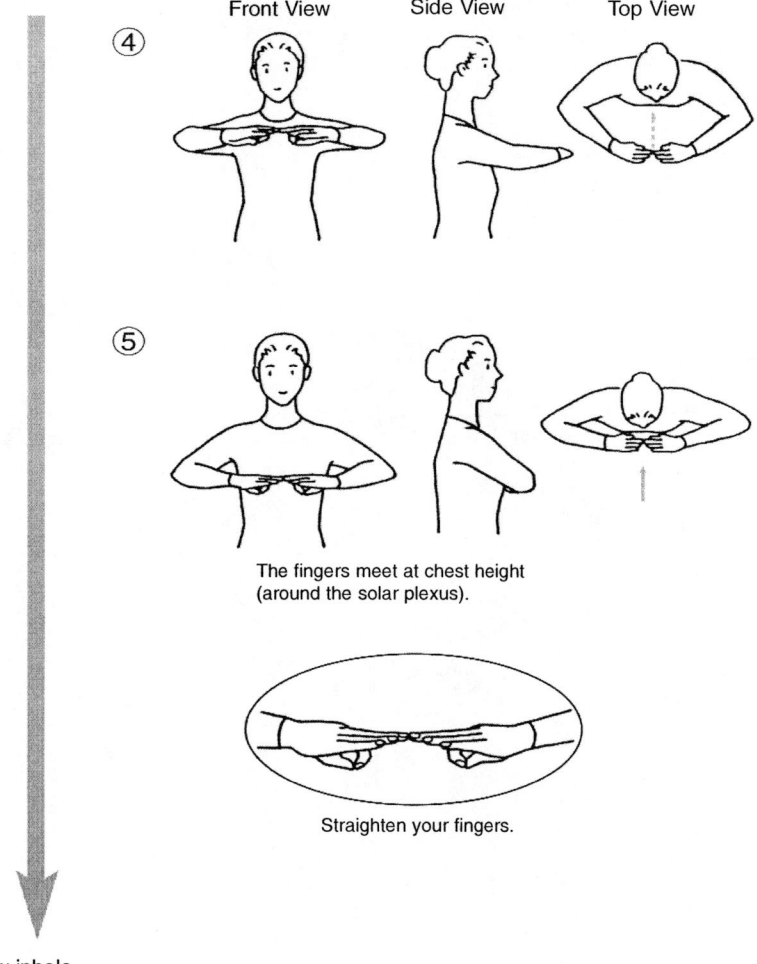

Front View   Side View   Top View

The fingers meet at chest height
(around the solar plexus).

Straighten your fingers.

now inhale
(after completing the movement)

8

While making the sound 'ku,' turn your palms up with your middle fingertips still touching. Extend your hands out in front of you, then spread them out widely to either side, palms still facing up. Gradually bring the hands down and cross them in front of the navel area, the right hand over the left.

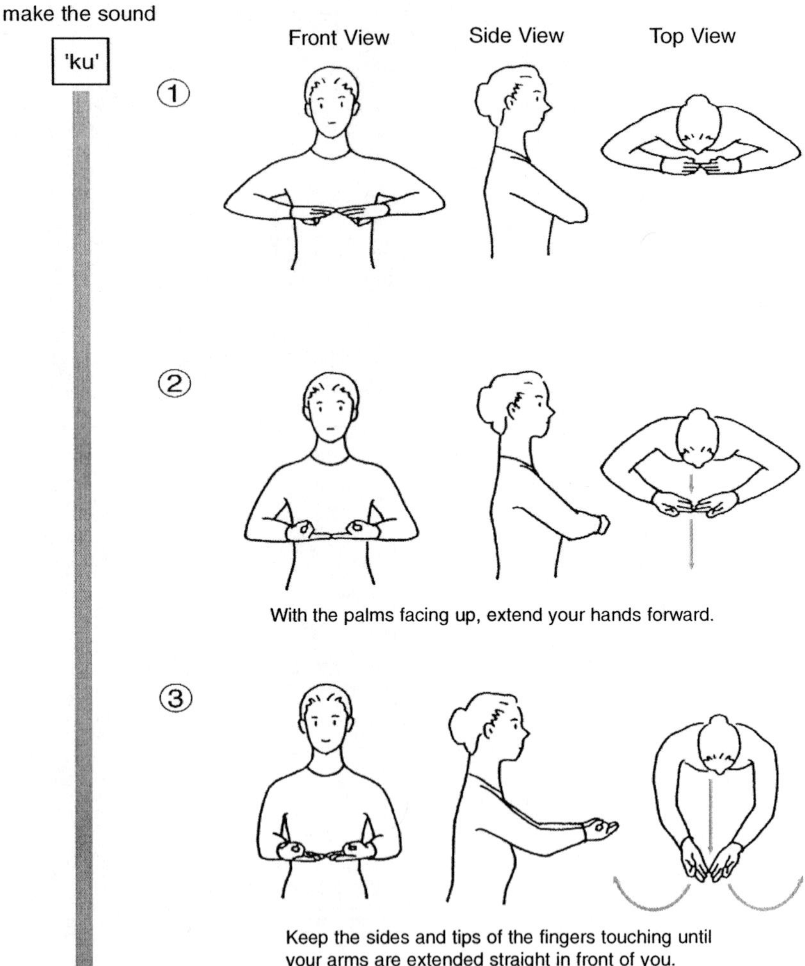

make the sound

'ku'

Front View   Side View   Top View

①

②

With the palms facing up, extend your hands forward.

③

Keep the sides and tips of the fingers touching until your arms are extended straight in front of you.

(continued on next page)

(continued from the previous page)

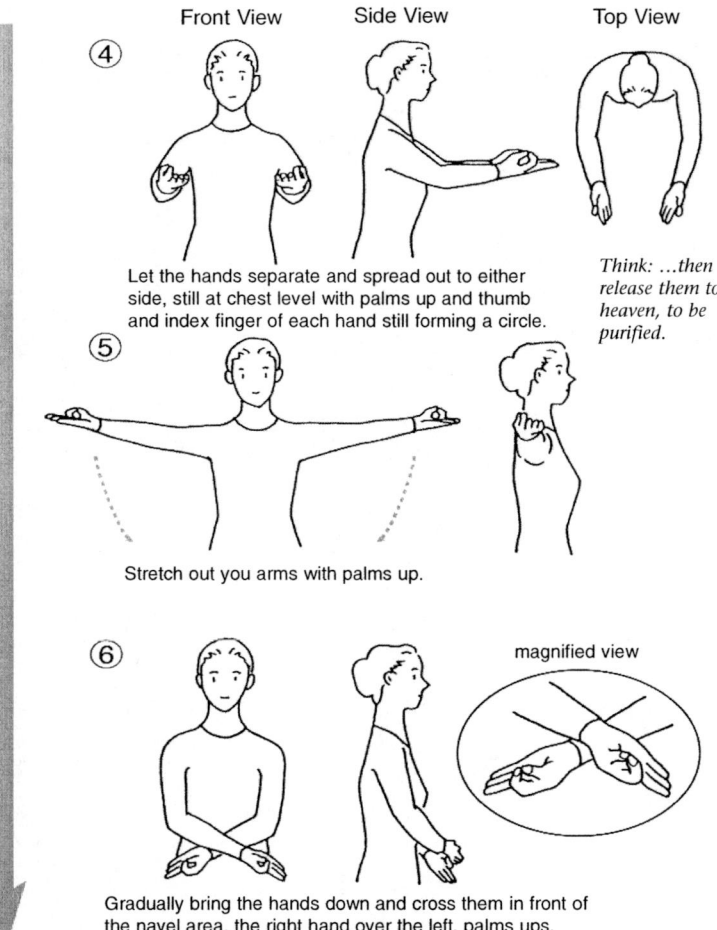

Front View   Side View   Top View

④ Let the hands separate and spread out to either side, still at chest level with palms up and thumb and index finger of each hand still forming a circle.

Think: …then release them to heaven, to be purified.

⑤ Stretch out you arms with palms up.

⑥ Gradually bring the hands down and cross them in front of the navel area, the right hand over the left, palms ups.

magnified view

now inhale
(after completing the movement)

While making the sound 'ka,' make a large, circular movement by lifting the arms upward on either side and crossing the hands above your head, palms facing inward with the inside of the left wrist touching the back of the right wrist. Continue the same sweeping, circular movement by bringing both hands downward in front of you and circling upward again until they extend straight out horizontally at either side (shoulder height, palms facing down).

make the sound

'ka'

Front View   Side View

①

Think: Each human being is reborn as infinite light itself, infinite love itself...

②   the big circle means infinity

line of vision

③   the palms face up

The palms face in. The right hand comes in front of the left.

(continued on next page)

(continued from the previous page)

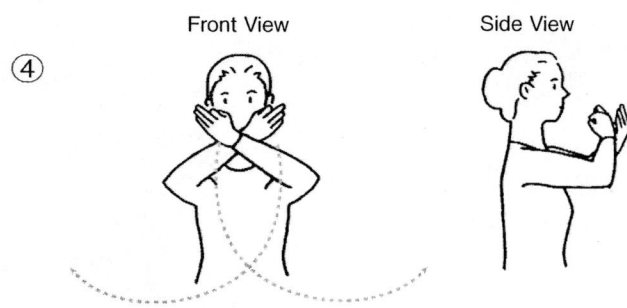

④ Front View   Side View

The right and left hands cross as
they move downward in a circling motion.

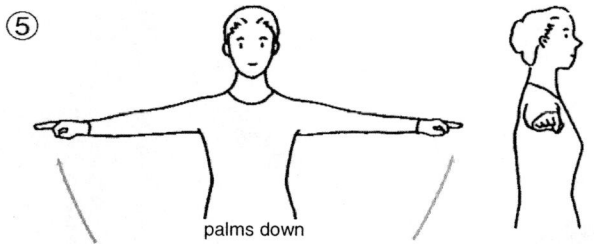

⑤

palms down

The arms sweep upward to either side, stopping at shoulder height.
The fingers extend straight out to the side, palms down.

now inhale
(after completing the movement)

10

While making the sound 'mi,' bring the hands downward in a circling movement. The hands cross in front of the navel area, the right hand under the left. As the hands cross, the palms of both hands turn outward. The circling movement continues until the hands cross above the head, with the inside of the left wrist brushing against the back of the right wrist. The circling movement continues downward until the arms extend straight outward to the sides at shoulder height, palms facing downward.

make the sound

'mi'

Front View   Side View

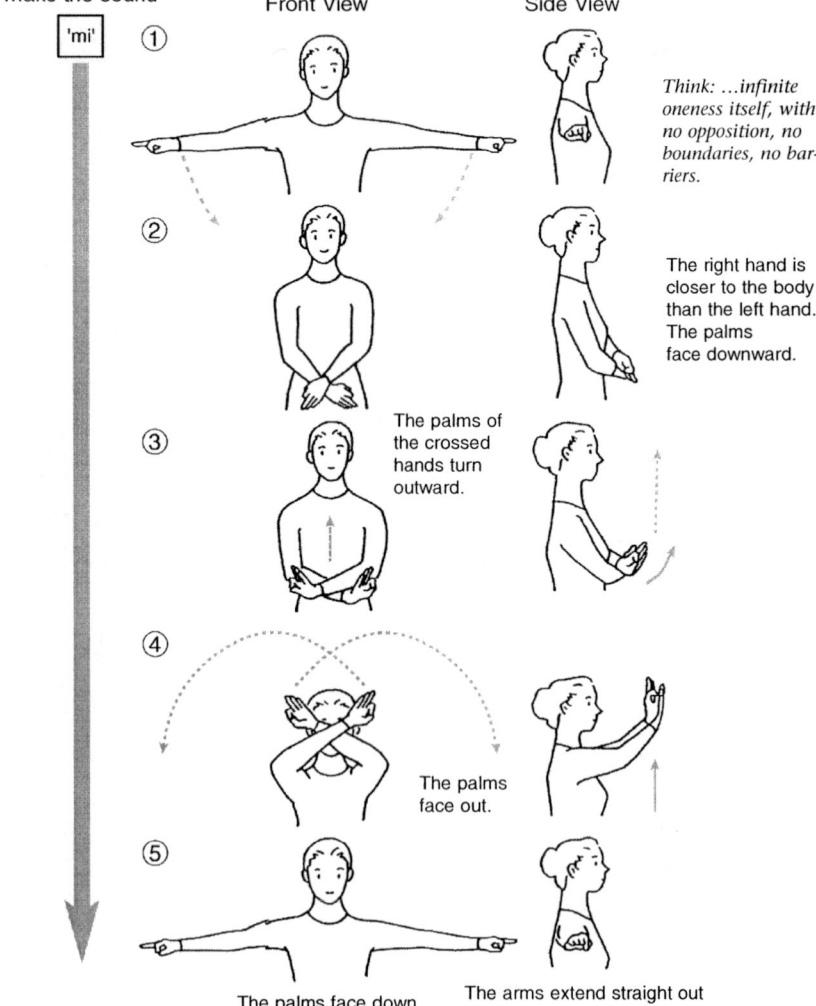

① Think: ...infinite oneness itself, with no opposition, no boundaries, no barriers.

② The right hand is closer to the body than the left hand. The palms face downward.

③ The palms of the crossed hands turn outward.

④ The palms face out.

⑤ The palms face down.   The arms extend straight out at either side. The fingers are extended.

now inhale
(after completing the movement)

328

11 While making the sound 'na,' lower your hands and bring them together in front of you. Then raise the hands as if scooping something up. When the hands are in front of the face, form circles made with the forefinger and thumb of each hand, and link the circles together. The palms and the fingers are pressed together.

make the sound

'na'

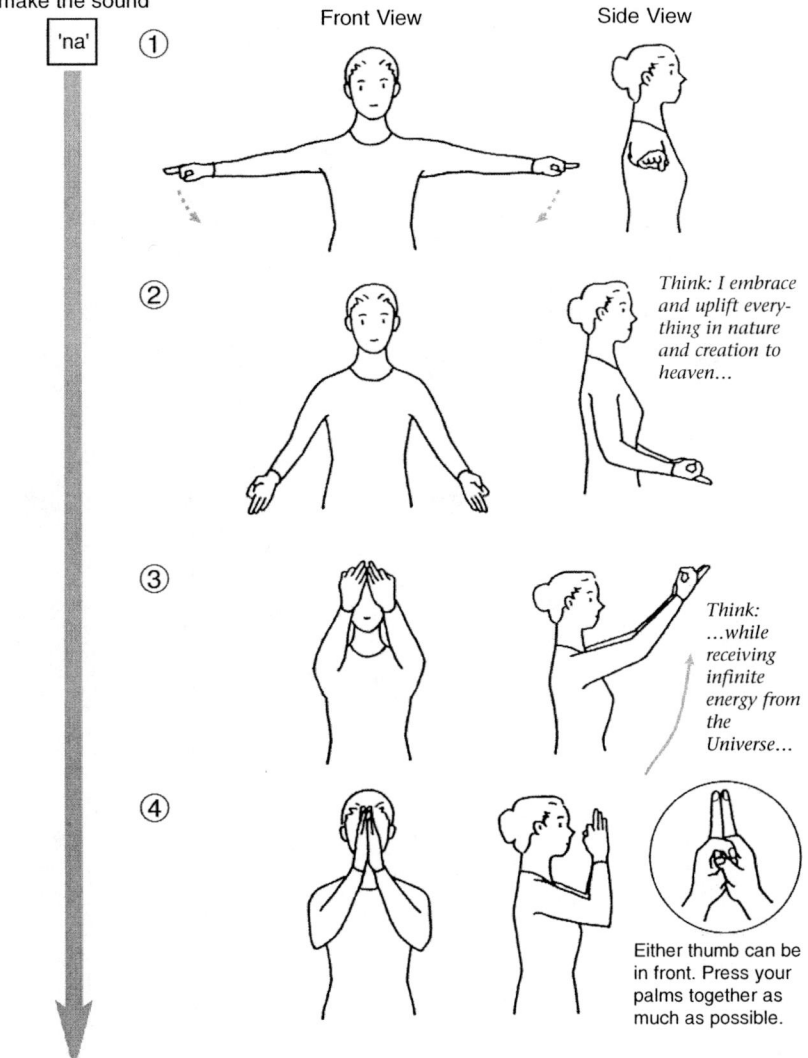

Front View   Side View

① ②

Think: I embrace and uplift everything in nature and creation to heaven...

③

Think: ...while receiving infinite energy from the Universe...

④

Either thumb can be in front. Press your palms together as much as possible.

now inhale
(after completing the movement)

12

While making the sound 'ri,' separate the hands and lower them to hip level.

make the sound

'ri'

Front View   Side View

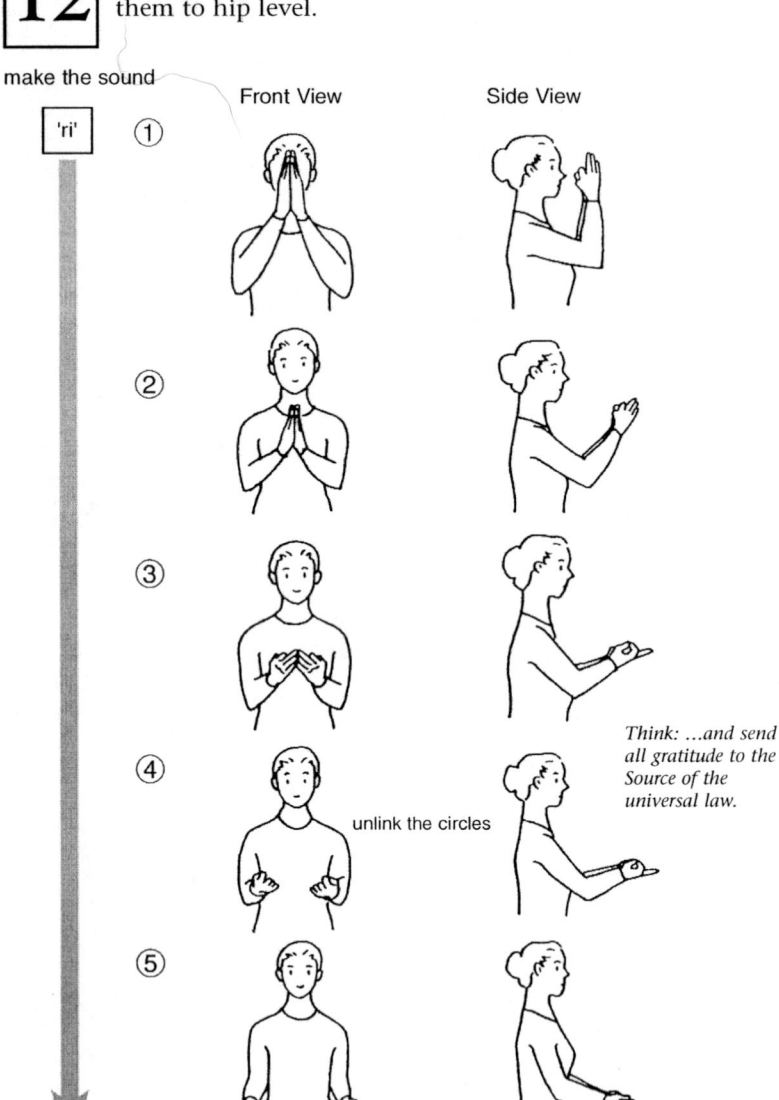

① ② ③ ④ ⑤

Think: ...and send all gratitude to the Source of the universal law.

unlink the circles

The palms are visible from the front.

now inhale
(after completing the movement)

13 While holding your breath, form a figure 7 (seven) with your index finger (a crossed seven, as written in European countries).

hold your breath   Front View   Side View

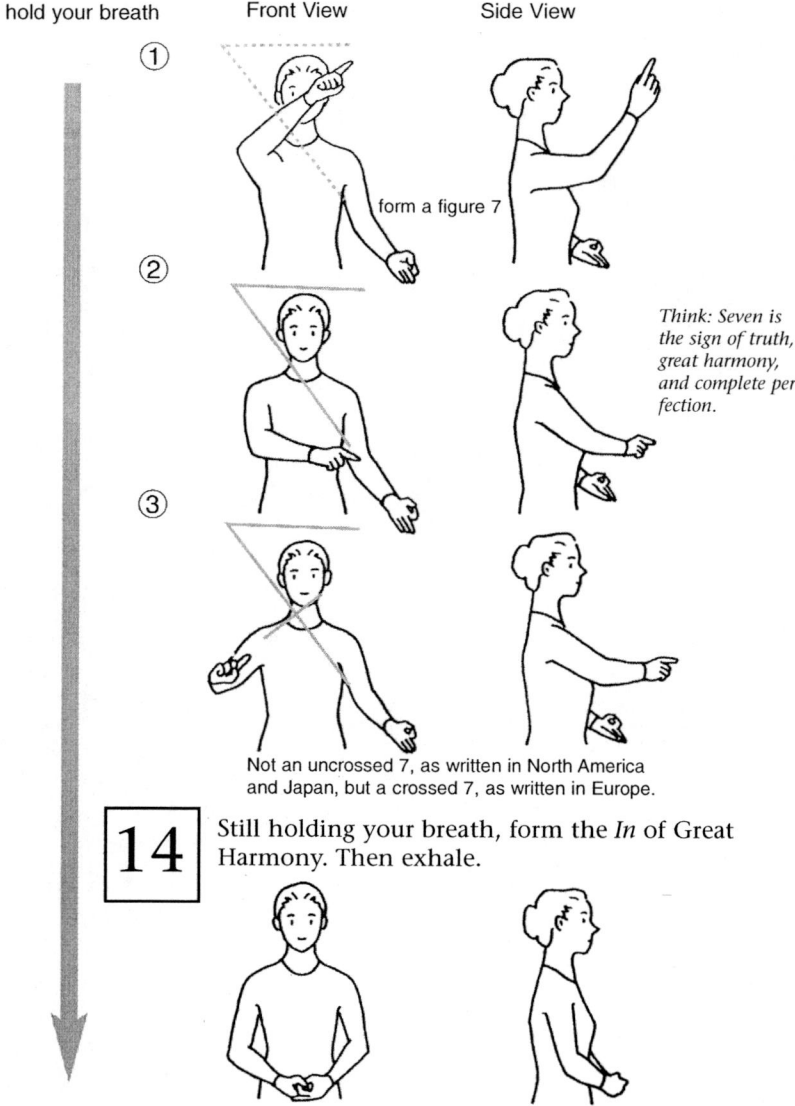

①   form a figure 7

②   *Think: Seven is the sign of truth, great harmony, and complete perfection.*

③

Not an uncrossed 7, as written in North America and Japan, but a crossed 7, as written in Europe.

14 Still holding your breath, form the *In* of Great Harmony. Then exhale.

exhale and resume normal breathing
(after completing the movement)

331

NOTES

1. George Adamski (1891-1965), co-author of *Flying Saucers Have Landed* (London, Werner Laurie, 1953).

2. Here, 'we' refers to the research group engaged in the pursuit of cosmic science. See Note 5.

3. *Goi Sensei* refers to Masahisa Goi (1916-1980), a Japanese philosopher who initiated an international movement of prayer for world peace. Refer to his works *God and Man* (Byakko Press, 2000), *The Spirit of Lao Tsu* (Byakko Press, 2001), and *The Future of Mankind* (Byakko Press, 1985). In Japanese, *Sensei* means teacher.

4. Holy Hill was a prayer center located in Ichikawa, Japan until May, 1999.

5. Cosmic science is a scientific study aimed at elucidating the principles and structures of the universe and all forms of life. It is attained by extinguishing the individual self and attuning oneself to higher dimensional principles.

6. An often-used wording of this prayer is *May Peace Prevail on Earth*.

7. Hideo Saito (1904-1984) was an accomplished artist, author, and student of Masahisa Goi.

8. The state of meditation described here is considered exceptional. The meditation method generally practiced at Holy Hill was to focus steadily on the prayer words *May Peace*

Prevail on Earth while praying in a group and throughout one's daily life.

9. The language referred to is Japanese.

10. In this work, 'karma' or 'karmic' refers to disharmonious thought vibrations that human beings have been emitting since they forgot their essential oneness with each other and with all living things.

11. *Kuu* is a Japanese word sometimes translated as 'stillness,' 'emptiness,' or 'nothingness.' Masahisa Goi explains: '*Kuu* is not a nihilistic or negative condition. It contains nothing, yet everything. It is the infiniteness of life itself—divinity itself—living vibrantly.'

12. An *In* is a means of attuning ourselves with harmonizing, higher dimensional energy and letting that energy flow through the physical plane. Through the centuries, various *In* have been practiced by holy people to bring specific benefits at certain times and places. Through the activities of cosmic science, two important *In* have recently been conveyed to human beings on Earth. These *In* are not intended for a few individuals, but for all people who can understand their meaning and purpose: to develop the inherent divinity of all human beings.

13. To read about the first Universal *In* being conveyed to Earth, see *You are the Universe* by Masami Saionji (Byakko Press, 2001).

ABOUT THE AUTHOR

Masao Murata was born in 1906 in Shiga prefecture, Japan. While serving as president of a small electric company, he spent his spare hours in support of the world peace prayer movement founded by his mentor and advisor, Masahisa Goi. When asked to describe Mr. Murata, Mr. Goi wrote:

> *During our association, Mr. Murata came to believe deeply in the love and protection of his guardian spirits and divinity. This lent much radiance to his prominent psychic abilities, and it deepened his experiences in the divine, spiritual, and subconscious realms which transcend the five senses. It also allowed him to communicate superbly with cosmic humanity. In his various reports on experiences aboard space vessels we find descriptions that are, in some respects, even more detailed than those of Adamski.*
>
> *One of the wonderful things about Mr. Murata is that, despite his many mystical qualities, he never lets any trace of the mystical show through in his bearing and personality. At all times he is never anything but a delightfully natural, usual person.*

Angels of the Cosmos is Masao Murata's first work published in English. His other works, published in Japanese, include *Communications with the Spiritual World* (Vol. I-V), *Children Who Went to the Spiritual World* (Vol. I-II), *Tales of Seven Hermits*, and *Cosmic Humanity and the Future of Earth*.

Masao Murata died peacefully at the age of eighty-nine and is affectionately remembered by his wife, colleagues, and friends.